Process Improvement
with
Electronic Health Records

A Stepwise Approach to Workflow and Process Management

MARGRET AMATAYAKUL

MBA, RHIA, CHPS, CPHIT, CPEHR, CPHIE, FHIMSS

CRC Press
Taylor & Francis Group
Boca Raton   London   New York

CRC Press is an imprint of the
Taylor & Francis Group, an **informa** business

A PRODUCTIVITY PRESS BOOK

CRC Press
Taylor & Francis Group
6000 Broken Sound Parkway NW, Suite 300
Boca Raton, FL 33487-2742

© 2012 by Taylor & Francis Group, LLC
CRC Press is an imprint of Taylor & Francis Group, an Informa business

No claim to original U.S. Government works

Printed in the United States of America on acid-free paper
Version Date: 20120323

International Standard Book Number: 978-1-4398-7233-8 (Paperback)

Visit the Taylor & Francis Web site at
http://www.taylorandfrancis.com

and the CRC Press Web site at
http://www.crcpress.com

Contents

Preface

Quality improvement is a cornerstone of health care. Yet managing the efficiency and effectiveness of workflow has not always been considered an integral part of healthcare quality improvement. This is especially true as electronic health records (EHRs) are being implemented. This new technology impacts clinicians in ways most never anticipated. There are many benefits from EHRs, but there have also been unintended consequences—often from lack of attention to workflows and processes and their connection points.

This book was written to overcome the paucity of guidance on workflow and process management specifically associated with EHR implementation, adoption, and optimization. Within the context of EHR then, workflow and process management is the application of a focused approach to understanding and optimizing how inputs (in any form—raw data, semi-processed data, and information from knowledge sources such as EBM) are processed (mentally or by computers using algorithms and clinical decision support [CDS] rules) into outputs (information) that contribute to an immediate effect or downstream effects (which also contribute to creation of further knowledge).

Workflow and process management for EHR focuses on mental processes, which have been described by Dr. Sam Bierstock as "thoughtflow," performed by knowledge workers. The clinical transformation that an EHR is expected to bring about is not just the movement from paper to electronic documentation. It is technology that contributes to a fundamental change in how medicine is practiced. The original Institute of Medicine (1991) study on computer-based patient records observes that "merely automating the form, content, and procedures of current patient records will perpetuate their deficiencies and will be insufficient to meet emerging user needs."

The chapters in this book introduce workflow and process management in health care and set the stage for a ten-step approach to applying workflow and process management principles at whatever stage a care delivery organization is in its EHR journey. Each chapter includes specific guidance and tools, as well as case studies. Healthcare knowledge workers are said to learn in a "see one, do one" mode. Stories bring reality to theory and practical advice.

Chapter 1: Introduction to Workflow and Process Management in Health Care introduces the topic to the healthcare environment, describing the clinical transformation that knowledge workers are expected to achieve in adopting EHR. Chapter 2: Workflow and Process Management Overview defines terms and compares workflow and process management for EHR to other continuous quality improvement (CQI) methodologies and to change management.

The ten steps for workflow and process management begin with Chapter 3, Step 1: Assess Readiness for Workflow and Process Management. It urges care delivery organizations to take a critical look at their culture, to educate all stakeholders, to set goals for EHR outcomes, and to provide a workflow and process management governance structure.

Knowing what processes need to be addressed in EHR workflow and process redesign is covered in Chapter 4, Step 2: Compile Process Inventory. Care delivery organizations may well have applied CQI techniques to various workflows and processes in the past, but the EHR environment often breaks down or combines processes differently than in the traditional departmental or task approach. Workflow and process management for EHR must be patient centered, not staff or task centered.

Chapter 5 covers Step 3: Select Tools and Train Team. EHR vendors often point out that workflow and process changes that come about as a result of EHR capabilities are the responsibility of the care delivery organization itself. Even though some support and guidance from experts can be helpful, it is likewise true that the people who know the current workflows and processes best are those who are currently performing them. Workflow and process analysis and redesign actually help initiate change management.

Chapter 6, Step 4: Current Workflows and Processes dives into the specifics of documenting current workflows. It discusses the level of detail necessary for workflow and process mapping to be effective in understanding "thoughtflows" and the information needs of clinicians.

Chapter 7, Step 5: Obtain Baseline Data describes the purposes and uses for collecting baseline data. Not all care delivery organizations opt to collect baseline data as they may not have an interest in or, in many cases, the patience, for later conducting benefits realization studies. Still, such activities can be motivational—and provide the evidence that knowledge workers especially require to adopt change.

Chapter 8, Step 6: Validate Workflow and Process Maps urges care delivery organizations to step back and ensure that current maps represent reality. Improvements cannot be effected on workflows and processes if workarounds and problems associated with current workflows and processes are not well understood. It does little good to map a current workflow and process as it is supposed to be performed. Part of validation is also capturing variations. And once again, engagement of all stakeholders helps them take ownership of changes to come.

Chapter 9, Step 7: Identify Process Redesign Opportunities describes the process for getting stakeholders to create, document, and validate new workflows and processes. It may seem like many steps to get to this point, but mapping current workflows and processes initiates changes that take considerable time to "gel." Mapping current workflows and processes also has valuable outputs of its own—it educates about EHR and helps the organization specify EHR requirements for vendor selection. The redesign of workflows and processes actually represents third and fourth outcomes that help the organization implement EHR and gain adoption, and later optimize use.

Chapter 10, Step 8: Conduct Root Cause Analysis to Redesign Workflows and Processes is a step that should be performed concurrently with Step 7, but may also be performed some period of time after redesigned workflows and processes have been implemented. Redesigned workflows and processes may be found to not work well, or require further change as the environment changes with ever new technology, new regulations, or new clinical research findings. Root cause analysis is not new to health care, but often has not been applied to IT issues.

Chapter 11, Step 9: Implement Redesigned Workflows and Processes is the culmination of the work in all previous steps, although as noted above may well not be the last time redesign and implementation is necessary. This chapter also dives more deeply into change management, discusses how to create change agents, and offers suggestions for using a few "tried and true" change management tools.

Chapter 12, Step 10: Monitor Goal Achievement with Redesigned Workflows "closes the loop" on the book and urges care delivery organizations to use continuous workflow and process management to celebrate their successes and to view course correction as not something bad but a part of the learning process that all relatively new technology implementations require.

Acknowledgments

A special thank you is extended to each and every organization that has written articles, been written about in news stories, or sought consultation about their successes and challenges with respect to workflows and processes in an EHR environment. These teachings have contributed to the rich experience base that compiling such a book requires.

Appreciation is also extended to the staff at CRC Press, especially Kristine Mednansky and Frances Weeks, for their expertise and patience with a passionate author. They say a bit of eccentricity is necessary to be creative, yet surely it tests the wits of those who must execute the product. By the same token, readers must be thanked as they are asked to be equally creative in their workflow and process designs while serious about achieving the goals for EHRs.

Two unsung heroes who likely are unaware of their status include Anita Cassidy and Keith Guggenberger who wrote *A Practical Guide to Information Systems Process Improvement* in 2001 under the same publisher. This book, with a general focus on information systems, was inspirational in its clear cut approach to workflow and process management. In fact, the connection to the publisher was made when an offer was extended to co-write a second edition or a companion book on process improvement for the EHR environment.

Finally, while writing a book the author is often immersed in a cocoon that is impenetrable to friends and family. My husband, Paul, deserves an extra special thank you for his indulgence that allows me to write what I am so passionate about and who has directed my career for over 4 decades.

About the Author

Margret Amatayakul is a health information management professional with a passion for automating medical records since her first professional job included creating a retinal disease registry on punch cards! She is currently president of Margret\A Consulting, LLC. The firm provides integrated delivery systems, hospitals, physician practices, vendors, health plans, their business associates, and the legal and investment communities with consulting, freelance technical writing, and educational programming to improve quality and cost-effectiveness of the strategic business of health care through IT. Margret is also adjunct professor in the health information and informatics management master's program at the College of St. Scholastica, and co-founder and member of the board of examiners of Health IT Certification, LLC. Margret has formerly held positions as the associate executive director of the American Health Information Management Association (AHIMA), associate professor at the University of Illinois Medical Center, and director of the medical record department at the Illinois Eye and Ear Infirmary. She is the author of numerous books, textbook chapters, and articles on electronic health records and HIPAA/HITECH privacy and security compliance. She has served on the board of directors of the Healthcare Information Management and Systems Society (HIMSS) and is active in several other professional health informatics organizations.

List of Figures

List of Tables

List of Case Studies

Chapter 1

Introduction to Workflow and Process Management in Health Care

> Many EHR implementations focus on the impressive features of the
> EHR software—ability to graph results, display images—rather than the
> workflow requirements of the clinician users.
>
> **—Barry P. Chaiken, MD, 2011**

This chapter sets the context for the importance of workflow and process management in health care, in general, and more specifically for optimal use of the electronic health record (EHR) and other health information technology (HIT). It describes the characteristics of knowledge workers who often challenge the ability to achieve benefits from EHR and HIT, and distinguishes knowledge management from heuristic thought and professional judgment that continue to be required as clinicians who are knowledge workers use computer systems. It provides case studies describing examples of workflow and process improvements, and how workflow and process management generates opportunities for further improvement.

Context of Workflow and Process Management in Health Care

It is well known that workflow and process management's roots are in manufacturing and industrial engineering, starting as early as the 1920s with process charts and work simplification. More recently, *business process management* (BPM) is being adopted as "a systematic approach to making an organization's workflow more effective, more efficient, and more capable of adapting to an ever-changing environment" (SearchCIO 2005). A business process is an activity that accomplishes a specific goal. BPM seeks to reduce human error and miscommunication and focus stakeholders on the requirements of their roles. SearchCIO includes in its definition that BPM is often a point of connection within a company between a line-of-business and the information technology (IT) department when the business process can be aided by IT.

Specific to health care, *quality improvement theories* such as Six Sigma, Total Quality Management, Business Process Reengineering, and Lean Systems have been embraced by a number of care delivery organizations (CDOs). In 2009, the Joint Commission created a Center for Transforming Healthcare focused on creating solutions to highest-priority healthcare quality and safety problems using Lean Six Sigma and change management tools with a focus on reliable measurement it calls Robust Process Improvement.™

Despite the widespread use of BPM in other industries and to some extent in health care in the face of specific needs, few CDOs or their IT vendors utilize these techniques in their implementation of EHRs and HIT. The result has been well-documented lower adoption rates of automation in health care than in other industries, less than ideal outcomes from EHRs and HIT, and even controversy over whether EHRs really can improve patient safety, quality, and cost of care. Yet where EHR vendors do use workflow and process management techniques, there appear to be better results, as evidenced by the frequency of acclaim the CDOs and their vendors earn (HIMSS Davies Award n.d.).

There is a critical need in health care to recognize that HIT is less about technology and more about its effect. In discussing the Centers for Medicare & Medicaid Services (CMS) (2010) incentive program for making meaningful use of electronic health records, David Blumenthal, MD (Wagner 2009), former director of the Office of the National Coordinator (ONC), observed that

> Meaningful use [incentive program for adopting certified EHR technology] is not a technology project, but a change management project. Components of meaningful use include sociology, psychology, behavior change, and the mobilization of levers to change complex systems and improve their performance.

The federal government is seeking to use Health Information Technology for Economic and Clinical Health (HITECH) and its Affordable Care Act (ACA) to achieve health reform: to enhance the quality of care, improve patient safety, expand access to care, and reduce the cost of care. The healthcare industry must find a way to make EHR and HIT successful.

Workflow and Process Management for Clinical Transformation

The term *clinical transformation* has been used to describe the scope of change needed in health care. While not the sole factor, automation plays an important

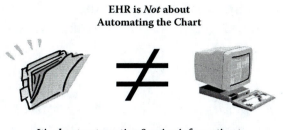

**EHR is *Not* about
Automating the Chart**

*It's about automating & using information to
achieve value*

Figure 1.1 The value of EHR technology. (From Copyright © Margret\A Consulting, LLC. With permission.)

role in such transformation. Barry Chaiken, MD (2011) notes, "As organizations rush to satisfy meaningful use criteria…, many are turning their focus to a rapid deployment of EHR systems. Unfortunately, EHR adoption is just one tool used to transform health care, and not the single transformative activity so many believe it to be." He goes on further to propose that

> Health care transformation requires a comprehensive vision of care delivery that understands the importance of effective workflow in delivering care. Technology expands the options available in designing workflow… Implementing IT using workflows designed for paper-based processes fails to leverage the benefits inherent in the technology… lead[ing] to severe inefficiencies and medical errors. Proper use of IT requires workflow redesign that safely leverages the technology to enhance processes and workflow while delivering higher levels of safe and efficient patient care.

Another way to put this is that an EHR is not about automating the chart; it is about automating and using information to achieve value (Amatayakul 2011) (Figure 1.1).

Challenges of Workflow and Process Management in Health Care

So why has it been so difficult to institute workflow and process management to achieve the clinical transformation that EHR and HIT are supposed to support?

Ball and Bierstock (2007) describe the issue that "Vendors long have developed systems based on presumptions about the way clinicians work, but without a clear understanding of how clinicians think. Although workflows are complex and varied, they can be observed, described, measured, and addressed." Dr. Bierstock has coined the term *thoughtflow* to describe the need to understand how clinicians think—and then work, to appreciate the process used to obtain, assess, prioritize, and act on information.

The notion of understanding how clinicians think with respect to how they may use a computer is, in itself, transformative. Workflows and processes that traditional computer systems are intended to perform are those that process vast amounts of data into information. Users then gain value from the rapid and tireless processing performed by the computer.

However, most clinicians do not view themselves as processing vast amounts of data that would require a computer to perform. They process mentally all the data they need to make decisions about a patient, and then document a summary of that information—largely for reimbursement and legal purposes. They neither want to take the time to record all the data, nor rely on a machine to generate an answer for them. In addition, the structured format of the information generated from a computer has generally not been conducive for later review or to relate to others the patient's story. To clinicians, then, a computer slows them down, disrupts their entire thought process, and does not generate useful information for them.

What often is not appreciated by clinicians, however, is that patient safety and quality-of-care improvements are expected to come from the application of *evidence-based medicine* (EBM), which is knowledge generated by a large amount of data from clinical trials. A specific patient's data can be processed against the EBM to aid the clinician in clinical decision support. Unfortunately, EBM is often viewed as cookbook medicine (Timmermans and Mauck 2005; Swensen et al. 2010), and has not always been well developed or disseminated in a manner that is necessarily useful to the clinician in an individual patient care situation (Tonelli 2006).

Many studies have described unintended consequences from the use of EHRs—factors that would steer anyone away from their use. However, Temple (2011) describes the importance of studying studies—including recognizing that many studies are based on the adoption of technology that existed in 2005–2007 or even earlier, and many of the studies acknowledge that workflows and processes were not considered in either the selection or implementation of the systems.

Perhaps Simmons (2011) sums up best the importance of analyzing workflow in making the EHR selection and implementation: "… the EHR system will only do what you tell it to do. If you don't fully understand the workflow and information process of your [organization], your EHR system won't provide you with the highest level of efficiency possible." Adler (2007) notes that many who have implemented EHR when asked what they would do differently say, "spend as much time as possible planning, which should cut down on surprises as the project proceeds." Planning includes workflow redesign both before selection and during implementation. In fact, Dr. Adler's article is illustrated with a picture captioned "The Swamp of Shoddy Planning." The full scope of what an EHR can and cannot be expected to do must be understood; and clinicians who are expected to use the EHR must understand how they can best take advantage of what the EHR can do for them.

Workflow and Process Management Defined for Health Care

Within the context of health care and EHR/HIT, then, *workflow and process management* must be considered the application of a focused approach to understanding and optimizing how inputs (in any form—raw data, semi-processed data, and information from knowledge sources such as EBM) are processed (mentally or by computer using algorithms and clinical decision support [CDS] rules) into outputs (information) that contribute to an immediate effect and/or downstream effects (which also contribute to creation of further knowledge) (Figure 1.2).

Although terms such as business process management, process redesign and process improvement are often used, this book makes an effort to use the term "workflow and process management" for some very specific reasons:

1. Despite that health care could benefit from adopting better business practices; "business" is a term that does not resonate well with clinicians—who are the primary focus of the clinical transformation needed in health care.
2. "Redesign" is a term that often implies to new users of EHR that the technology will force them to change how they work—and, frankly, this is neither necessarily true nor desired. Redesign of workflows and processes should be

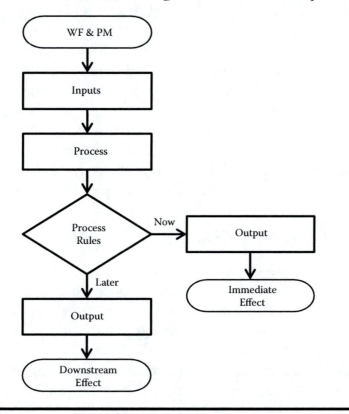

Figure 1.2 Workflow and process management in health care. (From Copyright © Margret\A Consulting, LLC. With permission.)

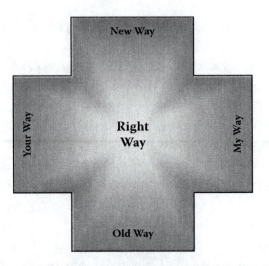

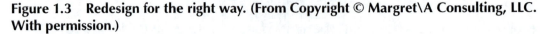

Figure 1.3   Redesign for the right way. (From Copyright © Margret\A Consulting, LLC. With permission.)

done because it is the right thing to do, not to get rid of the old (paper) way, do things only your way, or do things only someone else's (vendor's) way (Figure 1.3).

3. "Improvement" is also a loaded term. In fact, many clinicians are beginning to chafe at what appears to be constant hounding to improve. Health care in the United States does need to improve on many fronts, but making the assumption that all workflows and processes in the old way are no good does not help those who generally are very well-intentioned. A constant focus on improvement rather than doing the right thing (which should automatically lead to improvement) could also put pressure on control processes that may seem too time-consuming for a "Lean" environment yet are critical to patient care.

A case study set in a healthcare environment illustrates the potential for workflow and process management in health care to reap positive results:

Case Study 1.1: Workflow for Preventive Screening

Between 2007 and 2010, the Centers for Medicare & Medicaid Services (CMS) conducted a study to improve preventive care services in clinics (specifically seasonal influenza vaccination, pneumococcal vaccination, colorectal cancer screening, and breast cancer screening) through the use of HIT. It engaged their Quality Improvement Organizations (QIOs) throughout the United States to study how EHRs could help improve the rate of preventive screening. After recruiting the required number of clinics, baseline data were collected. Then workflows and processes were documented, and potential opportunities for redesign were reviewed with the clinics. Specific refinements necessary in the EHR also were discussed with EHR vendors. In addition, clinics were supplied with educational material for both providers and patients, as well as support for ongoing data collection and reporting (McGann 2007).

Although there may well have been a Hawthorne effect that contributed to the observed improvement, a number of workflow and process changes were identified that contributed to the desired level of improvement set by CMS. These varied by vendor and clinic, but included the following (Amatayakul 2010):

- Ability to generate a report of preventive service performance (i.e., some EHRs were not able to perform this basic function initially). Several clinics distributed these "report cards" regularly to their clinicians; and in some cases posted them in public areas for patients to be reminded of the importance of such screenings, setting up both a competitive environment for clinicians and reinforcement for patients.
- Ability to generate reminder letters or postcards; and in one instance to link to a telephonic system for automated calls to patients.
- Ability to record when a patient self-reported that a preventive service was performed elsewhere (e.g., flu shot at the grocery store) so that the clinic was given "credit" for checking on the screening.
- Ability to record preventive services performed on the clinic's patients by staff at health fairs via a smart phone app.
- Making a change in the software to provide the list of preventive screening measures due at the time the physician recorded the patient's assessment and plan in the EHR rather than at the time the physician first opened the patient's record (i.e., thereby addressing the patient's primary concern first but still being reminded of outstanding screenings).
- Making a change in the software to split the list of preventive screening measures to appear as more specific alerts when different members of the clinic used the EHR—hence dividing the workload as appropriate for the type of patient (e.g., the scheduling clerk could remind any patient with a previously recorded flu shot that one was needed; the nurse at check-in could discuss the need for a mammogram with female patients according to age and medical history; and the physician would discuss the need for a colonoscopy at the conclusion of a visit).
- Receiving a feed from the state's immunization registry to pre-populate childhood immunizations. (Even though this study was directed to Medicare beneficiaries, many clinics identified they needed help with other screening reminders as well.)
- Developing a policy that required specialists to refer patients due for a screening to their primary care provider. This included a hyperlink back to the check-out desk that would trigger staff to offer to make an appointment for the patient.

In Case Study 1.1 described above, either or both a *workflow* (sequence of steps or hand-offs performed) and a *process* (manner in which work was performed)

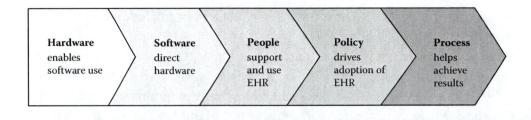

Figure 1.4   EHR system components. (From Copyright © Margret\A Consulting, LLC. With permission.)

were addressed. The result often entailed a combination of workflow and process redesign along with an organizational policy or procedure update and some change management tactics to ease people into understanding and adopting the changes.

A key factor, then, in appreciating workflow and process management for health care as it adopts EHR and HIT is that a system of hardware, software, people, policy, and process is necessary. A *system* is a set of elements that work together to achieve a common goal or purpose. Some experts suggest that, following the *80/20 rule*, hardware and software contribute only 20 percent, and some suggest even only 10 percent, of what makes an EHR successful; while change management, executive management commitment, and workflow and process management contribute at least 80 percent. Unfortunately, such a system has been difficult to achieve in the United States, as suggested by the US Department of Health and Human Services (HHS.Govarchives, n.d.):

> The health care 'system' in America is not a system. It's a disconnected collection of large and small medical businesses, health care professionals, treatment centers, hospitals, and all who provide support for them. Each player may have its own internal structure for gathering and sharing information, but nothing ties those isolated structures into an interoperable national system capable of making information easily shared and compared.

While hardware and software are the technical underpinnings for HITECH and health reform, it is people, policy, and process that really make the difference in how well the technology is used and how effective it is in creating health and healthcare value (Figure 1.4).

Workflows and Processes Performed by Knowledge Workers

In 1959, Peter Drucker made popular the phrase "knowledge worker" when he described a shift in workforce trends from manual laborers to those who accumulate and use expertise in a given domain. Socialcast (2011) observes that knowledge workers are becoming the fastest-growing sector of the world's workforce, while lamenting that with only 40 percent of Americans obtaining a college degree, an imminent shortage of knowledge workers in the United States is looming. Lesser (2011), however, suggests that the knowledge worker who is skilled at "gathering and synthesizing knowledge into coherent and useful observations" will become increasingly obsolete in the years ahead—because knowledge is becoming increasingly ubiquitous. In fact, today, the concept of knowledge management has less to do with managing knowledge workers and more to do with compiling knowledge and making it readily available. In health care, Alvai et al. (2010) define knowledge management as "the use of IT to enhance and facilitate evidence-based clinical decision making"—suggesting, it is believed, that

- *Knowledge management* is the compilation of knowledge, which can be performed by machine
- *Knowledge workers* apply knowledge, which still requires heuristic thought and professional judgment by a human

Lesser sees the knowledge worker being replaced by the "insight worker," who he describes as "a person who is able to translate observations into insights that can deliver impact." Perhaps it is not the terminology applied to these workers that is important, but that they can effectively apply knowledge (whether internalized or through using knowledge resources) in complex situations, often under extreme time pressures, and with a high degree of uncertainty—which is how Stead and Lin (2009) have characterized the current state of health care. EHR vendors in their hold-harmless contract clauses often use the term *professional judgment* in describing that EHR technology does not make clinical decisions and is not a substitute for competent, properly trained, and knowledgeable staff to analyze the information presented by the software. There is currently much debate about just how much trust can and should be put into HIT—and if one cannot trust the technology, why buy it? Alternatively, EHR or other HIT that is viewed as a medical device would come under the Food and Drug Administration (FDA) regulatory powers, a move they are strongly considering and one that has many concerned about the impact that would have on product sales and innovation.

Still, it must be acknowledged that understanding knowledge workers within the context of workflow and process management for HIT is important because knowledge is generally considered the product of data being processed into information with human experience applied to that as illustrated in Figure 1.5. Some extend this continuum to add wisdom—the evaluation of whether the knowledge is of value (Ackoff 1989). Weinberger (2010) even questions the oversimplification of the continuum in favor of a more complex knowledge-generation process that is social, goal driven, contextual, and culturally bound.

Appreciating what knowledge workers do and how that impacts their use of IT has a direct impact on managing workflows and processes in such an

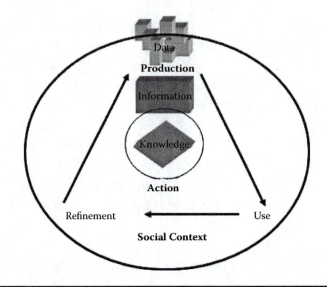

Figure 1.5 Data–information–knowledge generation. (From Copyright © Margret\A Consulting, LLC. With permission.)

environment. A key difference lies in the fact that in generating and applying knowledge, there are few visual clues present that make the workflows and processes apparent. In a manual worker environment, every step in a process and the sequence of those steps can be seen. Where the paper chart on a door in a clinic was an indicator that the room contained a patient, the paper chart no longer exists. Printed and color-coded forms served similar purposes. The challenge now is to understand the world where knowledge workers or insight workers look into the "black box" that is the vast resources of the computer and process that knowledge in their own "black box" that is the equally mysterious brain. Consider the following Case Study 1.2.

Case Study 1.2: Diagnosis–Drug Selection

A physician (endocrinologist) who had used an EHR for several months was desirous of using it "better." He was not sure what that meant, but he was convinced that he was not using it to its full potential. As a result, he sought a consultant skilled in workflow and process management to observe him as he performed his work with his patients. The first patient visit observed was an immediate challenge. The patient had come for one of her regular three-month diabetes check-ups, but also complained of having a urinary tract infection that was getting worse, despite that her primary care physician had given her a prescription a few days prior. As the primary care physician was now on vacation, she asked her endocrinologist for help.

The endocrinologist was highly sympathetic, and stated he would give her a different prescription. He called up the woman's universal medication list on his EHR and identified with her which drug she was taking for the infection.

The consultant could not see what the endocrinologist was thinking next, but could see him move his mouse to a link to the Internet from his EHR, then pull away from the link. He next picked up a paperback *Physician Desk Reference* and flipped through it—not stopping on any given page. Finally, he opened his e-prescribing screen and selected a drug. The screen showed a "green light" that the drug was on formulary for the patient's pharmacy benefits, and no alert appeared that the drug was contraindicated. The endocrinologist asked the patient if she still wanted to go to the retail pharmacy identified in the system, and upon her positive response struck a key invoking the prescription transaction to be sent to the designated pharmacy. He told the patient to be sure to see her primary care physician if the new drug did not solve the problem or seek emergency care in the event of any significant reaction.

After the patient left and the endocrinologist and consultant debriefed, the endocrinologist acknowledged that, not being a urologist and so not knowing other choices of suitable drugs for this patient, he was frustrated by the fact that he could not use the EHR to perform a search for a better choice of drug given her diagnosis and symptoms. He stated that he considered calling a colleague, but decided he had neither the time nor the inclination to expose his lack of knowledge in front of his patient, so he simply entered a drug he knew from his medical school days that was in the same class of drugs as the one she was taking and hoped that the system would alert him to any serious issues. While fortunately in follow-up with the endocrinologist the patient did get better on his choice of drug, it was observed that at that time there was no EHR that had the type of clinical decision support he was seeking. His only other alternative was to review a list of drugs by class in his *Physician Desk Reference* or automated drug knowledge base, reading about each drug in turn to make a potentially more informed decision.

While in Case Study 1.2 the potential for redesigning the process was not positive, it illustrates both the difficulty in "seeing" the process and the need for a better product that would make knowledge easier to extract and use. (As an aside, studies have repeatedly shown that clinicians have significant informational needs that are not met in their practices, with estimates that one clinical question arises per patient visit, and as many as 70 percent of these questions go unanswered (Ketchell et al. 2005; Ely et al. 2007).)

Challenges and Needs for Workflow and Process Management for Knowledge Workers

Understanding knowledge workers and the knowledge-management challenges they face is important not only to appreciate how difficult it is to understand and redesign their workflows and processes because they cannot be seen, but also to appreciate what workflow and process challenges they face and how the characteristics of knowledge workers may impact their ability to adopt new workflows and processes even when they are right for them.

Clearly, from the two case studies described already, workflows and processes performed by clinicians as they acquire data, process it into information, and apply their experience to generate and apply knowledge are largely performed mentally. It should also be clear that "little things" mean a lot. Consider the following Case Study 1.3 summarized from The Health Care Blog (Pullen 2010).

Case Study 1.3: Sequencing of Data in an EHR

Ed Pullen, MD, observes on The Health Care Blog that EHRs "have a bad reputation among many physicians for generating progress notes that are so verbose and filled with standard phrases that they are nearly useless to other physicians, and even to the physician who produced the note in the first place." He observes that EHRs are very good, and possibly too good, at creating documentation to assure payment and reportedly good at standing up to legal scrutiny because they are generally more complete and follow standards of practice. However, he notes that EHRs have been engineered to intentionally create a "SOAP note" familiar to physicians from years of use of paper charts. As a result, **S**ubjective and **O**bjective information are described first, then **A**ssessment and **P**lan. However, most consultants or physicians who want to refresh their memory of the patient generally want a quick understanding of the patient's condition and treatment, not the details of how the diagnosis and treatment plan was determined. Dr. Pullen suggests that having to scroll down to see the end of notes, which tend to be longer in the EHR, is time-consuming and may be missed if a reader is unwilling or forgets to scroll down. He suggests that the EHR be designed to obviously capture the information in the existing sequence, but to display it in reverse order, as APSO. He concludes his post with, "We need to modify our work processes to make our technology work for us, not try to use the technology to electronically reproduce previous workflows."

Responses to the post described in the above Case Study 1.3 were positive, with one commenter reporting on an anonymous survey of pediatricians who acknowledged making at least one diagnostic error a month, and just under half stating that at least once a year an error was made that harmed patients. When asked to identify the reasons for the diagnostic process errors, about half cited a lack of information in the patient's medical history or failure to review the medical chart. While obviously both can be attributed to human error, the workflows and processes associated with EHR should make documenting in and reviewing of the chart easier.

The Institute of Medicine in its first patient record study report (Dick and Steen 1991) described the notion that EHRs "encompass a broader view of the record than today, moving from the notion of a location for keeping track of patient care events to a resource with much enhanced utility." It is such enhanced utility that must be designed into products and adopted into workflows and processes.

Unfortunately, part of the issue with adoption of EHRs is that clinicians are only now just beginning to understand the potential for what enhanced utility can be afforded by an EHR. Knowledge workers often display certain traits, or characteristics, that may preclude them from taking advantage of such enhanced utility. Knowledge workers

- Are able to work on many projects at the same time
- Learn in a creative, inquiry-driven, and self-controlled manner
- Are able to multiply the results of their efforts through soft factors such as emotional intelligence and trust
- Need to be empowered to make the most of their deepest skills
- Make decisions autonomously, where traditional command-and-control paradigms are not effective for them to contribute to achievement of organizational interests

Students of physicians, and many physicians themselves, agree with many, if not all, of these characteristics. Physicians routinely go from the diabetic patient with a urinary tract infection if "only" to another diabetic patient but this one with cancer. They have mastered much knowledge, but do so on their own terms. Never put them in a classroom with other physicians to learn how to use the EHR, as each will feel that he or she is the only one who does not know how to use a computer, will be extremely embarrassed, and essentially shut down their learning process until they can apply their intuition to learn on their own. It is often said that other than their knowledge, physicians' only assets in caring for patients are time and trust; take either of those away and they will perform well below their potential. Both CDOs and patients have put physicians on a pedestal because of their skills; yet because physicians fear failure (and the threat of a malpractice lawsuit) perhaps more than anything else, they often appear to be ultra-conservative, plodding, and resistant to change.

Atler (2005) as well as Matson and Prusak (2010) describe the need to better manage knowledge workers (in all industries) because they are the key source of growth and opportunity. Atler notes, however, that because "they don't like to be told what to do, they enjoy more autonomy than other workers, [and] much of their work is invisible and hard to measure," they are left alone without the process improvement that other workers benefit from. This reinforces the notion that knowledge management is not managing knowledge workers, but supplying knowledge that knowledge workers can tap into to better perform their work—but that they often get no help to use and that they resist when such help is made available to them.

The result then is very much about the *law of supply and demand.* If clinicians do not demand such functionality and usability, there is no incentive for vendors to supply it. Interestingly, while a corollary may seem to be if clinicians do not know what to demand, there will surely be no supply, this is not quite the case. In many cases, as clinicians start to adopt EHR, they envision much greater functional capabilities than the system can supply—sometimes leading to product improvement; but unfortunately more often, it seems, disappointment and what are considered failed implementations with no feedback to vendors.

This discussion may suggest that physicians are the only knowledge workers in health care, and that is certainly not true. However, it does seem that others who could and should be characterized as knowledge workers in health care often operate in the shadows of physicians and thus do not display and sometimes do not operate as knowledge workers. Conrad and Sherrod (2011) urge nurse managers to "develop knowledge worker skills related to data gathering, analysis, and identifying clinical trends and patterns … As unit leaders, nurse managers need to equip themselves with skills to harness the power of electronic data systems and rapidly translate patient findings and information into knowledge that informs and produces quality patient-care outcomes."

More advanced forms of BPM, and ideally workflow and process management for HIT, "incorporate human interaction management so that many people and systems interact in structured, ad-hoc, and sometimes completely dynamic ways to complete one to many transactions" (Vom Brocke and Rosemann 2010). In describing Ochsner Health System's EHR implementation, Belmont (Guerra 2011) observes that they adopted the mantra that "integration will trump preferences." He observes that while this did not mean the vendor's way was the only way, it did mean that when someone said, "I want to do it my way," this was a signal to "sit down and say, 'Can you live with the integrated version of this?'"

Key Points

- The economic and clinical health of America depends on health reform, aided by **health information technology**. The U.S. healthcare system is in need of a clinical transformation that focuses on using **electronic health records** in the **right way**.
- To optimize use of **hardware** and **software** that may aid in creating an effective and efficient healthcare system, management of **workflow** and **process** performed by **people** who are knowledge workers and within the context of an integrated **policy** structure is vital.
- **Knowledge management** and **business process management** alone are insufficient to meet emerging **knowledge worker** needs. **Integration** is needed at every level, from system interoperability to sharing health information across the continuum of care and engaging all stakeholders in the value proposition.

References

Ackoff, R.L., 1989. "From Data to Wisdom." *Journal of Applied Systems Analysis*, 16: 3–9.

Adler, K.G., 2007 (Feb.). "How to Successfully Navigate Your EHR Implementation." *Family Practice Management*, 33–39.

Alavi, M. et al., 2010. "IT-Enabled Knowledge Management in Healthcare Delivery: The Case of Emergency Care." *ICIS 2010 Proceedings*, Paper 124.

Amatayakul, M., (2010). Personal experience performing services for Stratis Health, Bloomington, MN.

Amatayakul, M., (2011). Core Course I: Overview of HIT, EHR, and HIE. Health IT Certification. See http://healthitcertification.com.

Atler, A., 2005 (Aug. 5). "Knowledge Workers Need Better Management." *CIO Insight*. Available at http://www.cioinsight.com/c/a/Expert-Voices/Knowledge-Workers-Need-Better-Management/.

Ball, M.J. and S. Bierstock, 2007 (Summer). "Clinician Use of Enabling Technology." *Journal of Health Information Management*, 21(3): 68–71.

Centers for Medicare & Medicaid Services (CMS), 2010 (Jul. 28). 42 CFR 412, 413, 422 et al. Medicare and Medicaid Programs; Electronic Health Record Incentive Program; Final Rule.

Chaiken, B.P., 2011 (Apr. 7). "Transforming Health Care Through Improved Clinician Workflows." *iHealthBeat*. Available at: http://www.ihealthbeat.org/perspectives/2011/transforming-health-care-through-improved-clinician-workflows.aspx

Conrad, S. and D. Sherrod, 2011 (Feb.). "Nurse Managers as Knowledge Workers." *Nursing Management*, 47–48.

Dick, R.S. and E.B. Steen, Eds., 1991. *The Computer-based Patient Record: An Essential Technology for Health Care*. Committee on Improving the Patient Record, Institute of Medicine, Washington, DC: National Academy Press, 3.

Drucker, P., 1959. *The Landmarks of Tomorrow*. New York: Harper & Row Publishers.

Ely, J.W. et al., 2007 (Jul./Aug.). "Patient-Care Questions that Physicians Are Unable to Answer." *Journal of the American Medical Informatics Association*, 14(4): 407–412.

Guerra, A., 2011 (Jun. 30). "Chris Belmont, System VP/CIO, Ochsner Health System, Chapter 1." Podcast Available at: http://healthsystemcio.com/2011/06/30/chris-belmont-system-vpcio-ochsner-health-system-chapter-1/.

HHS.Govarchive, n.d. "Value-Driven Health Care." Available at: http://archive.hhs.gov/valuedriven/

HIMSS Davies Award, n.d. Nicholas E. Davies Award of Excellence, Chicago: Healthcare Information Management and Systems Society. See http://www.himss.org/davies.

Joint Commission, 2009. Center for Transforming Healthcare. Available at: http://www.centerfortransforminghealthcare.org/service/faq.aspx

Ketchell, D.S. et al., 2005 (Sep.-Oct.). "PrimeAnswers: A Practical Interface for Answering Primary Care Questions." *Journal of the American Medical Informatics Association*, 12(5): 537–545.

Lesser, R., 2011 (Feb. 2). "Are Knowledge Workers Being Replaced by 'Insight Workers'?" *Huffpost Business*. Available at: http://www.huffingtonpost.com/rich-lesser/post_1664_b_817400.html

Matson, E. and L. Prusak, 2010 (Sept.). "Boosting the Productivity of Knowledge Workers." *McKinsey Quarterly*. Available at: http://www.mckinseyquarterly.com/Boosting_the_productivity_of_knowledge_workers_2671

McGann, P., 2007 (Oct. 23). "The QIO 9th Scope of Work: A Content Overview." QualNet, 2007, Baltimore, MD.

Pullen, E., 2010 (Apr. 11). "APSO needs to replace SOAP in EMRs." The Health Care Blog. Available at: http://thehealthcareblog.com/blog/2010/04/11/apso-needs-to-replace-soap-in-emrs/

SearchCIO, 2005. "Business Process Management (BPM)." Available at http://searchcio.techtarget.com/definition/busness-process-management.

Socialcast, 2011 (May 3). "The Evolution of the Knowledge Worker." http://blog.socialcast.com/e2sday-the-evolution-of-the-knowledge-worker/

Simmons, J., 2011 (Jun. 15). "The Importance of Analyzing Your Workflow Before EHR Selection." Available at: http://jaysimmons.org/2011/06/15/the-importance-of-analyzing-your-workflow-before-ehr-selection/.

Stead, W.W. and H.S. Lin, Eds., 2009. *Computational Technology for Effective Health Care: Immediate Steps and Strategic Directions*. National Research Council, Washington, DC: National Academies Press, S-2.

Swensen, S.J. et al., 2010. "Cottage Industry to Postindustrial Care — The Revolution in Health Care Delivery." *The New England Journal of Medicine*, 362(5): e12.

Temple, R., 2011 (Feb. 1). "EHR Value & the Importance of Studying Studies." Healthsystemcio.com. Available at: http://healthsystemcio.com/2011/02/01/ehr-value-the-importance-of-studying-studies/

Timmermans, S. and A. Mauck, 2005 (Jan./Feb.). "The Promises and Pitfalls of Evidence-based Medicine." *Health Affairs,* 24(1): 18–28.

Tonelli, M., 2006 (Feb.). "Clinical Case: Evidence-Based Medicine and Clinical Expertise." *Ethics Journal of the American Medical Association*, 8(2): 71–74.

Vom Brocke, J. and M. Rosemann, 2010. *Handbook on Business Process Management 2: Strategic Alignment, Governance, People and Culture*. Berlin: Springer.

Wagner, R., 2009 (Nov. 19). "Blumenthal: Patient Care, Not Tech, Will Drive Meaningful Use." *InformationWeek*, Available at: http://www.informationweek.com/blog/healthcare/229204271?printer_friendly=this-page

Weinberger, D., 2010 (Feb. 2). "The Problem with the Data-Information-Knowledge-Wisdom Hierarchy." Kellogg School of Management: The Conversation. Available at: http://blogs.hbr.org/cs/2010/02/data_is_to_info_is_not.html

Chapter 2

Workflow and Process Management Overview

The efficacy of the electronic health record (EHR) is determined in part by its integration with the work of the clinician; and the policies, norms, constraints, and tasks of the organization and the larger health-care industry.

—Paraphrased from Ben-Tzion Karsh, PhD, 2009

This chapter provides an overview of the nuts and bolts of workflow and process management. It defines terms, identifies stakeholders, draws relationships to quality improvement theories and methodologies, discusses the importance of workflow and process management to change management, and describes the key points at which workflow and process management should be performed to successfully impact EHR and HIT selection, implementation, adoption, and optimization. Finally, this chapter introduces the steps in workflow and process management that then are covered in the remainder of the book.

Definitions of Terms: Workflow and Process Management

Workflow and process management was defined in Chapter 1 within the context of health care in general and EHR (electronic health record) and health information technology (HIT) specifically as

The application of a focused approach to understanding and optimizing how inputs are processed into outputs that contribute to an immediate effect and/or downstream effects.

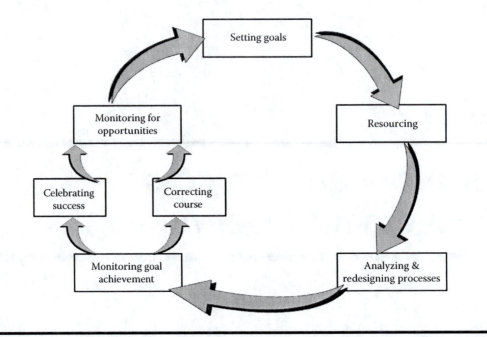

Figure 2.1 Workflow and process management. (From Copyright © Margret\A Consulting, LLC. With permission.)

Breaking down this definition assures an appreciation for the fact that workflow and process management is a focused approach. It is a form of management, which implies the ongoing organization and coordination of *people, policy,* and *process* for the achievement of defined *goals.* Within the context of this book, workflow and process management will focus on helping to achieve clinical transformation through the adoption of EHR and HIT.

Workflow and process management as an overall approach such as illustrated in Figure 2.1 must include

- Setting goals and expectations for their accomplishment
- Planning for, providing, and organizing resources to accomplish the goals
- Documenting and analyzing current workflows and processes and redesigning them to aid in achieving the established goals
- Monitoring goal achievement and putting in motion the feedback mechanisms to celebrate success and correct course where necessary
- Continuously be on the alert for and rapidly respond to opportunities or needs to adjust workflows and processes

Because goals imply a target for improvement, workflow and process management may also be called *continuous process improvement,* or *continuous quality improvement* (CQI). As previously noted in Chapter 1, with the extreme pressures of time, uncertainty, and complexity of medical care today (Stead and Lin 2009), knowledge workers often develop norms of denial, blame, and cover-up regarding stress, fatigue, and errors (Lundblad 2003). As a result, they tend to lack trust in goal setting. In fact, the landmark Institute of Medicine (IOM) work *To Err Is*

Human: Building a Safer Health System (Kohn, Corrigan, and Donaldson, Eds. 1999) was a wakeup call for the industry, not only recognizing for the first time the magnitude of medical errors, but that "silence surrounds this issue… [where] providers perceive the medical liability system as a serious impediment to systematic efforts to uncover and learn from errors." In the minds of many knowledge workers, failure is black and white, not shades of gray. They generally see no going back from a failure—if the patient dies, you cannot bring the person back to life. Hence, when missing a target by one if the goal is to reduce the ten serious diagnostic errors made per year to two errors per year, knowledge workers will focus on the failure to meet the goal rather than appreciate the forward progress and seek additional ways to get closer to the goal.

The IOM urged "designing a better health *system* as a more effective way to reduce errors than blaming individuals (some experts, such as Deming, believe improving processes is the *only* way to improve quality)." Stead and Lin's work also acknowledges that where "today's health care fails to deliver the most effective care and suffers substantially as a result of medical errors [and] many medical interventions undertaken today are in fact not necessary…these persistent problems do not reflect incompetence on the part of healthcare professionals—rather, they are a consequence of the inherent intellectual complexity of health care taken as a whole and a medical care environment that has not been adequately structured to help clinicians avoid mistakes or to systematically improve their decision making and practice."

With a focus on inputs, processes, and outputs and an emphasis in this book on EHR and HIT, workflow and process management may suggest solely an information system focus. However, it should be remembered throughout the discussion that adoption of EHR and HIT has a broader perspective and must be performed within a context of continuous quality improvement in a positive way. Similarly, implementing EHR and HIT is not "just" an IT project, but part of an ongoing commitment to transform health care. Every workflow and process that is performed using information—whether physical or mental, paper based or automated, to treat one patient or to create evidence-based medical knowledge—is the subject of workflow and process management within the context of EHR and HIT.

Definitions of Terms: Process and Workflow

Workflows and processes are the focus of workflow and process management. In Chapter 1 the following definitions, elaborated upon here, were introduced:

Process is the manner in which work is performed. In order to manage the overall work of an organization, unique processes are often identified. A process is usually constrained by a logical separation—by level of skill, or credential, needed to perform the work; by the nature of the product or service being provided (i.e., by function; by location where the service is provided); and often a combination of these. Consider a house that has separate rooms, one in which guests are entertained, another in which certain people cook food, etc. Each room has constraints with respect to who may use the room, for what purpose the room is used, and possibly the geographic location in which the house exists. So, too, a care delivery organization (CDO) will have a patient registration area, rooms where patients can be afforded privacy when being interviewed and examined, units where patients stay for a period of time so they can be closely monitored by nursing staff, specialized rooms for performing procedures, back offices where billing occurs, etc. Different functions are performed by nurses, physicians, laboratorians, phlebotomists, registration clerks, coders, finance officers, etc. Given the nature of the patient's illness or injury, not all locations or types of workers will be needed because not all services will be performed on every patient.

Workflow is the sequence of steps or hand-offs within a process and between processes. Consider a physician office visit. There is a specific sequence to the process the physician uses to greet the patient, ask questions about the nature of the illness or injury that is the reason for the visit, examine the patient, reach a conclusion about what is wrong, and decide on a treatment regimen. Even this process could be divided into smaller processes, such as history taking, physical examination, assessment and plan, and writing a prescription. This sequence is rarely altered. As a result, the addition of any new step, such as adding preventive screening reminders such as described in Case Study 1.1 or the requirement for the patient to be given a clinical summary at the conclusion of an office visit as required under the Centers for Medicare & Medicaid Services (CMS) (2010) incentive program for making meaningful use of EHR can present quite a significant redesign challenge.

Workflow also entails hand-offs within and between processes. For the physician office visit, there is also a registration process that is different than, but connected to, the check-in process where the nurse takes vital signs and prepares the patient to be seen by the physician. Any change in a process, such as the addition of preventive screening or clinical summary distribution, may focus on only one process or potentially impact more than one. In Case Study 1.1, the clinic decided to distribute preventive screening reminders to different types of staff.

In care delivery organizations (CDOs), there are many workflows and processes, from creating a bill to selecting a drug to treating a patient. Two simplified examples are provided in Table 2.1 and Table 2.2.

Taking a process inventory for the organization is recommended as an important step in workflow and process management (further described in Chapter 4). It is not uncommon for CDOs to have as many as twenty to fifty clinically related processes that might be associated with implementing an EHR or other HIT. While each process is generally documented separately, it is likely that if one were to document every process in a CDO, there would be many connection points between them. For example, there could be documentation of drug

Table 2.1 Hospital Billing Workflow and Process Example

1. Various source systems, such as laboratory information systems, radiology information systems, etc. collect charges each time a process (e.g., lab test, x-ray) is performed.
2. The source systems send charges to the patient financial system.
3. The patient financial system collects all charges for a patient during the admission.
4. On discharge of a patient, diagnosis and procedures codes are identified in the health information management department and entered into the patient financial system.
5. When the patient financial system determines the bill is complete, it generates an X12 837I claim transaction.
6. The claim transaction can be transmitted either to a clearinghouse or health plan directly.

Table 2.2 Ambulatory Care Prescription Workflow and Process Example

1. After interviewing and examining a patient,

2. The physician will think about the patient's:
  a. Diagnosis
  b. Lab results

3. Determine the class of drug used to treat the patient's condition
4. Recall variations within the class to identify the specific drug

5. Consider the patient's:
  a. Allergies
  b. Other medications being taken
  c. Insurance benefit formulary

6. The physician then opens the e-prescribing system to:
  a. Select the patient
  b. Enter the name of the drug being considered
  c. Respond to any drug contraindication warnings with an alternative choice of drug
  d. Discuss any alerts that the drug is expensive or not on the patient's insurance benefit formulary
  e. Check with the patient as to which retail pharmacy the prescription should be sent
  f. Command the system to create a prescription transaction that is sent directly to the patient's retail pharmacy of choice

7. If the prescription is for a controlled substance, the physician must generate a paper prescription from the e-prescribing system, sign it, and give it to the patient.

selection in a hospital performed by a physician where a charge is applied by the billing department for the drug having been administered to the patient.

Workflow versus process relates to technical reasons to focus on workflow rather than the entire process. From a technical perspective, *workflow* refers solely to the flow of work within a process, and *workflow management* refers to the business logic rules that direct that flow. Workflow in this context can be automated, and *workflow systems* are available to do so (Webster 2005). Frequently, workflow systems are associated with *electronic content and document management* (ECDM) systems that encompass document scanning, incorporation of digital content into a database, and assignment of work on the documents and/or digital content based on business rules. For example, in health care and even with an EHR, there often remain many documents handwritten on paper and/or dictated and transcribed into a digital format. These may be indexed based on certain attributes or content and distributed to staff for coding, then billing, then quality review, etc.

Dataflow is another term sometimes associated with workflow and process management, especially when the focus is to use automation to effect improvement. Dataflow refers to the way data are transformed as various operations within a process and across processes are performed (Simsion and Witt 2004; Bowman 2009). Dataflow modeling and analysis is a specific examination of how the value of a specific variable is changed during processing and how that impacts the value of other variables (Cohen 2010). Case Study 2.1 is an example of a dataflow that went very wrong.

Case Study 2.1: Poor Dataflow Yields Medical Error

In 2011, the *Chicago Tribune* (Graham and Dizikes 2011) reported on the death of baby Genesis. A consequence of a series of errors ultimately resulting in a massive overdose of sodium chloride killed the newborn infant. Although not all the details were described pending litigation, it appears that a physician entered a correct order for the drug into the hospital's computerized provider order entry system (CPOE). However, while the ordering system is connected to the hospital's pharmacy information system, it was not yet connected to the automated IV compounding machine that prepares intravenous bags for low-volume, highly individualized orders. As a result, a pharmacy technician transcribed the order from the CPOE system into the compounding system, making a data entry error that resulted in an amount of sodium chloride sixty times what was ordered. Although the data entry error could have been identified by automated alerts on the IV compounding machine, the alerts were not activated. The outermost label on the IV bag administered to the baby did not reflect its actual contents because the admixture would have required too many separate labels. Also contributing to the problem was that a blood test was performed on the infant showed abnormally high sodium levels, but the lab technician reviewing the results for quality control assumed the reading was so high it had to be inaccurate and did not take steps to investigate further.

Subsequently, it was reported that the hospital has activated alerts for IV compounding machines, strengthened "double-check" policies for all medications leaving the pharmacy, and implemented additional upgrades to electronic systems. Electronic communication gaps are common, often not addressed, or requiring custom-made software to exchange data. Experts have called for more oversight for EHR and other HIT that connect with medical devices, much as the Federal Aviation Administration (FAA) investigates every plane crash. The Food and Drug Administration (FDA) does not currently regulate EHR, nor does it have mandatory reporting of adverse events (only pharmaceutical manufacturers are required to report problems with drugs). The FDA created a working group to study the matter in 2009 (Ropes and Gray 2009), with no definitive resolution at time of this writing. Still, while better oversight of technology may be appropriate, many of the issues identified in this case study and others are those related to "people, policy, and process"—and to a lesser extent the technology.

Business process management software may yet be another tool that the healthcare industry should evaluate more closely. Today, such software is used extensively in the financial services industry, including banking and insurance. Gartner (Sinur and Hill 2010) has identified some sixty such products worldwide, of which it includes twenty-five in its "Magic Quadrant" analysis. The software enables "in-flight" changes to processes, such as changing data requirements for a business transaction (e.g., birth date is no longer required for opening a savings account), eliminating tasks (e.g., only one supervisor instead of two need to approve loans under $500), redirecting the work item (e.g., one staff member is in line for the next customer but is taking longer than normal so give another staff member the next customer), etc. The extent to which such software could have detected each of the problems in the workflow and associated dataflow described in Case Study 2.1 can only be speculated upon as such software has yet to be demanded by or developed for the healthcare industry.

Definitions of Terms: Workflow and Process Mapping

Workflow and process mapping is a term often used to describe the documentation of processes and their workflows. Other terms that may be used to describe such documentation may be process diagramming, flowcharting, or simply documenting workflows and processes. The intent of workflow and process mapping is to create a visual representation of a process and its workflow. Ideally, this should include the current way the process is performed, sometimes called the "*as-is*" map, as well as a redesigned, or "*to-be*" map.

Current process does not imply only a paper-based process, but any process that may need redesign for any reason. There are bottlenecks, delays, hassles, or errors occurring—even in a process that will not be automated, such as a surgical procedure or directing a patient to one or more destinations throughout the CDO. With respect to EHR and HIT, current maps of the paper-based or semi-automated processes may be documented prior to vendor selection to help identify desired functionality in the new system. A current process may also be a previously redesigned process that is not producing desired results. Finally, a process may also be considered current in light of an upgrade or modification that needs to occur, such as may result from a new regulation, availability of new technology, or organizational or governance structure changes.

Process analysis is the act of studying a current process to identify opportunities for improvement or ways that changes necessitated by external factors can be accommodated. Some opportunities for redesign or improvement result from the observations listed in Table 2.3.

Redesign refers to the result of analysis of the current process. It is a reflection of the collective wisdom of the stakeholders about how a process may be improved or needs to be changed to best take advantage of what is new. While it is generally the goal to make the best redesign possible, it must be remembered that anything new will have some unknowns. Educated guesses can be made as to what will work in the new situation, but there is always the potential that a redesigned process may need to be "tweaked" or further redesigned to achieve even better results. Sometimes further redesign is referred to as *optimization* because an early redesign may be such that only the basic or fundamental

Table 2.3 Observations That Are Opportunities for Redesign or Improvement Bottlenecks

• Delays
• Inconsistent data entries
• Invisible changes or correction to data
• Lack of adherence to standards of practice
• Lack of information
• Lack of quality controls
• Long cycle time
• Rework due to errors
• Role ambiguity
• Sneakerware (i.e., manual entry of data output from one system into another due to lack of connectivity between systems)
• Unnecessary duplications
• Unnecessary steps
• Variations across individuals, nursing units, sites, organizations

Source: Copyright © Margret\A Consulting, LLC. With permission.

changes are addressed, with later changes taking advantage of the more subtle and sophisticated changes that are possible. Finally, redesign should focus on optimizing processes, not making a change only because automation requires it, and certainly not only to replicate existing processes in an automated environment (McCoy 2011).

Annotation tools in different forms are available for documenting workflow and process mapping. While these tools are discussed in depth in Chapter 5, it is worth reflecting on the use of a diagramming tool in comparison to a simple listing of steps, such as illustrated in Table 2.1 and Table 2.2. The key difference between using a diagramming tool and a list to annotate a workflow and process is that the production of a picture via a diagramming tool is often considered "worth a thousand words." Workflow, especially where there are logical branches in decision making or variations in performance, is often better illustrated using a diagramming tool. Logical branching or variation is not as effectively illustrated in a list, such as "*when* this happens do this, but if that happens do something else."

Process mapping software is available to use in diagramming. Software ranges from simple to complex. In addition, almost every word processing, spreadsheet, and presentation application has some workflow and process annotation support as well. There are also add-on utilities that can boost the process mapping power of these applications. Unfortunately, there is no software package that will automatically generate a current workflow and process map or analyze and redesign a workflow and process for a CDO. It requires people to devote effort to create workflow and process maps as part of the overall workflow and process management program.

Relationship of Workflow and Process Management for EHR and HIT to Other CQI Methodologies

This book uses the term "workflow and process management" as an approach, or methodology, to document, analyze, redesign, and continuously monitor workflows and processes in relationship to goal achievement. There are other CQI theories and methodologies that in many ways are similar, but also have distinguishing features. A brief summary of a few of the most common that have been adopted in health care include:

■ ***Six Sigma*** is a business management strategy with its origins in the quality improvement work of pioneers such as Shewhart, Deming, Juran, Ishikawa, and others. Motorola was among the first US companies to use the statistical tools from which Six Sigma derives its name—that a Six Sigma process is one in which 99.99966% (or 3.4 million opportunities) of the products manufactured are statistically expected to be free of defects ("zero defects"). GE subsequently built training programs and created the hierarchy of Belt certifications (Green, Black, and Master) whose holders drive projects with clear financial targets set by the organization (Keller 2011). Six Sigma projects utilize the DMAIC (Define, Measure, Analyze, Improve, and Control) methodology to define a business process, analyze root causes of defects, and institute control systems to maintain performance. A key focus of Six Sigma in general is to establish a culture of process improvement from executive leadership down to all workers. Its criticisms often lie in its intensive solution approaches where there is no room for intuition, thus sometimes stifling creativity. There are also concerns that the model assumes that process data always conform to the normal distribution, and as such may not operate optimally or cost effectively for all processes. An example is that a heart pacemaker process may need higher standards than a direct mail advertising campaign (Antony 2004).

■ *Lean* is a set of tools, such as Value Stream Mapping (material and information flow mapping), Five S (organizing workspace), Kanban (pull systems), and Poka-Yoke (error-proofing) designed to reduce waste and inefficiency. It is a management philosophy derived primarily from the Toyota Production System (TPS), which focused on improving the flow, or smoothness, of work (through level loading [Heijunka]) to gain efficiencies, rather than solely waste reduction in transport, inventory, motion, waiting, overproduction, overprocessing, and defects—which have been translated for health care into errors and waste of talent (Womack et al. 2005). Lean also supports sustainment through visual controls (sometimes incorporating principles from the Balanced Scorecard approach to CQI), huddles (short stand-up sessions at the beginning of the day to anticipate the work of the day and obtain updates, often characterized as leadership rounding), assessments (audits), Gemba walks (regularly scheduled walkthroughs as a learning place to see what is happening), culture change, Improvement Model (Deming's Plan-Do-Study-Act [PDSA]), and Kaizen Improvement Events (time-limited, structured event, often lasting one to five days, in which a team focuses on determining best solutions for a particular process or problem). Criticisms of Lean appear to derive from an extreme focus on reducing waste, staff, and other cost-cutting measures. Some also observe that in using Lean, leadership often falls into the "command-and-control" type of management approach that does not serve knowledge workers well (Nelson 2011).

■ *Lean Six Sigma*, as the name implies, is a combination of Six Sigma and Lean, perhaps to overcome each of its criticisms, although also to achieve the best of both methodologies. With Lean focusing on improving process flow and Six Sigma designed to focus on process variation, both have proven compatible. IBM is a strong proponent of the combination of Lean and Six Sigma, suggesting that this approach drives organizations "not just to do things better but to do better things." (Byrne et al. n.d.) There is clearly a need for improvement, but there is also a critical need for innovation.

■ *Balanced Scorecard* is a set of strategic performance management tools (with a dashboard at the core) with roots in performance management.

Organizational mission, values, vision, and strategy drive specific performance measures, targets, and initiatives (viewed by executive leadership from a business or enterprise dashboard). There are also cascading measures for all departments and individuals. Dashboards may be linked to budget reporting, compensation, and process improvement strategies. In its first generation of design, the Balanced Scorecard focused on four perspectives: financial, customer, internal business processes, and learning and growth. In subsequent generations of the approach, dashboards have included any measure deemed important by the organization. As with all methodologies, there has been criticism surrounding technical flaws, early applications, few empirical studies, and perhaps most importantly a forced distribution of people that may lead to a "one-size-fits-all" strategy to performance management—especially as the tool has been widely used to support incentive-based pay (Walker and Dunn 2006; McLaughlin and Hays 2008).

■ ***Business Process Management*** (BPM) is a technique designed to help organizations fundamentally rethink how they do their work in order to improve customer service, cut operational costs, and become more competitive. A key driver for this technique has been automation. Much like Balanced Scorecard, the approach embodied by BPM is to start with a high-level assessment of mission and strategic goals. Also called business process reengineering, this assessment defines work processes that execute decisions. In order to effect better alignment between mission and strategic goals, technology is employed to support processes. It assumes that technology cannot support improvement in a process if it is fundamentally inefficient or outmoded (Jeston and Nelis 2008). Lack of focus on the human dimension has been the primary criticism of this approach to process improvement, including that management thinking—often described as the largest cause of failure in an organization—never changes as a result of BPM (Davenport 1996).

■ ***ISO 9000 Quality Management System*** is a set of internationally recognized standards, updated to ISO 9001 in 2000, that affords greater applicability to service industries, moving from a system-based management approach to one that is more process-based (Sweeney and Heaton 2000). In discussing ISO 9000 Quality Management applicability to health care, Crago (2000) notes that ISO defines *quality management* as "all activities of the overall management function that determine the quality policy, objectives, and responsibilities and implement them by means such as quality planning, quality control, quality assurances, and quality improvement within the quality system." It defines *quality system* as "the organization structure, procedures, processes, and resources needed to implement quality management." ISO 9000 essentially provides a methodology and framework to evaluate whether an organization has efficiently and effectively defined, organized, integrated, and synchronized its operational resources to produce continuous quality improvement. ISO 9000 forms the basis for a registration and certification process that many companies find useful. Although Crago describes ISO 9000 as complementary to Six Sigma and Joint Commission accreditation in health care, there has been some interest in seeking ISO 9000 registration as an alternative to the Joint Commission accreditation, with proponents citing high cost and disruption of service inherent in the Joint Commission accreditation process (Diamond 1998).

In considering these different approaches, it would appear that each has strengths and weaknesses, including how well the approach itself is used to carry out its goals. It is also clear that combinations of these approaches have been tried as a means to overcome singular weaknesses and capitalize on strengths. A post to *Harvard Business Review's* Blog Network titled "Uniting the Religions of Process Improvement" (Power 2011) is a testament to both the intense need for process improvement and the complexity of making it happen. The blog suggests that taking the best from each approach and creating a tailored program that fits a particular organization could better institutionalize continuous improvement that is sustainable for decades. Commenters to this blog acknowledge that characterizing the approaches as religions may be a useful metaphor that emphasizes the dogmatic nature of some organizations' approaches to adopting one or another approach exclusively. However, several commenters suggested that creating yet another, albeit tailored, approach could be only creating another dogma. One commenter specifically suggested that any dogma that exists or emerges is not a suitable substitute for thinking; and that continuous improvement is about thinking, not a tool that will by itself solve problems for an organization.

It is hoped that this book does not create another dogma or spin on an existing dogma. Its goals are to first convince CDOs making an investment in EHR and HIT to address process improvement, and second to provide tools that have been helpful in doing so. Whether or not an organization has already adopted one of the common approaches to process improvement, it is sincerely hoped that attention will be given to the people, policy, and process aspects of implementing EHR and HIT. If nothing else, this brief journey through process improvement approaches should highlight that all organizations need process improvement that attends to the human element.

Healthcare Workflow and Process Management Timing

Workflow and process management has already been described as a *management* approach, meaning a continuous process and culture of embodying right. Because of the enormity of the investment that is EHR and HIT, not only in dollars but in time and level of change, determining what is right needs to begin at the beginning and be carried throughout the duration not only of implementation but also ongoing use of the EHR and HIT. It is therefore suggested that

CDOs consider applying an intensive effort to workflow and process management at five stages with respect to EHR and HIT:

1. **Early planning** for EHR and HIT should encourage simultaneous attention to workflows and processes known to be broken. Even if the organization ends up never acquiring EHR or HIT, there will be benefit from fixing broken processes; and the exercise will also contribute to creating desire for improvement, potentially through automation.

2. **Prior to selection** of EHR and HIT, a CDO can benefit from mapping all current workflows and processes that will be impacted by the technology, again not only to stimulate interest in EHR and HIT, but also to analyze them and identify the desired functionality and usability characteristics that will result in improvement with automation. It is noted that certification of EHR technology for the federal incentive program does not afford this level of functionality detail and does not address usability at all. In fact, the preamble to the incentive program regulations indicate that "Certification criteria represent the minimum capabilities EHR technology needs to include and have properly implemented in order to achieve certification. Certification criteria do not preclude EHR developers from including additional capabilities that are not required for purposes of certification" (CMS 2010). The certification criteria do not get to the level of detail that would reflect how the functionality fits into a CDO's workflows and processes, the necessary control points, connection points, and other aspects of design that both vary significantly among vendors and that are vital to effective use.

3. **During implementation**, whether or not the EHR/HIT vendor supports workflow and process mapping, a CDO should study its newly redesigned workflows and processes and ensure that they can be carried out with the EHR and HIT. In this case, however, the CDO needs to realize that some redesigned workflows and processes may represent an ideal situation that the vendor does not yet address and was a compromise by the CDO in its selection process. In this case, the CDO needs to work with the vendor to find a suitable workaround and urge the vendor to address the process in functionality built into future versions. There may also be functionality within the vendor product that had not been anticipated by the CDO and that may enable further improvement in workflows and process than expected. Finally, at each of these steps, the redesigned workflows and processes must be modified to reflect the latest design. These should then be used in system testing and training.

4. **Adoption** is the stage during which end users start to use the EHR and HIT. During this stage, basic functionality must be used by all so early milestones can be achieved. The redesigned workflows and processes should be used as a guide by end users and management to monitor workflow and process performance. Once again, however, these workflows and processes should not be considered as "cast in stone." Despite best efforts, the workflows and

processes may not work as intended; or they may work but still not be followed appropriately, so that retraining and reinforcement on the new workflows and processes are needed.

5. **Optimization** is the stage in which users who have successfully mastered the basic functionality and are reaching early milestones seek to improve their use of the system—yet another opportunity for applying workflow and process management.

Healthcare Workflow and Process Management Stakeholders

The key people needed within a CDO must be identified for each aspect of workflow and process management. Stakeholders include everyone from executive leadership to those who perform processes on a day-to-day basis, along with supervisors, information managers and technologists, process analysts and auditors, consultants and facilitators, vendors, and customers.

Executive leadership commitment is essential to successful workflow and process management. A culture of continuous quality improvement assures the necessary goal setting and resourcing. Adler (2007), previously cited in Chapter 1 as a strong supporter of workflow and process management, is also a strong supporter of setting goals and expectations to achieve them. He further observes that "if your practice is broken, you need to fix it before you try to bring an EHR on board. Dysfunctional organizations are likely to have dysfunctional implementations. Excellent communication, clear lines of authority, and an explicit decision-making process promote success." Such guidance is applicable to every type of CDO.

End users are those who use a product, such as an EHR, as opposed to those who design, sell, purchase, or implement a product. In the context of healthcare workflow and process management, end users include anyone who utilizes information in the course of providing services and who will be a user of EHR and HIT. It is the end user who ultimately is impacted by any workflow and process redesign. As a result, it is end users who must be "at the table" for workflow and process mapping, analysis, and redesign. Consider Case Study 2.2, which describes redesigning a patient room for a new hospital.

Case Study 2.2: Redesigning a Patient Room for a New Hospital

An existing hospital was building a replacement. It would contain the same number of beds but would conform to the latest building construction codes, be more spacious, provide single rooms for all patients, and allow room for outpatient and special procedures expansion. An architect specializing in hospital design was engaged. Early in the process, the architect visited the old facility and spoke with staff about what they liked and did not like. The architect recommended that workflows be studied, and time and motion studies be conducted to collect baseline data. The architect also brought several designs that were circulated widely for staff to see and on which to provide input. Finally, the building was constructed and in the later stages of interior construction, a mock patient room was created and a vendor supplied an example of the latest technology for patient beds. To approach the room safely during construction, a temporary walkway with walls was constructed, and a whiteboard lined the entire length of the walls—to be used for staff to write comments about the room. Many people, from physicians and nurses to housekeeping and dietary staff, visited and recorded their remarks. The rooms and equipment were then settled upon and constructed and installed, respectively. All appeared to be going well, and staff felt they had been given many opportunities for input.

Shortly before moving day, representatives from the IT department went to the new hospital to finalize plans for moving computer equipment. They observed that the nursing department had yet to decide whether to use carts with computers (called wireless on wheels, or WOWs), which also accommodate bar code readers and medication trays, or tablets they would carry on a sling. Nursing staff thought the tablets might be more convenient as they had found the WOWs they had in the old hospital heavy to push. However, it was found that the patient rooms did not accommodate wheeling in a WOW, nor was there any shelf or furniture on which to place a tablet, wireless bar code reader, and medication while administering to the patient. In their reviews of the mock room, clinicians had not considered that they would be significantly enhancing their use of HIT, and had focused solely on clinical aspects, such as how easy it was to view monitors, where to hang IV bags, the proximity of the sink to the patient, how easily patients could call for a nurse, etc.

So while this case study illustrates the excellent opportunity afforded everyone for input and thus illustrates that process maps can also be posted on walls or shared via groupware for such input, it also describes the need for potential users of what is new to be fully educated and guided to include all aspects of the workflows and processes being performed. Chapter 5 further discusses workflow and process teams and team governance to ensure that such input is considered.

Process analyst is an individual who is skilled in workflow and process mapping. While it is not necessary for a CDO to have a process analyst on staff to gain the benefits of process mapping and redesign, such an individual can help make the connection between executive leadership and end users. Case Study 2.3 illustrates a scenario where a process analyst was cultivated from within the CDO.

Case Study 2.3: Clinic Staff Mapping the Refill Process

A large clinic was planning to select an EHR. It recently had a positive experience with using a CQI methodology to streamline patient registration and improve staff leveling by creating multiple, standardized pods throughout the facility so that clerical and nursing staff could move easily between the pods, as demand for staff varied during a day and over time. They were interested in adopting a similar approach to their automation project. Physicians had not previously been part of the CQI project, but had appreciated the impact the results had on their work and so were willing to participate.

The clinic started with creating physician-nurse teams and used a staff member from the patient registration area who had been actively engaged in the previous project as the facilitator. They decided to start with the prescription refill process because physicians were anxious to acquire a stand-alone e-prescribing system for their smart phones to take advantage of the federal e-prescribing incentive that had just been initiated. Throughout the course of documenting their workflows, they discovered many interesting practices—some of which could be adopted by all, a few variations that would have to be accommodated, and other practices that were deemed potentially dangerous and needed significant redesign. One of the physicians took on the role of being the steward for standardizing the refill process to the extent feasible, both to continue to take advantage of their new staff leveling structure and to ensure that physicians could cover for one another as their patients may have needed prescriptions renewed during a vacation. Another physician who had previously used the EHR at a VA hospital during training commented that ultimately the EHR would enable a universal medication list that would aid patient safety. The registration supervisor/process facilitator also observed that the EHR would support an integrated master person index that would reduce errors that were frequently occurring as result of creating duplicate paper records.

For the CDO described in this case study, the staff were well prepared to take on the task of mapping their workflows and processes, and appeared to gain not only improved processes as a result, but also improved understanding of what life would be like with EHR. In this case the person designated to facilitate the process came to the task with some on-the-job training and positive results that encouraged teaming among all stakeholders. CDOs can cultivate their own process analysts in this way. If, however, there are team-building and change-management tasks that must also be associated with the workflow and process management, a professional analyst may be needed. Table 2.4 provides a sample job description for a process analyst job.

Many people who are new to workflow and process mapping find that it takes them a while to get the right level of detail for what they are mapping, and they often miss steps because they process them so naturally today. These missed steps are often those that are performed mentally—and those that are related to decision making that form the basis for clinical decision support (CDS) in EHRs. Omitting decision-making steps from a workflow and process map can cause them to be overlooked in the actual implementation of an EHR, and may result in unintended consequences (Han et al. 2005). The Agency for Healthcare Quality and Research (AHRQ) maintains a Patient Safety Network providing primers for various safety targets, including over 300 articles describing unintended consequences of CPOE systems and ways to overcome such occurrences.

Table 2.4 Process Analyst Job Description

Job Title: Process Analyst
Job Summary: The process analyst will be part of an ongoing effort to continuously improve workflows and processes in the care delivery organization's quest for providing value-based health care. The scope of responsibility of the analyst will include, but not be limited to, the optimization of the electronic health record and other health information technology.
Job Responsibilities:
1. Manages the organization's workflow and process management charter.
2. Conducts workflow and process discovery efforts through interviews, job shadowing, and other effective methodologies.
3. Creates and maintains accurate and complete "as is" workflow and process documentation.
4. Facilitates collaborative efforts to analyze, determine root cause of problems, and evolves "as is" workflows and processes into more effective, efficient, and compliant "to be" processes.
5. Helps develop training courses, workshops, and other methods to support workflow and process management.
6. Aids management in effecting change.
7. Participates in other workflow and process management activities as necessary.
Job Requirements:
1. Good listener and natural leader; good interpersonal skills; strong verbal and written communication skills.
2. Facilitation skills at every level of the organization; comfortable with creating collaborative and cooperative work environments.
3. Strategic thinker; ability to think analytically and problem solve.
4. Attention to detail, while seeing the big picture; ability to simplify complex things for wider understanding.
5. Bachelor's degree required (health administration, statistics, or other equivalent domain preferred).
6. Experience in workflow and process mapping. Lean Six Sigma background preferred.
7. Facile with Microsoft Office and Visio or other annotation software.

Source: Copyright © Margret\A Consulting, LLC. With permission.

One way to assure a more complete workflow and process mapping experience is by having the person who performs the process draw a map and then have someone who does not know anything about the process attempt to fully understand it. Wherever there are questions about "how did you get from A to B?", it is very likely that detail has been omitted. This review, however, can be resource intensive. While a process analyst is not totally immune from overlooking important details, it is much more likely that a skilled analyst will be able to ask those performing the process key questions to assure completeness. The process analyst in this role serves as a *process auditor.*

Finally, a process analyst who is not intimately involved in actually performing the process can be much more comfortable in asking the "tough questions" when it comes to analyzing current workflows and processes and offering recommendations for redesigning processes. A neutral third party can diffuse the "blame game."

Other stakeholders in workflow and process management have unique roles, but also cautionary notes with respect to their roles:

■ *Supervisors* should serve as extensions of executive leadership and provide support for workflow and process management. They generally should avoid being the front-line process mappers. Even where supervisors are "working supervisors," their role in process mapping will often be perceived as one of oversight, where the result frequently is a process map that only reflects the documented policy and procedure, and does not include all the variations, workarounds, and other "warts" that individuals may not want to reveal in front of their supervisors, but which need to be included in order to accurately characterize the current workflow and process. Without these being recognized, there will be less opportunity for analysis to achieve successful redesign.

■ *Consultants* can be brought in from outside the organization to train and support workflow and process management. Consultants should not be used as substitutes for executive leadership commitment or end-user engagement. Without these "bookends," workflow and process management may be viewed as an exercise focused on a specific project and not an ongoing management approach.

■ *Vendors* are identified separately from consultants because in the context of workflow and process management for EHR and HIT, such vendors have been notably absent with but a few exceptions. Many vendors have been reluctant to get into workflow and process management because their price point, and hence their staffing resources, often do not permit them to devote time to non-installation activities. In addition, workflow and process management may be valued by the vendor, but viewed as an internal management issue. While there is some merit in this perspective, EHR and HIT vendors who at least encourage their buyers to attend to workflow and process management are being realistic about the fact that "people, policy, and process" are the primary contributing factors to success with the EHR and HIT. Vendors who sell at a higher price point and embrace workflow and process management typically set the expectation that they will direct workflow and process mapping, analysis, and redesign.

■ *Customers* must also be considered stakeholders in workflow and process management, even if they do not directly engage in the activity themselves. For CDOs, the ultimate customer is the patient and his or her family or other caregivers. Health care is becoming a much more competitive industry, and patients do notice workflows and processes as embodied in wait times, lost clinical documentation, privacy and security with respect to EHRs, customer service "attitudes," and to a growing extent the notion that a CDO is adopting new technology to improve their service delivery and quality of care. Patients as customers can be indirectly engaged in workflow and process management through satisfaction surveys, focused interviews, comment cards, and report cards.

Caution must be applied in defining the customer beyond the patient. Sometimes CDOs pay greater attention to physicians as customers. Such physician customers, however, are end users of the EHR and other HITs. The Institute for Healthcare Improvement, in its Framework for Engaging Physicians in Quality and Safety (Reinertsen et al. 2007), recommends making physicians partners, not customers. Engaging physicians in workflow and process management takes some ingenuity and perseverance (Caldwell et al. 2005). Jackson (2009) notes that "we physicians are not necessarily resistant or obstructionist when it comes to Lean or quality improvement efforts…[but] success will be [achieved] when you find the ways to align the Lean principles with the physicians' goals—they are not incompatible. The true transformation in the medical culture will be achieved when this alignment results in trust and cooperation among all providers of patients' care." Table 2.5 lists some critical success factors in engaging physicians in workflow and process management.

Table 2.5   Engaging Physicians in Workflow and Process Management

1. Engage physician and board leadership in creating a charter for physician engagement in workflow and process management. Call the charter a quality agenda.
2. Include in the charter a plan to educate leaders, identify champions, fully support the masses, and work to turn around laggards and resisters.
3. Involve physicians from the beginning, visibly acknowledging their participation. Do not appoint non-physicians to lead physicians, or allow non-physicians to substitute for physicians.
4. Communicate early and often, in an open and candid, but respectful manner.
5. Value physicians' time with equivalently ranked persons' time in support.
6. Find ways to engage physicians that do not require meetings; where meetings are necessary, stick to a short, action-oriented agenda with documentation supplied well in advance and follow up documentation to all.
7. Provide a return for the physicians' investment. Focus on what is important to the physician: clinical quality, patient safety, and personal productivity, not financial metrics or personal promotion of administration.
8. Garner trust, and expect verification.
9. Focus on the 80/20, and not more. Do not assume that one size fits all or that there will be agreement on all standards, but expect integration.
10. Exhibit the courage of one's convictions. Provide back-up all the way to the board of directors as may be necessary.

Source: Copyright © Margret\A Consulting, LLC. With permission.

Other customers of CDOs in health care may include health plans, accrediting agencies, the population of the community in which the CDO exists, and others. It is important to remain cognizant of these customers' needs, while not displacing the ultimate customer, which is the patient.

Finally, end users in their role as ultimate users of the redesigned workflows and processes really have two roles. Their role in documenting how they currently perform their workflows and processes is essential. They are vital to analyzing and redesigning processes because they know their processes best. But, as professionals, they also have a role in the management of workflow and process. End users should view themselves as stewards of workflow and process, and be guided in and expected to contribute to the ongoing effort to manage workflows and processes.

Relationship and Importance of Workflow and Process Management to Change Management

The previous discussion clearly introduces the notion that workflow and process management is closely related to change management. While different, workflow and process management can be seen as a way to initiate change management; and certainly change management is a necessary component of workflow and process management.

Change management in the context of organizations and workflow and process management is an approach to transitioning people from a current state to a desired future state. Change management is as much a set of principles as techniques; philosophy and psychology. Change management principles include understanding the *system,* that is, the environment, culture, vision, goals, planning, communications, training, processes, relationships, behaviors, resistance management, feedback analysis, celebration, and course correction.

Steps in Workflow and Process Management

In preparation then to move forward with workflow and process management, the following steps are discussed in the remainder of this book:

1. *Prepare for workflow and process management.* In this step, the CDO should understand and, if necessary, cultivate its organizational culture for continuous quality improvement. It should evaluate its leadership and change management capacities and take the necessary steps to improve upon them. Designate a governance structure, including a workflow and process management charter described further in Chapter 3, for the focused workflow and process management associated with the EHR and HIT project. While some organizations may approach EHR as solely a government mandate,

Table 2.6   National Health Priorities

• Improve quality, safety, and efficiency and reduce health disparities
• Engage patients and families
• Improve care coordination
• Improve population and public health
• Ensure adequate privacy and security protections for personal health information

Source: Summarized from National Priorities Partnership, National Quality Forum, 2010.

others will want to embrace it for what it should be—a means to support a clinical transformation that achieves the nation's health priorities, identified in Table 2.6. Whatever the purpose, the CDO should envision the future state with EHR and HIT and set specific, measurable goals to monitor success. It can be helpful to assess end user readiness for the clinical transformation about to occur. Finally, develop a plan for documentation of workflow and process mapping, analysis, and redesign.

2. *Take a process inventory.* CDOs tend to have many of the same processes, as will be outlined in Chapter 4, but there are variations, depending on the type of CDO and its unique mission. Confirming existing processes and identifying new processes desired helps the CDO scope the workflow and process-mapping project for each stage. These can then be prioritized and resourced. A database for the workflow and process maps helps manage the output and enables the CDO to make the connections between each of the processes to minimize gaps.

3. *Select tools and train those who will perform the workflow and process mapping, analysis, and redesign.* While the choice of tool may be dictated by a formal approach already existing in the organization, some CDOs prefer to take a purposeful approach to selecting tools that will most help them with workflow and process management within the context of automation. Some CDOs prefer to standardize on a tool so they may have more universal utility; others may find that a mix of tools will get the job done better for them. Whatever tool or tools will be used as described in Chapter 5, those who will perform the mapping or provide input should have the appropriate level of training. To make this determination, clarify roles for each of the stakeholders.

4. *Map current workflows and processes*, as described extensively in Chapter 6. Document all process steps, including and especially those performed mentally on information, in the sequence as performed. Subsidiary documents may also need to be created, such as decision tables for complex decision-making or protocols that describe a standard set of criteria always applied to an operation. It is advisable to collect all forms and reports that are associated with each step in the process. These will serve to support selection and implementation. This is especially important where the CDO has special data or reporting requirements.

5. *Obtain baseline data.* Although not all CDOs will incorporate performance metrics, further defined in Chapter 7, in workflow and process mapping for EHR and HIT, it is an important element of process improvement, an aid in setting goals, and a means of measuring progress toward their achievement. To obtain baseline data, the CDO should define metrics, develop data collection tools, determine an appropriate sampling methodology, collect the data, assess reliability and validity of the data, and then document the baseline data for use in subsequent monitoring of goal achievement.

6. *Validate workflow and process maps.* Post maps in an accessible location for all stakeholders to provide input. Have them review the maps for completeness, clarity, variations, connection points, scope, and, above all else, the decision steps in the process. If necessary, a process auditor may be used to further validate the maps, such as described in Chapter 8. Finalize the current, or "as-is" maps.

7. *Analyze the "as-is" maps and identify redesign opportunities.* Obtain from stakeholders opportunities they see for improvement. Utilize the six quality areas promoted by the Institute of Medicine in its *Crossing the Quality Chasm* work identified in Table 2.7 to help the analysis with respect to quality of care and patient safety. Consider other opportunities for improvement, such as improving productivity, reducing hassle factors, new ways to generate revenue, assuring compliance, supporting continuity of care, etc. Other redesign aids are supplied in Chapter 9.

8. *Conduct root cause analysis to redesign workflows and processes.* While there may be many apparent opportunities for improvement, it is important to understand whether a proposed redesign is directed at a symptom or the underlying cause of a problem. Both must be addressed, but only addressing symptoms will not achieve as complete or sustainable improvement as desired. Utilize root cause analysis tools as described in Chapter 10 to help identify underlying problems to be addressed; then redesign the workflows and processes to address all issues.

9. *Implement redesigned workflows and processes.* At whatever stage the CDO is in its planning, selecting, implementing, gaining adoption, or optimizing EHR and HIT, implementing redesigned processes will require change management strategies, such as described in Chapter 11.

Table 2.7   IOM Crossing the Quality Chasm: Six Quality Areas

• Safe	• Timely
• Effective	• Patient centered
• Efficient	• Equitable

Source: Institute of Medicine, 2001. Crossing the Quality Chasm: A New Health System for the 21st Century. Washington, DC: National Academy Press.

10. *Monitor goal achievement.* To "close the loop," assure that milestones toward goals are met in a timely manner. Celebrate their successful achievement. Correct course if necessary by reviewing how the redesigned workflows and processes are being carried out. Make adjustments as needed and continue to monitor, using tools such as those described in Chapter 12.

Key Points

- How work is performed (**process**), including its sequence (**workflow**) and the credentials of the person performing the work is the focus of **workflow and process management**. Within the context of making a clinical transformation aided by EHR and HIT, workflow and process management focuses on understanding and optimizing how inputs are processed into outputs that contribute to a positive effect.
- There are many **stakeholders** in workflow and process management and these must especially include executive management and end users, including physicians and other knowledge workers who will be directly impacted by the change that EHR and HIT bring to their practice of medicine.
- A variety of approaches as well as tools for **continuous quality improvement** exists, and one or more may already be used by a CDO. Do not get mired down in the process of improvement; choose a set of techniques that assures you attend to the **human elements** of process and technology, and then "**just do it**"—early and often!

References

Adler, K.G., 2007 (Feb.). "How to Successfully Navigate Your EHR Implementation." *Family Practice Management*, 14(2): 33–39.

AHRQ, n.d. "Patient Safety Primers: Computerized Provider Order Entry," AHRQ Patient Safety Network. Available at: http://psnet.ahrq.gov/collectionBrowse. aspx?taxonomyID=662

Antony, J., 2004. "Some Pros and Cons of Six Sigma: An Academic Perspective." *The TQM Magazine*, 16(4): 303–306.

Bowman, D., 2009. Data Mapping and Data Movement: Extract Transform and Load (ETL). Information Management Architect. Available at: http://www.information-managmeent-architect.com/data-mapping.html

Byrne, G. et al., n.d. "Driving Operational Innovation Using Lean Six Sigma." IBM Institute for Business Value. Available at: http://www-935.ibm.com/services/uk/ bcs/pdf/driving_operational_innovation_using_lean_six_sigma.pdf

Caldwell, C. et al., 2005. The Role of Senior Leaders: Engaging Physicians. *Lean Six Sigma for Healthcare*. Milwaukee, WI: ASQ Quality Press, 135–142.

Centers for Medicare & Medicaid Services (CMS), 2010 (July 28). 42 CFR 412, 413, 422 et al. Medicare and Medicaid Programs; Electronic Health Record Incentive Program; Final Rule.

Cohen, G., 2010 Agile Excellence for Product Managers: *A Guide to Creating Winning Products with Agile Development Teams.* Silicon Valley, CA: Super Star Press.

Crago, M.G., 2000 (Nov.). "Patient Safety, Six Sigma & ISO 9000 Quality Management." *Quality Digest.* Available at: http://www.qualitydigest.com/nov00/html/patient.html

Davenport, T.H., 1996. "The Fad That Forgot People." Fast Company. Available at: http://www.rotman.utoronto,ca/~evans/teach363/fastco/reengin.htm

Diamond, F., 1998 (Nov.). "The Mountain Named JCAHO Meets the Tremor Called ISO." *Managed Care Magazine.* Available at: http://www.managedcaremag.com/archives/9811/9811.iso.html

Graham, J. and C. Dizikes, 2011 (June 27). "Baby's Death Spotlights Safety Risks Linked to Computerized Systems." *Chicago Tribune.* Available at: http://articles.chicagotribune.com/2011-06-27/news/ct-met-technology-errors-20110627_1_electronic-medical-records-physicians-systems

Han, Y.Y. et al., 2005 (Dec.). "Unexpected Increased Mortality After Implementation of a Commercially Sold Computerized Physician Order Entry System." *Pediatrics*, 116(9): 1506–1512.

Institute of Medicine, 2001. *Crossing the Quality Chasm: A New Health System for the 21st Century.* Washington, DC: National Academy Press, 39–40.

IOM. 1999. *To Err Is Human: Building a Safer Health System.* Washington, DC: National Academy Press, 2, 4.

Jackson, M., 2009 (Sept. 15). "Engaging Physicians in Lean Transformation." NC State of Business, North Carolina State University. Available at: http://blogs.ies.ncsu.edu/NCStateofBusiness.php/2009/09/15/engaging-physicians-in-lean-transformation/

Jeston, J. and J. Nelis, 2008. *Business Process Management, second edition.* Oxford: Butterworth-Heinemann.

Karsh, B., 2009 (June). "Clinical Practice Improvement and Redesign: How Change in Workflow Can Be Supported by Clinical Decision Support." AHRQ Publication No. 09-0054-EF. Rockville, MD: Agency for Healthcare Research and Quality.

Keller, P., 2011. *Six Sigma Demystified, second edition.* New York: The McGraw-Hill Companies, Inc.

Lundblad, J.P., 2003 (Winter). "A Review and Critique of Rogers' Diffusion of Innovation Theory as it Applies to Organizations." *Organization Development Journal.* Available at: http://findarticles.com/p/articles/mi_qa5427/is_200301/ai_n21341140/

McCoy, M.J., 2011. "Change Management and Process Redesign." *ACOG*: Health Information Technology. Available at: http://www.acog.org/departments/dept_notice.cfm?recno=47&bulletin=4844

McLaughlin, D.B. and J.M. Hays, 2008. *Healthcare Operations Management*, Chicago, IL: Health Administration Press, 70–96

National Priorities Partnership, 2010 (Oct. 14). Input to the Secretary of Health and Human Services on Priorities for the 2011 National Quality Strategy, Washington, DC: National Quality Forum.

Nelson, M., 2011. Sustaining Lean in Healthcare: Developing and Engaging Physician Leadership. Boca Raton, FL: CRC Press.

Power, B., 2011 (Mar. 7). "Uniting the Religions of Process Improvement." HBR Blog Network. Available at: http://blogs.hbr.org/cs/2011/03/uniting_the_religions_of_proce.html

Ropes & Gray, 2009 (Apr. 2). FDA Creates Working Group on Regulation of Electronic Health Record Systems. Rope & Gray LLP: News & Publications. Available at: http://www.ropegray.com/fdaregulationofelectronichealthrecordsystems/

Reinertsen, J.L. et al., 2007. "Engaging Physicians in a Shared Quality Agenda." Institute for Healthcare Improvement, Innovation Series 2007.

Simsion, G.C. and G.C. Witt, 2004. Data Modeling Essentials, third edition. San Francisco: Morgan Kaufmann Press.

Sinur, J. and J.B. Hill, 2010 (Oct. 18). "Magic Quadrant for Business Process Management Suites," Gartner Publication: G00205212.

Stead, W.W. and H.S. Lin, Eds., 2009. Computational Technology for Effective Health Care: Immediate Steps and Strategic Directions. National Research Council, Washington, DC: National Academies Press, S-2.

Sweeney, J. and C. Heaton, 2000. "Interpretations and Variations of ISO 9000 in Acute Health Care." International Journal for Quality in Health Care, 12(3): 203–209.

Walker, K.B. and L.M. Dunn, 2006 (Annual). "Improving Hospital Performance and Productivity with the Balanced Scorecard." *Academy of Health Care Management Journal,* 2: 85–110.

Webster, C., 2005 (Feb. 14). "EHR Workflow Management Systems in Ambulatory Care." *2005 HIMSS Annual Conference,* Dallas.

Womack, J.P. et al., 2005. "Going Lean in Health Care," *Innovation Series*, Cambridge, MA: Institute for Healthcare Improvement.

Chapter 3

Step 1: Assess Readiness for Workflow and Process Management

Effective leaders help others to understand the necessity of change and to accept a common vision of the desired outcome.

—John P. Kotter

This chapter initiates the steps in workflow and process management when applied to improving the quality of health and health care through use of automation. It describes strategies for determining the readiness of a care delivery organization (CDO) to manage the level of change that EHR and HIT require of knowledge workers. It provides specific, practical tools for assessing an organization's culture and change capacity, visioning, assessing and addressing end-user needs with respect to EHR and HIT adoption, and setting goals in support of a continuous quality improvement (CQI) program. It urges CDOs to establish a workflow and process management governance structure explained in a project charter.

Understand Organizational Culture for Change

Why spend time on understanding readiness for EHR and HIT when their meaningful use is being mandated by the federal government?

There are many potential answers to this question, but the bottom line is suggested by the question itself. An EHR must be *meaningfully used;* it must be fully integrated into the fabric of how CDOs perform their work and many believe that requires an organizational culture that truly embraces continuous quality improvement and supports their workers in making the transition to new workflows and processes. An EHR that is fully utilized represents a *clinical transformation* in which not only is the healthcare documentation process changed, but how information is gathered and used in the practice of medicine to support clinicians in their decision making.

Generally speaking, the federal incentive money for EHR—which is a voluntary program—is unlikely to cover the full cost, and certainly not the level of effort it takes to ensure that the right EHR is selected for the organization and implemented in a manner that will enable it to be optimally used. Repeatedly it is heard from those who have previously implemented an EHR: if they had to do it over again, they would spend more time planning in order to spend less time backfilling, dealing with workarounds, cajoling resisters, and fixing broken workflows and processes that should have been fixed at the start.

And, yes, there could be better product. It is sad, but probably true, however, that it will not be until the majority of CDOs adopt current EHRs that those modifications will be made such that EHRs truly support cognitive processes. In intensively studying eight of what are considered among the nation's best implementations of EHR, the National Academy of Sciences (Stead and Lin 2009) found that

> IT applications … are often designed in ways that simply mimic existing paper-based forms and provide little support for the cognitive tasks of clinicians or the workflow of the people who must actually use the system. Moreover, these applications do not take advantage of human-computer interaction principles, leading to poor designs that can increase the chance of error, add to rather than reduce work, and compound the frustrations of executing required tasks.

Perhaps the Academy's study results sound like a testament to wait for better product. But that really is not the answer because even if the products were better today, it would still take considerable effort to replace paper-based processes with automated ones. It is very likely that not until another generation of product is implemented where the transition is from an old form of automation to a new form of automation will such implementation be easier. It is interesting, however, to see that despite the longer-term existence of automation in other industries, there continues to be a need for continuous quality improvement that requires supporting workers with the transition.

So with all that having been said, the assumption moving forward is that human factors, what this book refers to as "people, policy, and process," significantly contribute to success with EHR and HIT. Addressing human factors does not have to take a long time and can be performed concurrently with other aspects of EHR and HIT implementation.

Human factors begin at the top, with the culture of the organization embracing continuous quality improvement and understanding how to effect change

(Boan and Funderburk 2003). Case Study 3.1 relates an experience that suggests the CDO's executive leadership—the "C Suite" of chief executive officer (CEO), chief operating officer (COO), chief information officer (CIO), etc.—truly created an effective culture.

Case Study 3.1: The Itinerant C Suite

A few years ago, a hospital believed it was ahead of the curve on adopting automation and thus applied for an HIT award. Part of the award process entailed a site visit. The contact person for the hospital was the CIO. When the visitor arrived at the hospital, the CIO greeted the visitor at the front desk. En route to the IT department, the CIO both chatted with the visitor and greeted or accepted greetings from a number of others walking by. The CIO asked a passing physician how a new technology was working; a nurse thanked the CIO for seeing that something on a patient care unit was fixed; a billing department staff member asked for help with something, and in exchanging greetings with the COO, the CIO introduced the visitor and noted the impending visit later in the day.

When settled into the CIO's office, the visitor commented on the congeniality of the organization and asked how the CIO kept track of everything. The CIO stated that the CEO's management philosophy was to "walk the talk." It was expected that every member of the entire management team—from CEO to supervisor—would not spend more than half time at their desk. It was also noted that the organization held few formal meetings; that most decisions could be made on the spot and the input gleaned from walking around enabled what meetings were held to be used very productively for priority setting and true strategic planning. There was a formal CQI program that was visible to all, including patients. Because issues could be immediately observed, they could be attended to right away with the right individuals involved, thereby reducing the likelihood of an issue growing into something much larger and requiring much more time. Finally, the CIO said, "And, I go home on time!"

How does an organization know if its corporate culture is effective? It might be suggested that if an organization has to ask such a question, the answer most likely is that its culture is not working well. However, many also suggest that cultures need to be adaptive. It is necessary to periodically revisit and reaffirm core values and associated behaviors (Heskett and Sasser 2008). Table 3.1 describes several specific ways to assess an organization's culture. While the tools can and are used by consultants, they are much more effective when used by managers themselves. This not only demonstrates their interest in understanding the culture of the organization, but also provides everyone with a clear signal that managers are serious about their mission to adapt the culture as necessary. The tools should be used frequently to continuously obtain feedback and reinforce organizational values.

Table 3.1 Organizational Culture Assessment Tools

Culture Assessment Tool	Purpose and Approach
Walk-throughs	*Purpose:* As described in Case Study 3.1, walk-throughs allow managers the ability to actually see for themselves how things are working. In addition to assessing the current culture, if this technique is adopted on an ongoing basis it can serve to help maintain and adjust the culture over time.
	Approach: Plan for managers to conduct frequent walk-throughs, at different times of the day or different days and in different locations as applicable to their scope of authority. Early in initiating such a process, managers may find a checklist of things to look for (see Table 3.2 for examples of observations) and/or maintaining a diary of findings and needed follow up (both for celebration and corrective action) necessary.
Focused interviews	*Purpose:* Interviews help managers learn about the organization's culture in a systematic manner, allow free-form questions to emerge that enhance information gathering, and enable behavior observation to validate responses. Interviews may be tailored to the target audience.
	Approach: Select small groups of physicians, staff, and patients, sometimes as separate groups and sometimes in integrated groups as appropriate. Plan to ask indirect questions (see Table 3.3 for examples of questions) that will get people to discuss their response rather than give yes/no answers.
Surveys	*Purpose:* Surveys (distributed via paper or online) help canvas a large number of people in a short period of time. Different surveys (including use of different modalities depending on level or automation in the organization) at different times and/or to different target audiences may be used to pinpoint areas needing further exploration through walk-throughs or focused interviews.
	Approach: Introduce the purpose of the survey in an open and respectful manner. Ensure a sufficiently large and random sample that responses will be valid. Construct the survey to be short and easy to respond to (see Table 3.4 for an example); test it with a small sample of the applicable population prior to administering.
Inventory	*Purpose:* An inventory is similar to a survey, but typically is a more standard set of attributes that people are asked to rank. It is often used in benchmarking against other organizations, but can be within an organization to evaluate the degree or strength of beliefs people hold and as a baseline to measure the effect of change.
	Approach: Utilize a standard inventory if planning to benchmark. These may be obtained from consulting firms, award program criteria, standards, etc. Otherwise, construct a set of attributes and administer in the same manner as a survey. In fact, the attributes may be drawn from the survey (see highlighted terms in Table 3.4).

Table 3.1 (continued)   Organizational Culture Assessment Tools

Culture Assessment Tool	Purpose and Approach
Assessment	*Purpose*: An assessment is generally a formal, in-person process conducted by a neutral third party (often a consultant) to evaluate and report to management.
	Approach: When considering an assessment for organizational culture change, it may be appropriate for executive management to introduce an overall program of culture change and sandwich the assessment between managers' use of other tools. Such a strategy strengthens the evidence that management is committed to making a change, not just hiring a consultant to make it happen, which rarely is sustainable.
Exercises	*Purpose*: Exercises help engage all members of the organization's "community" more fully than by simply responding to questions in an interview, survey, or inventory. It allows both managers and other stakeholders to "practice" the culture change and obtain critique.
	Approach: Exercises are often automated simulations, but can be conducted as an in-person activity with a facilitator. They can be constructed by the organization, but may require someone skilled in instructional design to provide development assistance and tools. An excellent example is created by Duke Center for Instructional Technology on the Duke University Medical Center Department of Community and Family Medicine website at http:// patientsafetyed.duhs.duke.edu/module_c/module_overview.html (Wiseman and Kaprielian n.d.)
Open forums	*Purpose*: Open forums imply the ability for anyone to provide input on anything within the scope of the forum's intent.
	Approach: Open forums may utilize social media or be conducted in a designated location within a facility. They may be formal or informal, accommodating many at a time or a few at a time, often depending on their purpose and timing. For example, when introducing a major change, it may be appropriate to have a more formal, large, open forum in an auditorium where managers can field any manner of questions after delivering a short description of the change. Alternatively, during the go-live of a new IT system, weekly bagel breakfasts or pizza lunches are an effective social occasion where new users often let down their guard and are much more forthcoming about their concerns and even offer ideas for improvement (Zafar and Kho 2006; Lombardo 2003). With respect to organizational culture, open forums may be staffed by managers, human resource personnel, consultants, clinical systems analysts, process analysts, or any combination thereof.

Source: Copyright © Margret\A Consulting, LLC. With permission.

Table 3.2 Sample Management Walk-through Checklist to Assess Organizational Culture

Management Walk-through Checklist

Manager: _____ Title: _____ Date: _____

Observation	Time	Location	Person(s)	Notes	Follow-Up
Are people helping each other?					
Do people approach me as I conduct my walkthrough?					
Do people look happy?					
Do people appear to be working on specific tasks?					
Are people using equipment and supplies as intended?					
Do people attend meetings on time?					
How do people respond to patients asking questions?					
How do people respond to fellow staff members asking questions?					
How do people respond to physician communications?					

Source: Copyright © Margret\A Consulting, LLC. With permission.

Table 3.3   Sample Focused Interview Questions to Assess Organizational Culture

Focused Interview	
Interviewer: _____ Title: _____ Date: _____	
Attendees' Initials and Credentials (e.g. JD/MD, MS/RN, KW/Pt):	
Questions	*Attributed Responses*
1. What would you tell a friend about the CDO if he or she thought about working/practicing here?	
2. What is the one thing you would most like to change about this CDO?	
3. Who is a hero here? Why?	
4. What kinds of people fail in here?	
5. What kinds of comments do patients make about the CDO?	
6. Do you refer people here? Why or why not?	
7. How would you characterize the quality of care provided here in relationship to care provided where you previously worked/practiced?	
8. Provide an example of a conflict in which you found yourself and how that was resolved.	
9. Describe your proudest moment while working/practicing here.	
10. Do you have any thoughts about whether the culture of the organization should and could change?	

Source: Copyright © Margret\A Consulting, LLC. With permission.

Change an Organization's Culture

Once the organization understands stakeholders' perceptions about its culture, it is important to follow up as promised in the communications surrounding the assessments. Changing an organization's culture where assessment findings reveal concerns is not an easy task. There are frequently subcultures within a CDO requiring different strategies. The following are some generic steps with respect to changing culture:

Table 3.4 Sample Survey Questions/Inventory Attributes to Assess Organizational Culture

Organizational Assessment

The purpose of this Survey/Inventory is to help <Name of CDO> learn how our stakeholders view the organization on key performance indicators. Over the coming months, we will be conducting a variety of additional assessments and with your help will be instituting changes to improve how we deliver quality care in an efficient and effective manner. Your responses are anonymous.

Please respond to each question to describe this CDO on the following attributes:	*I don't know*	*Superior*	*Good*	*Average*	*Fair*	*Poor*
1. How would you rate the **quality of care and patient safety** delivered here?						
2. What is the **image in the community** of <Name of CDO>?						
3. How would you rate the **supervision** afforded by management here?						
4. How would you rate the **employment practices** here?						
5. How would you rate the **staffing and workload** here?						
6. How would you rate the organization's overall **communications**?						
7. How would you rate the **general morale** here?						
8. How would you rate **pay and benefits** here in comparison to comparable organizations where you have worked?						
9. How would you rate the **cohesiveness** of <Name of CDO> staff, managers, and physician community?						
10. How would you rate the **use of automation** here in comparison to other organization in which you worked?						

Source: Copyright © Margret\A Consulting, LLC. With permission.

1. ***Understand the organization's leadership and change management capabilities***, especially with respect to making a clinical transformation through the use of EHR and HIT. It may be possible for the organization to mandate the use of EHR by nurses and other clinical staff, but that same posture may not work for physicians. And even within the staff community, an outright mandate may result in disgruntled employees and staff turnover even where staff may say they are positive toward EHR. Under contract from the California Health Care Foundation, the California Community Clinics has created an excellent EHR Assessment and Readiness form. It is available from a variety of websites, including the Agency for Healthcare Quality and Research, the National Association of Community Health Clinics, and the National Opinion Research Center, which also supplies a description of the context for the tool (http://www.norc.org/6275/Module2/Community%20 Clinic%20EHR%20Readiness%20Assessment%20Tool.pdf). It is suitable for any type of CDO. On each readiness area, the CDO rates its preparedness as "not yet," "moderately," or "highly prepared." A scoring methodology is supplied. Where an organization finds it is not highly prepared, it is advisable to follow the suggestions in the "highly prepared" category to improve readiness.

2. ***Determine the organization's strategic direction***. Review the CDO's mission, vision, and values and make adjustments as necessary. For example, if a mission is to be "committed to excellence in patient care," it may be helpful to define a bit further what excellence means. Reading further between the lines, is the CDO focused only on the ill and the injured, or also on wellness and preventive services? Does it incorporate teaching and/or research in its mission? Does it seek to focus on a certain type of patient or want to offer services beyond acute care? Will this mission statement carry them over to a more coordinated and shared risk model of health care that health reform holds? These may seem like broad-brush concepts in light of a specific EHR and HIT agenda, yet they truly impact the clinical transformation that the EHR is intended to support. For example, if clinicians struggle with information sharing—as many do—certain types of HIT may not be sought and the resultant impact on the CDO could keep it from participating in certain incentive programs or effectively managing its revenue stream in other ways. Specific visioning techniques, such as listed in Table 3.5, help an organization create a more specific, meaningful vision that can embrace technology and other factors that can contribute to success. Visioning should then lead to goal setting that supports the continuous quality improvement cycle.

3. ***Change behavior to create the desired organizational culture***. Changing behavior in an existing organization is more difficult than creating a culture in a new organization (Heathfield n.d.). To change a culture within an existing organization, executive management must unlearn old

Table 3.5   Visioning Techniques

General:

- Environmental scanning/trend analysis
- Force field analysis
- Normative group process
- Scenarios, or use cases
- "Pain points"
- "A day in the life of"
- "Through the eyes of your patients"
- Current state/future state

Specific to EHR and HIT:

- What does EHR mean to me as a user?
- What does EHR mean to my organization?
- What does EHR mean to our patients?
- What does EHR mean to others in our community?
  - Referring providers
  - Public health
  - Health plans
  - Employers
  - Others

Source: Copyright © Health IT Certification, LLC. With
permission.

values, assumptions, and behaviors before they can adopt new ones. Some executives seeking to effect such change seek a coach (Crane 2005). Others participate in a formal learning collaborative where executives from different organizations undertake a series of learning sessions intermingled with specific exercises that are shared with the group and upon which they receive feedback. As executive management changes, a mentoring program can be adopted for lower-tier managers so that the new culture is infused throughout the entire CDO (Whitmore 2009). The result of such behavior change should be a culture of empowerment where managers become leaders (see Table 3.6).

Assess End-User Readiness for the Clinical Transformation That EHR and HIT Represent

One additional assessment that can contribute to a CDOs planning arsenal is an assessment of end-user readiness for the clinical transformation that EHR and

Table 3.6   Managers Becoming Leaders

Managers believe...	*Leaders believe ...*
In doing things right.	In doing the right things.
Their power lies in their knowledge.	Their power lies in their vulnerability.
In creating structure and procedures for people to follow.	In creating a vision and promoting flexibility through values as guidelines for behavior.
In delegating responsibility.	In modeling accountability and empowering people to assume authority.
In solving problems and making decisions.	In facilitating others to solve problems and make decisions.
Their job is to point out errors.	Their job is to celebrate success and support course correction.
They know the answers.	They must seek the answers.
They should talk at people by telling, directing, and lecturing.	They should engage in dialogue with people by asking, requesting, and listening.

Source: Adapted from *Becoming a Coach for the Teams You Lead*, Thomas G. Crane. 2005.

HIT represent. Determining attitudes and beliefs toward EHR and HIT can help an organization identify where education is needed and where there is a need to begin the change management process early. Table 3.7a provides a survey that the author has developed and used effectively for over ten years.

Despite seeking responses to only twelve statements, the tool has provided significant insights into end users' concerns and how they view EHR. The statements are designed to require the reading of each statement. Most organizations distribute the tool anonymously, but require end users to categorize themselves as specified by the organization. Categories might include administration, members of the medical staff, other clinicians, and other staff, depending on the size of the organization. Table 3.7b supplies a stoplight structure to assess where responses suggest risk. After tallying the number of responses to each statement, analyze the result by considering where most respondents rated the statements. In some cases, both strong agreement and strong disagreement suggest risk because such extremes may represent lack of knowledge or unrealistic expectations. For example, when administered to a moderate-sized clinic, if the statement that "EHRs reduce staffing requirements" has physicians responding in strong agreement (designated red) and administration in strong disagreement (also designated red), then there is clearly a disconnect in expectations that must be addressed. In some cases, the stoplight assessment suggests moderate risk (yellow) and potentially also at both sides of the rating scale. For example, strong disagreement with "their alerts can be annoying" is unrealistic because if the organization does not set the sensitivity of the alerts appropriately, they can

Table 3.7a Attitudes and Beliefs Survey for End Users

Concerning Electronic Health Records (EHR):	*Strongly Agree*	*Agree*	*Neutral*	*Disagree*	*Strongly Disagree*
1. They increase efficiency.					
2. They are not as secure as paper records.					
3. Our patients are expecting us to use them.					
4. They will improve my personal productivity.					
5. They are difficult to learn how to use.					
6. Their use in front of patients is depersonalizing.					
7. Their cost is beyond our budget.					
8. They improve quality of care.					
9. They reduce staffing requirements.					
10. Their alerts can be annoying.					
11. We are in an age where we must electronically exchange data with other providers, payers, and patients.					
12. Health care is too complex nowadays without access to evidence-based support.					

Source: Copyright © Margret\A Consulting, LLC. With permission.

be annoying even to the biggest EHR champion. On the other end of the scale, strong agreement suggests the need to educate end users that alert sensitivity should be able to be set.

CDOs that have used the "Attitudes and Beliefs Survey for End Users" early in the process of planning for automation have also found it helpful to use reworded statements on the same topics as a means to assess end-user satisfaction with the EHR after a period of acclimation (see Table 3.7c). It has been especially interesting to see the movement in statements 11 and 12, where often these garner disagreement early in the planning stages and greater interest after some period of using the EHR.

Table 3.7b   Attitudes and Beliefs Stoplight Assessment View

Concerning Electronic Health Records (EHR):	Strongly Agree	Agree	Neutral	Disagree	Strongly Disagree
1. They increase efficiency.	G	G	Y	R	R
2. They are not as secure as paper records.	R	R	Y	G	G
3. Our patients are expecting us to use them.	G	G	Y	Y	R
4. They will improve my personal productivity.	G	G	Y	R	R
5. They are difficult to learn how to use.	R	G	G	G	Y
6. Their use in front of patients is depersonalizing.	R	R	Y	G	G
7. Their cost is beyond our budget.	R	G	G	G	Y
8. They improve quality of care.	G	G	Y	Y	R
9. They reduce staffing requirements.	R	Y	G	G	R
10. Their alerts can be annoying.	Y	G	G	G	Y
11. We are in an age where we must electronically exchange data with other providers, payers, and patients.	G	G	Y	R	R
12. Health care is too complex nowadays without access to evidence-based support.	G	G	Y	R	R

Source: Copyright © Margret\A Consulting, LLC. With permission.

Note: R = Red, Y = Yellow, G = Green.

Educate Stakeholders about EHR and HIT

The outcome of all the assessments should be educational opportunities to address key needs. Specific to introducing changes that will occur with EHR and HIT, educational programming should help stakeholders better understand and be realistic about the automation and its purpose. More informed stakeholders are much more amenable to contributing to subsequent planning efforts and supporting implementation.

Early education about EHR and HIT should be targeted to the needs of each group of stakeholders. Education was described for executive management

Table 3.7c   Use of Attitudes and Beliefs for End-User Satisfaction Survey

Concerning Our Electronic Health Record (EHR):	Strongly Agree	Agree	Neutral	Disagree	Strongly Disagree
1. It has increased efficiency.					
2. It is not as secure as paper records.					
3. My patients are comfortable with me using it.					
4. It has improved my personal productivity.					
5. It was difficult to learn how to use.					
6. Use in front of my patients is depersonalizing.					
7. Cost was beyond our budget.					
8. It has improved quality of care.					
9. It should have reduced staffing requirements.					
10. Its alerts are annoying.					
11. I appreciate the ability to electronically exchange data with other providers, payers, and patients.					
12. I appreciate having access to evidence-based support.					

Source: Copyright © Margret\A Consulting, LLC. With permission.

as a means to help adapt the culture of the organization to continuous quality improvement. End users obviously will be trained on the EHR and HIT they are expected to use. But all stakeholders, including executive management, end users, and everyone in between or playing a supportive role should receive appropriate education early in the planning, selection, and implementation stages of adopting EHR and HIT:

◾ Executive leadership, including the board of directors, needs to understand the context in which changes are being made—the need for continuous quality improvement as the United States continues to lag behind in key quality indicators such as infant mortality and life expectancy; health reform to improve quality and reduce cost; the scope of automation and realistic expectations for what it costs and what it can help accomplish; and above all, to respond to questions that will lead to ongoing commitment and support.

- End users must be kept informed, have myths debunked, and learn more intimately about what EHR and HIT can and cannot do. Different groups of end users will likely need different types of both content and delivery mechanisms. Physicians often want to see a system in action to develop trust—so site visits, even outside of the context of selection, can be helpful. Nurses, whose average age in hospitals is around forty-six years old (AACN 2011) often have very limited experience using a computer and appear to want much more specific information about how a computer works and what applications will be implemented in order to alleviate their fears surrounding their potential to break the system, downtime, privacy and security, and how it will impact their work and their performance reviews (Barrameda 2011). Other end users may actually be more comfortable with technology but may need expectation leveling.

- IT and other supporting staff also need early education to orient them to clinician attributes and other clinical hurdles. For example, many IT staff find it extremely difficult to appreciate that a nurse may never have used a computer, or at least not in an employment context. IT staff may never have had an opportunity to work with physicians and may not recognize unique attributes of knowledge workers that must be considered in orienting them to EHR and HIT.

Coordinating education among all stakeholders will also help them learn, create trust, build bridges, and reduce the stovepipe (or silo) mentality that is so prevalent in CDOs. They will gain a greater appreciation for the need to integrate data, workflows, and processes.

In addition to the site visits mentioned above, which generally are reserved for selected individuals (and physicians may be expected to pay for such visits themselves), there are a variety of other educational activities that can help inform and alleviate concerns:

- Demonstrations—both web based and live — brought to an organization can help stakeholders get as close to the "real deal" as possible early in the educational process. Although few hospital-oriented EHR vendors have demos on the web, many vendors targeting the ambulatory and other specialty care markets do have such demos. It is recommended that those shown these demos have a facilitator present to help them bridge the gap between their own organization and the vendor's target audience. Even when a vendor may conduct the demo, via the web or in person, such a facilitator should be present to ensure that the demo is educational and not sales focused. The facilitator can also guide new users to features and functions they may overlook, point out the relationship of EHR to thought processes, and respond to questions. It should be noted that when conducting these demos, CDOs should stress that they are educational, and not for the purpose of selecting a product or receiving training on how to use a given system. Demos will be conducted for these purposes as well, but early demos should serve to orient stakeholders to become informed consumers.

■ Literature review and web surfing should be encouraged as an educational process. Some CDOs have found it helpful to approach EHR education as a book club, requiring each member of a work team or unit to find articles or news of interest on the web and report on these as brief parts of regularly scheduled meetings. Summarization of these can also be posted to an educational section of the organization's intranet; and if a discussion board is available, stakeholders can exchange views about what they are seeing. This gives future end users experience in using a computer, and the selection of articles can reflect upon their potential concerns as well.

■ Trade shows, conferences, and seminars can be helpful, although, as with site visits, costly and generally limited to a specific purpose and representative few persons. Proceedings of conferences, however, are often posted to the web or made available through CDs; and, of course, those attending should be expected to return to the CDO with information to be disseminated in a variety of ways.

Set S.M.A.R.T. Goals

The planning steps described in this chapter support the CDO's ability to identify specific, measurable goals and set expectations for achieving them. Such goals support the organization's continuous quality improvement cycle. For CDOs, whether selecting, implementing, or optimizing EHR and HIT, goal setting serves multiple specific purposes as identified in Figure 3.1.

Goal setting is often difficult for CDOs, for many reasons. Previously it was described that CDOs exist with a cultural norm of considering failure to be all or nothing, and—realistically and legitimately—fearing the huge repercussions that often occur from a patient care failure. Although a patient's life may not be at stake with respect to every goal that could be set for an EHR, the fear of failure mentality often precludes clinicians from being comfortable setting goals for an EHR. In addition, clinicians often do not fully understand EHR and HIT, or at least have no experience using automation. They may feel they do not have the knowledge base to set realistic goals. Goal setting is important for the reasons cited in Figure 3.1, but should not be undertaken until more positive cultural norms are supported and stakeholders are more informed about EHR and HIT. Once that occurs, all stakeholders should have input into the goals, at least through a process that represents all stakeholder interests and is open and transparent to all. Goals then need to be S.M.A.R.T. and reflect the outcomes of using the EHR and HIT in workflows and processes that have been adapted accordingly.

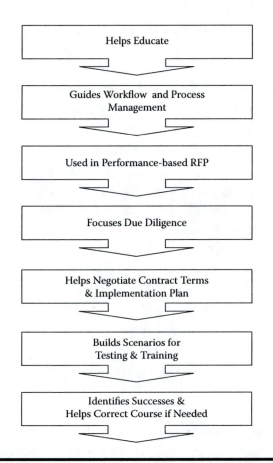

Figure 3.1 Purposes of goal setting for EHR and HIT. (From Copyright © Margret\A Consulting, LLC. With permission.)

Writing goals as Specific, Measurable, Achievable, Realistic, and Time-based (S.M.A.R.T.) statements helps the organization get specific about goals. They describe a future state where it is feasible to determine whether the goal has been met. The acronym S.M.A.R.T. has a number of variations. The following alternative terms help define the concept:

- **S**pecific, significant, stretching—goals should be described by who, does what, where, why, how, and when. Anyone reading the goal should be able to ascertain its meaning.
- **M**easurable, meaningful, motivational—specific metrics are critical to goal setting. Without measurement, it is impossible to determine if the goals have been met.
- **A**chievable, agreed upon, attainable, acceptable, action oriented, account-able—all of these terms hold great importance in relationship to the ultimate goal of accomplishing one's goals. While a goal itself cannot be accountable, accountability—and the consequences for not achieving the goal—should be made clear in the goal statement.

- ■ **R**ealistic, relevant, reasonable, rewarding, results oriented, reliable, resourced—for a goal to be achievable, it must be able to be accomplished; otherwise it is considered a dream, not a goal!
- ■ **T**ime based, timely, tangible, trackable—even when it may be necessary to establish milestones in order to achieve the goal, the milestones must be clearly described. Dates, time periods, or events can be used to describe when a goal, its milestones, or its subparts should be met.

When CDOs start to write goals for EHR and HIT, they often find themselves writing feature and function specifications, rather than outcomes. This may suggest that the stakeholders do not fully understand EHR and HIT even after education and personal exploration. One physician summed this up as only a physician could:

> My colleagues understand EHR at the intellectual level, but not at the intestinal level.

> **—Robert G. McDonald, MD**
> *P.S. Rudie Medical Clinic, Duluth, Minnesota*

It is also possible to write too many goals, where they become checklists of short-term things to do, more like a project plan than a set of over-arching objectives. These become difficult to prioritize and later to measure results. Goals should also be set within the context of what is feasible. Although it may seem that this leads to setting minimalistic goals, a common failing in setting goals in CDOs is to seek the "moon and the stars." In fact, because the EHR is so complex and takes considerable time to learn and become accomplished at using, it may be appropriate to, indeed, set some minimalistic goals in order to create some early wins. Case Study 3.2 is a slightly embellished, real experience that illustrates many of the things that go right in setting goals, and some cautions as well.

Case Study 3.2: On-Board and Overboard with Goal Setting

Dr. E. Record was the EHR champion for her ten-physician office. She wanted to "do things right" in selecting and implementing an EHR, including setting goals. Her first thought about what goals to set was that many colleagues in other offices indicated they reduced transcription expense using EHR. She decided to set a goal that the EHR should include speech dictation, which would enable physicians to dictate directly into the EHR so they could get rid of their transcription service costs.

However, she decided she wanted to see speech dictation in action, and thus visited the radiology department at her hospital where radiologists used this technology to document reports. She was disappointed to learn that if the office got rid of their transcription service, the physicians would have to correct any errors made in the speech-to-text translation process themselves. She felt this would slow them down tremendously. She also learned that the dictation did not result in structured data that was required for the federal EHR incentive program. Yet she also was concerned about the format of the EHR output she had received from colleagues, where information was presented in long lists of facts—not conducive to reading or learning about her colleagues' feelings about their patients.

Dr. Record then wondered if all products yielded such output, so she viewed several demos and was relieved to find there were feasible options, although next she expressed concern about how she would ever be able to write a goal that covered all the features and functions she wanted in an EHR. It was finally discussed with her that the purpose of writing goals was to convey the intended outcome *after* the EHR had been implemented. The goal statement should contribute to, but be more than, a statement of functional requirements. She realized she also needed to include some metrics. She initially considered the elimination of transcription expense within a month of go-live. After a bit more discussion, she agreed this might be unrealistic, and so set a goal of 50 percent reduction by the end of the first year of use and 85 percent reduction by the end of the second year of use. She was then shown the S.M.A.R.T. goal-setting tool in Table 3.8, and was happy she could include some verbiage describing for her partners what key features and functions would enable them to achieve the goal.

Interestingly, before she showed this goal to her partners, she wanted to add that if by the end of the second year every physician was not meeting the goal, those who were behind would be required to pay for transcription services out of their own pockets. While this is a relatively common practice that has actually been quite effective, it was suggested to Dr. Record that, while she had done a great job researching and refining the goals to be S.M.A.R.T., she needed buy-in

Table 3.8   S.M.A.R.T. Goal-Setting Tool with Example

Goal Elements	Example	
Specific	Reduce provider dictation to minimize transcription expense and ensure structured data to earn federal incentives and receive clinical decision support.	
Measurable	by 50% to accommodate the learning curve	by 85% to accommodate lengthy or unusual notes or referral letters
Achievable	using templates in the EHR that wrap narrative text around structured data and provide comment fields for short description of subjective information	
Realistic	which are reviewed and approved by physician users, who are aided with one-on-one end-user support during go-live	
Time based	by the end of the first year after go-live.	by the end of the second year after go-live or risk paying for transcription service out of pocket.

Source: Copyright © Margret\A Consulting, LLC. With permission.

from her partners and other stakeholders—getting input from them. When she then took what she learned about EHRs and the S.M.A.R.T. tool, but not the goal statement, to her steering committee, the result was essentially the same as what she had written, including the consequence for not meeting the goal! In addition, the health information manager suggested specification of what exceptions would be permitted to comprise the 15 percent remaining dictation. Table 3.8 supplies this finalized example. Now everyone in the office felt they had developed, agreed to, and could envision achieving the goals.

Workflow and Process Management Governance

A final step before going full speed ahead into mapping current processes, and analyzing, redesigning, and implementing redesigned processes for EHR and HIT is to create a workflow and process management governance structure. A **governance structure** is the management framework within which decisions are made. When a specific project is undertaken, a project governance structure identifies the responsibilities and accountabilities for project decision making. As suggested by case Study 3.2, it is critical to remember that all stakeholders need to be engaged in a project such as EHR and HIT, and it is vitally important to have a process that ensures useful results.

A **project charter** often is created to establish the governance structure and set the ground rules for how the project will be accomplished (PMI—Central Iowa Chapter 2009). Table 3.9 supplies the components of a charter and an example. Note that the example specifies that the project only focuses on documenting current workflows for the purposes of contributing to EHR functional requirements, refining EHR goals, and contributing current maps to the redesign activity to be performed following vendor selection. This hospital is separating documentation of current process from redesign in anticipation that the EHR vendor to be selected will likely aid in conducting the redesign effort. As noted previously, while not all vendors can be expected to provide such services, the example hospital has apparently decided to consider only vendors that do include this service. Whether or not their selection process will yield such an outcome, when the redesign of the workflows occurs, the hospital should expect to construct another project charter.

For small CDOs, such as critical access hospitals, small physician offices, long-term care facilities, etc., it may not be necessary to adopt as formal a charter as described in Table 3.9, however, making decisions about each element and documenting pertinent parts can be extremely helpful. If nothing else, it provides satisfaction that the work being performed has been completed, and it provides documentation when needed, such as for implementation, training, and optimization.

Table 3.9   Workflow and Process Management Project Charter

Project Charter Component	*Description*	*Example for EHR Workflow and Process Mapping in a Hospital*
Description and purpose	States the work of the project and its intended outcomes.	This project will map current workflows and processes; collect baseline data associated with current workflows and processes; and analyze current workflows and processes to contribute to EHR functional requirements specifications, aid in refining goals for EHR outcomes, and identify opportunities for improvement that may yield immediate results. The current maps will enable the CDO to redesign workflows and processes to support effective and efficient use of the EHR during its implementation.
Scope	Describes the boundaries and constraints of the project.	Only workflows and processes associated with use of an EHR will be mapped and analyzed for the purposes specified. Workflows and processes outside of this scope will be referred to the CQI Team.
		This project will contribute its output to the redesign project once an EHR vendor is selected.
		Opportunities for immediate improvement in a workflow and process are expected to be addressed by respective managers and supervisors. Their implementation will not be tracked as part of this project, but if they are implemented, a revised "current" workflow and process must be submitted to the current workflow and process database.
Critical success factors	Identifies factors that must be present to achieve the intended outcomes.	Every stakeholder group associated with a process will be represented in the project and individuals' work on the project will be considered part of their regular job duties.
		Physician stakeholders as applicable to a given process will participate directly and will not substitute others for their participation.

continued

Table 3.9 (continued)   Workflow and Process Management Project Charter

Project Charter Component	Description	Example for EHR Workflow and Process Mapping in a Hospital
		All participants will be identified in the Directory of Project Participants (Appendix A) and are expected to collaborate in their work.
		All participants will be trained on workflow and process mapping and will be expected to demonstrate competency in order to proceed on their team. Appendix B supplies the training materials and competency requirements.
		As workflows and processes are mapped, they will be validated by the broadest possible range of stakeholders and their interoperability will be verified by cross-departmental teams to ensure completeness, accuracy, and feasibility for accomplishing changes.
		At the completion of each workflow and process mapping and analysis, functional requirements derived from the activity will be posted to a master EHR functional requirements tool on the project's intranet site.
Leadership	Identifies the project's oversight authority, executive sponsor, and either actual leader or process to identify leaders as applicable.	The chief operating officer, chief medical informatics officer, chief information officer, and director of CQI will serve as executive sponsors. There will be a lead process analyst internal to the organization who may be assisted by a consultant as budgeted.
Participants	Identifies the actual participants or process to identify participants as applicable.	A formal team-building process will be used to identify individuals to work on the project. Each team will be trained by the lead process analyst, and one member of each team will be designated its deputy lead process analyst.
Timeline	Provides a completion date and milestones to reach that date.	A process inventory (Appendix C) will be compiled within one (1) month of project initiation.

Table 3.9 (continued)   Workflow and Process Management Project Charter

Project Charter Component	Description	Example for EHR Workflow and Process Mapping in a Hospital
		A detailed project plan (Appendix D) will be established within one (1) week of the process inventory being completed.
		All current workflows and processes will be mapped using the documentation requirements specified in Appendix E within three (3) months of the process inventory being made available.
		Baseline data collection will be conducted simultaneously with the workflow and process mapping and documented as specified in Appendix F.
		All current workflows and process will be analyzed to contribute to the functional requirements specification (see Appendix G) within three (3) months of current mapping completion.
		Redesign of processes will occur after EHR vendor selection.
Resources	Sets forth budget, time allocation for staff, and other resources needed to achieve intended outcomes.	A budget, as provided in Appendix H, has been allocated for 75 percent of the process analyst time, two (2) weeks of BPM consulting time, expenses associated with creating an electronic discussion board, refreshments for team meetings and celebration of accomplishments, and 10 percent contingency factor. The hallway between the employee entrance and the IT department will be designated the comment wall. It is expected that the majority of process mapping will be performed by individuals contributing to a collective process, and that team communications will occur via the discussion board and comment wall after initial training with the exception of a validation session.

continued

Table 3.9 (continued)   Workflow and Process Management Project Charter

Project Charter Component	Description	Example for EHR Workflow and Process Mapping in a Hospital
Reporting requirements	Specifies when and to whom feedback must be supplied on project status; and requires use of an issues log and escalation procedure in the event the project gets off course.	Team meeting dates, times, locations/call-in numbers, agendas, and applicable documents will be posted to the intranet project site at least two days prior to their occurrence. Executive sponsors will randomly participate in parts of at least 25 percent of team meetings, will contribute comments to posted maps, and will review project status regularly. The process analyst will post a status update daily to the intranet project site. Any issue requiring sponsor assistance to resolve will be copied to the executive sponsor team. Any issue not resolved within the allotted time will be escalated to the CQI Team for assistance in resolution. All managers and supervisors as applicable will communicate project goals and status to stakeholders on a regular basis, seeking input from the broadest possible range of stakeholders under their authority.
Documentation	Provides specific requirements for what documentation represents the final outcome of the project, what documentation may be intermediary, how and where all documentation is maintained, and the documentation's retention period.	All process maps will be documented using the systems flowchart technique on which participants will be trained (referred to Appendix B). Each map will include metadata as described in Appendix E. Maps will be accompanied by any supporting documentation, including but not limited to current forms and reports, associated policies and procedures or clinical protocols, and metrics to define baseline data collection. Baseline data collected may utilize any applicable techniques approved by the process analyst and in consultation with the CQI Team. Documentation of key data collection findings should be incorporated into the systems flowcharts and the full set of data collected appended to the maps.

Table 3.9 (continued)   Workflow and Process Management Project Charter

Project Charter Component	Description	Example for EHR Workflow and Process Mapping in a Hospital
		All maps being worked on must be maintained on the project's intranet site with applicable supporting documentation. Once current maps are complete, the lead process analyst should be notified who will contribute them to the project database and maintain them for one (1) year after the redesign of the workflow and process has been implemented.
Versioning	Requires that a formal process for identifying each version of a document be created and adhered to.	The metadata for each workflow and process map requires version specification. The lead process analyst will maintain version control and will receive written requests and provide approval for new versions as applicable.
Appendices	Includes points of contact, history of revision to the charter, and any other material that may need to be referenced within the charter.	Appendix A: Directory of Project Participants (see Chapter 5) Appendix B: Training for Workflow and Process Mapping (see Chapter 5) Appendix C: Process Inventory (see Chapter 4) Appendix D: Project Plan Appendix E: Documentation Requirements (see Chapters 5, 6, and 8) Appendix F: Baseline Data Collection Process (see Chapter 7) Appendix G: EHR Functional Requirements Specifications (see Chapter 4) Appendix H: Project Budget

Source: Copyright © Margret\A Consulting, LLC. With permission.

Key Points

■ Determining a CDO's readiness for the **clinical transformation** that can be aided by EHR and HIT is an absolute precursor to making the change happen. Assessing readiness is necessary at all levels, from **executive managers** to **end users** (not to imply that clinicians are at the "bottom" of the organizational structure).

■ **Culture** has a powerful effect on an organization. Making a change in a CDO's culture and its capacity for **change management** requires flexibility and adaptability, **education** to sufficiently understand the factors of change so that effective **visioning** of the future state with those factors present can be performed, and the creation of **leadership** in all stakeholders throughout the organization.

■ Envisioning the future not only aids in addressing organizational requirements to effectively and efficiently manage change, but also prepares an organization to set **S.M.A.R.T. goals**. Many change management experts refer to Lewis Carroll's *Alice in Wonderland* and Alice's conversation with the Cheshire cat:

> *Alice:* "Would you please tell me which way I ought to go from here?"
> *Cat:* "That depends a good deal upon where you want to get to."
> *Alice:* "I don't much care where."
> *Cat:* "Then it doesn't matter which way you go."
> *Alice, as an added explanation:* "—so long as I get somewhere."
> *Cat:* "Oh you're sure to do that. If you only walk long enough."

■ Part of readying the organization when specific factors are being implemented to effect change is creating a **project governance** structure, often documented in a **project charter**.

References

AACN, 2011 (July). "Fact Sheet: Nursing Shortage." American Association of Colleges of Nursing. Available at: http://www.aacn.nche.edu/media/factsheets/nursingshortage.htm

Barrameda, M. 2011 (Jan. 24). "EHR Lessons for Nurses: Nurse CIO of Generations+/ Northern Manhattan Health Network Offers Tips for EHR Success." *Advance for Nurses*. Available at: http://nursing.advanceweb.com/Columns/Nursing-Informatics/ EHR-Lessons-for-Nurses.as...

Boan, D. and F. Funderburk, 2003 (Nov. 3). "Healthcare Quality Improvement and Organizational Culture: Literature Review. "*Insights*. Delmarva Foundation. Available at: http://w.delmarvafoundation.org/newsAndPublications/reports/documents/ Organizational_Culture.pdf

California Community Clinics EHR Assessment and Readiness. 2008 (June 19). Available at: http://www.norc.org/6275/Module2/Community%20Clinic%20EHR%20 Readiness%20Assessment%20Tool.pdf

Crane, T.G. and L.N. Patrick, 2005. The Heart of Coaching: Using Transformational Coaching to Create a High-Performance Coaching Culture. San Diego, CA: FTA Press, 122–123.

Health IT Certification, LLC, 2011. "EHR Visioning." Core Course III: HIT, EHR, and HIE Goals and Migration Path. Available at: www.healthitcertification.com

Heathfield, S.M., n.d. "How to Change Your Culture: Organizational Culture Change." About.com. Available at: http://humanresources.about.com/od/organizationalculture/a/culture_change.htm

Heskett, J. and W.E. Sasser, 2008. *The Ownership Quotient: Putting the Service Profit Chain to Work for Unbeatable Competitive Advantage*. Boston: Harvard Business School Publishing Corporation, 141–167.

Lombardo, R., 2003. CRM for the Common Man: The essential guide to designing and planning a successful CRM strategy for your business. Las Vegas, NV: PEAK Sales Consulting, 121–132.

PMI — Central Iowa Chapter, 2009 (Jan. 16)."Program Charter," Version: 1.4. Available at: http://www.pmi.org/pmief/learningzone/PMI-CIC_Collaborate_to_Succeed.pdf

Stead, W.W. and H.S. Lin, Eds., 2009. *Computational Technology for Effective Health Care: Immediate Steps and Strategic Directions*. National Research Council, Washington, DC: National Academies Press, S-3.

Whitmore, J., 2009. Coaching for Performance: GROWing Human Potential, fourth edition. Boston: Nicholas Brealey Publising, 9–20.

Wiseman and Kaprielian, n.d. Patient Safety—Quality Improvement: Culture of Safety. Duke Center for Instructional Technology, Duke University Medical Center Department of Community and Family Medicine. Available at: (http://patientsafetyed.duhs.duke.edu/module_c/module_overview.html)

Zafar, A. and A. Kho, 2006 (May 15)."Practical Considerations for Applying Informatics Techniques to your PBRN." AHRQ Practice-based Research Network Research Conference, Bethesda, MD. Available at: http://pbrn.ahrq.gov/portal/server.pt?open=18&objID=810141&qid=1163760&rank=9&parentname=CommunityPage&parentid=0&mode=2&in_hi_userid=8762&cached=true

Chapter 4

Step 2: Compile Process Inventory

A matter that becomes clear ceases to concern us.

—Friedrich Wilhelm Nietzche, Philosopher

This chapter provides clarity around the processes to be mapped. While Step 1 prepares the care delivery organization (CDO) to undertake process mapping by assessing and attending to organizational readiness, Step 2 organizes the process mapping work so that the focus shifts to each specific process. There should be no further concern that there is a process that has been missed. Compiling a process inventory also breaks up the work into manageable components. It provides clarity about how the process is coordinated with one or more other processes to ensure system-wide interoperability.

Process Inventory Description and Purpose

A **Process Inventory** is a list of processes and their descriptions, often categorized as assets and prioritized by importance and value to an organization (Lehmann n.d.). Within the context of planning for EHR and HIT, the purpose of the process inventory is to enumerate those processes that will be impacted in any way by the EHR or HIT. In this way, no process is missed and it is clear who needs to be involved in mapping, analyzing, and redesigning the process. Processes not impacted by EHR and HIT may benefit from workflow and process improvement, but often must be put aside during readiness for EHR and HIT, as there simply may not be organizational resources to address them simultaneously.

Creating a list of processes should begin with a review of what is workflow and process:

Table 4.1 EHR and HIT Process Characteristics

- Who: Process participants
- Does: Operations
  - How: Action steps
  - Why and when: Decision steps
  - Sub-steps
  - Connections (i.e., workflow)
- What: Object of operation (to produce outputs)

Process is the manner in which work is performed.

Workflow is the sequence of steps or hand-offs within a process and between processes.

With respect to EHR and HIT, a process has certain characteristics, as illustrated in Table 4.1. These characteristics generally answer the questions who does what, and including how, why, and when. When compiling a Process Inventory, the set of related inputs, operations, and outputs performed by individuals or systems is one process to be mapped, analyzed, and ultimately redesigned as applicable.

Process Inventory Worksheet

While generic lists of processes typically found in CDOs are supplied in this chapter, it can be helpful to begin identifying processes using a **Process Inventory Worksheet**, and then use the generic list to check that a process has not been forgotten. There is no absolute right or wrong set of processes or standard size of processes. A good rule of thumb is to consider a process as a set of related activities and determine if they are almost always performed together, or if there are sub-processes that reflect a variety of exceptions or variations. Where there are many sub-processes, the primary process may be too large to consider as a single process (Reardan 2010). In actuality, the size of the process is more an artifact of convenience in managing the process.

Each CDO may find that its set of processes is slightly different from that of another CDO. For example, many hospitals have moved the admission process that used to be performed at the time the patient presented to the hospital to a period prior to the patient's arrival. The process may now be performed by different people than originally, and include different inputs, operations, and outputs. Likewise, many physician offices have not had a formal check-out process. When the physician is finished seeing a patient, he or she often just departs. Some offices are beginning to consider adding a check-out process as a means to ensure that co-pays are collected, follow-up appointments are made on a timely basis, written instructions for treatment regimens are provided, and now, as a new step from the federal incentive program for making meaningful use of EHR, the patient is given a summary of the visit.

Table 4.2 Process Inventory Worksheet Template with Examples

Process	Participants	Connects from	Begins with	Ends with	Connects to
Patient Intake (Clinic)	• Nurse • Patient • Registration Desk	• Patient Check-in • Patient Interview	• Registration desk notifies nurse patient is ready	• Nurse notifies physician patient intake is completed	• Physician Chart Review, or
Physician Chart Review (Clinic)	• Physician • Nurse	• Patient Intake	• Nurse notifies physician patient intake is completed	• Physician enters patient exam room	• Patient Interview
Quality Reporting (Hospital)	• Clinical Data Abstractor (CDA) • Clinical Effectiveness Department (CED) Manager • Quality Committee • Medical Director of CED • Patient registration, admission, discharge, and transfer department • Health Information Management Department • IT Report Writing Programmer	• Patient Admission, and • Patient Discharge	• CDA reviews daily admissions against CED criteria for point of care record review, and • CDA reviews daily discharges against CED criteria for data abstraction completion	• CDA submits abstracted data for transmission to vendor	• Quarterly Clinical Effectiveness Review (CER)

Source: Copyright © Margret\A Consulting, LLC. With permission.

Table 4.2 provides a template for a Process Inventory Worksheet suitable for identifying processes associated with EHR and HIT. Two case studies that discuss the examples within the template follow the description of how to construct the Worksheet.

In using the Process Inventory Worksheet, the first column is used to identify the process by name. The second column should list all participants in the process, generally with the person (or system) performing the bulk of the process listed first. This is often described as the "process owner" (NC-DENR 2006). The "Connects from" column identifies the process that directly precedes this process. The "Begins with" and "Ends with" columns are used to identify the specific steps that initiate and conclude the process, respectively. The "Connects to" column then identifies the process that directly follows this process. Once the inventory is completed, every process listed in the "Connects from" and "Connects to" columns should be listed in the "Process" column with its own description. Some process analysts recommend adding performance goals, definitions, and exceptions to a Process Inventory Worksheet (UN/CEFACT and OASIS 2001). If a CDO finds that it is struggling still to establish boundaries around processes, these further attributes may be helpful.

Case Study 4.1: Clinic Processes

A small clinic with two physicians started listing its processes with the Patient Intake and Physician Chart Review processes. The Patient Check-in process is identified as the process that directly precedes the Patient Intake process. This process has not been described yet, but when the Process Inventory Worksheet is completed, it should precede the Patient Intake process in sequence.

The Patient Intake process connects to either the Physician Chart Review process or the Patient Interview process. This variation reflects different physician preferences, as well as different characteristics of the patients one of the physicians sees. One physician prefers to review the charts of all patients prior to entering the exam room and beginning the interview with the patient, with the exception of patients who are returning regularly for chronic disease follow-up. The other physician does not want to take the time between seeing patients to review the chart and believes it is important to review the record with the patient anyway.

Based on what the clinic documented so far on its Process Inventory Worksheet, where the physicians review charts does not appear to impact the Patient Intake "Ends with" step, as the nurse notifies the physician that the patient intake is completed, whether or not the physician chooses to review the chart in advance. However, after reviewing the Worksheet again, the clinic questioned the accuracy of this because the nurse actually notifies the physicians in different ways, depending on the physician's preference. For example, where the physician will review the chart in advance requires the nurse to place the chart in the physician's office in comparison to on the door of the exam room when chart review will not precede the patient interview.

This case study highlights the importance of deciding on the level of detail in the ultimate mapping process. How the nurse makes the notification and where the chart is placed will obviously change with an EHR or HIT. In fact, once the nurse completes the Patient Intake process, it is possible that the EHR will automatically trigger a notification to the physician's dashboard that the patient is ready, eliminating a step for the nurse to have to perform. In this case, the physician can decide whether or not to review the chart before entering the exam room. However, the workflow here is important to document so that applicable decisions can be made—perhaps also about the type of input device the physicians want, or when the physicians return to their offices. (Some clinics have actually found that once a clinic adopts an EHR, physicians rarely spend any time in their offices and some have eliminated offices in place of a single staff lounge, saving space or generating additional exam rooms.)

Case Study 4.2: Hospital Processes

A hospital chose to list on its Process Inventory Worksheet "Quality Reporting" as one of many processes performed in the hospital. Unlike the clinic example (or other examples that could have been chosen for a hospital), this example is not directly related to the direct delivery of patient care, but to the overall operations of the hospital. Every CDO will have some of both types of processes.

In the Quality Reporting example, two potential "Connecting from" processes and associated "Begins with" steps were listed. The Process Inventory Worksheet is not intended to enumerate all steps in every process, so the hospital creating this inventory knew that the majority of the process was performed in the same manner whatever the starting point. The ending step is for the clinical data abstractor to submit data for transmission to the (Core Measures) vendor. This process connects to the Quarterly Clinical Effectiveness Review, which, while not shown, probably aggregates the data and contributes to an executive dashboard so that outliers may be further investigated.

Generic Lists of Processes

To aid CDOs in ensuring they have fully identified all processes impacted by EHR and HIT by means of the Process Inventory Worksheet, Tables 4.3a and 4.3b provide lists of generic processes for hospitals and ambulatory care facilities (i.e., physician offices, clinics, outpatient departments). For other care delivery settings (such as nursing homes, home health agencies, behavioral healthcare facilities, etc.), which are many and varied, the two lists can be mixed and matched. Although not a direct CDO, health information exchange organizations (HIOs) are playing an increasingly important role in aiding the exchange of data across (disparate) organizations. A set of basic and advanced processes for HIOs is provided in Table 4.3c.

Compiling the Process Inventory

The hospital example in Table 4.2, especially in comparison to the generic list of processes in Table 4.3a, also highlights the need for clarity in describing unique processes. "Quality Reporting" may actually be too large a process to consider as one. For example, unless the clinical data abstractor is actually reviewing records at the point of care to begin the data abstraction process, there may be three separate processes here. One process may be clinical data analysis, or clinical

Table 4.3a Generic List of Hospital Processes

• Patient Registration
• Admission, Discharge, Transfer/Bed Control
• Care Coordination/Case Management
• Nursing Assessment
• History and Physical Examination
• Differential Diagnosis/Problem List
• Care Planning
• Physician Ordering
• Order Communications

• Medication Management
  • Medication Reconciliation
  • Medication and Medication Allergy Lists
  • Drug Selection
  • Pharmacy Evaluation and Distributing
  • Medication Administration

• Diagnostic Studies Results Review and Management
  • Laboratory
  • Radiology/Diagnostic Imaging
  • Required Reporting

• Surgery/Procedures
• Medication Administration
• Patient Monitoring/Vital Signs
• Patient Education
• Patient Discharge Instruction

• Revenue Cycle
  • Eligibility Verification
  • Documentation Improvement
  • Coding
  • Billing
  • Claims Status
  • Remittance Processing
  • Collections
  • Value-based Purchasing

• Patient Follow Up

Table 4.3a (continued)   Generic List of Hospital Processes

• Health Information Management
  • Master Person Index
  • Electronic Document Management
  • Release of Information
  • Transfer Records
  • Health Information Exchange
  • Privacy
  • Security
  • Breach Notification

• Quality Measurement, Reporting, and Improvement
• Registry Maintenance
• Risk Management
• Executive Decision Support
• Marketing/Fund Raising
• Research
• Education
• Personal Health Record

Source: Copyright © Margret\A Consulting, LLC. With permission.

Table 4.3b   Generic List of Ambulatory Care Processes

• Pre-visit Registration
• Scheduling
• Patient Check-in
• Patient Intake
• Physician Chart Review
• Medical History Interview
• Physical Examination
• Assessment
• Diagnosis
• Care Planning
• Health Maintenance/Preventive Screening
• Staff Tasking
• Procedures

continued

Table 4.3b (continued)   Generic List of Ambulatory Care Processes

• Prescribing
    • Drug Sample Management
    • Controlled Substances

• Diagnostic Studies Ordering
• Coding
• Charge Capture and Billing
• Patient Accounts Receivable Management
• Referral Management
• Patient Instructions
• Visit Summary
• Patient Check-out
• Nurse-Only Visits
• Same-Day/Urgent Care Visits
• Annual Physical Exam
• Occupational Medicine
• Consultation
• Nursing Home Support
• Diagnostics Studies Results Review and Management
• No Show Management
• Prescription Refill/Renewal Requests
• Phone Calls/E-mail/E-visits
• Patient Follow-Up/Recall
• Release of Information
• (School, Camp, Employment, Other) Forms Completion
• Electronic Document Management
• Chronic Disease Management
• Quality Measurement, Reporting, and Improvement
• Required Reporting
• Personal Health Record
• Clinical Trials Recruitment and Participation
• Value-Based Purchasing

Source: Copyright © Margret\A Consulting, LLC. With permission.

Table 4.3c   Generic List of Health Information Exchange Processes

Basic Processes
• Participant Data Sharing Management
• Patient Identification
• Record Location

• Identity Management
   • Authorization for Access
   • Authentication
   • Access Control
   • Audit Logging

• Consent Management
   • Patient Opt-in/Opt-out
   • Release of Information
   • Patient Authorization

• Document/Data Transmission
   • Security
   • Standards Conversion

• System Integration
Advanced/Special Processes
• Personal Health Record
• Data and Code Set Mapping
• Registry Services
• De-identification
• Data Aggregation
• Data Analytics
• Quality Measurement, Reporting, and Improvement
• Biosurveillance/Population Health
• Emergency Response
• Temporary/Permanent Data Storage
• Contingency Services
• Disability Processing

Source: Copyright © Margret\A Consulting, LLC. With permission.

documentation improvement; another process may be case management; and a third process might be quality data abstraction. It may not be until all processes are listed on the Process Inventory Worksheet and connection points made that it becomes clear that adjustment is needed.

A process inventory is the means to ensure that ultimately all processes impacted by EHR and HIT are mapped, analyzed, and redesigned. Sometimes the CDO's organizational chart may "get in the way" of adequately separating unique processes, or identifying where unique processes cross organizational boundaries. Health information management and revenue cycle management processes are examples where there are a number of associated processes frequently performed by several different departments. Bringing members of these teams together to enumerate the processes and recognize connection points not only serves to ensure completeness of the Process Inventory, but also promotes **process interoperability**. The standards development organization that creates many of the protocols for exchange of data across disparate healthcare systems, Health Level Seven (HL7), uses the term "process interoperability" as the third tier in scoping interoperability for health care (HL7 2007). (The first two tiers include technical interoperability and semantic interoperability, as illustrated in Figure 4.1.) A common understanding of the relationships and dependencies among and between processes achieves greater coordination and leads to efficiencies and greater effectiveness. Process interoperability embodies the human/social element—workflow, process rules, protocols, user roles, etc. (Benson 2010).

It is generally advisable to list (and map) current processes completely before moving to analysis and redesign of processes. However, where it can be anticipated that a process will change dramatically with EHR and HIT, it may be advisable to expand the scope of the process, especially where it is cross-departmental—at least until such time that sub-processes can be clearly delineated and the full range of participants return to review and validate the process in its entirety. If significant changes in job duties are anticipated, expanding the scope of the process can also help identify the new or enhanced job duties, helping

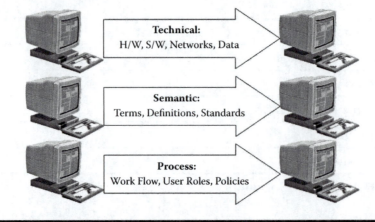

Figure 4.1 Importance of process interoperability. (From *Coming to Terms: Scoping Interoperability for Health Care*, HL7, 2007.)

to alleviate concerns about loss of jobs. (At this time also it may be prudent to engage labor leaders or union representatives to plan for upcoming changes. For example, nurses in many hospitals are organized and the EHR could impact the scope of their jobs.)

As an example from Case Study 4.2, if the EHR truly captures structured data for the majority of its documentation and includes alerts where data for quality improvement reporting is required, there may be no need for a clinical data abstraction process, or even a clinical data analysis/clinical documentation improvement program—or at least not for the limited scope of Quality Reporting. After all, data standards must be met for direct patient care (e.g., clinical decision support), reimbursement, and other purposes. Individuals who perform current quality *reporting* functions could be utilized more effectively in quality *improvement* aspects, where they interpret trends, help in redesigning clinical processes, improve screen design, contribute to automated protocol development, monitor use and make adjustments in clinical decision support, and continuously educate about quality.

Managing the Process Inventory

Although the Process Inventory Worksheet, once completed, can serve as the CDO's Process Inventory, the contents of the Worksheet may be stripped down for the Process Inventory to just list the process names, or possibly the names and process owner. Alternatively, the contents of the Worksheet may be loaded into a database with other workflow and process management project activities associated with the processes, such as the name of the deputy lead analyst for each process, due date, etc.

In whatever manner the CDO chooses to store its Process Inventory, use of the Worksheet should result in a list of processes to be mapped, analyzed, and redesigned—the Process Inventory. In addition to the primary purpose of ensuring a complete list of processes to be mapped for EHR and HIT, the Inventory can also be used to prioritize process mapping if desired.

Just as with the EHR itself, some CDOs prefer a "big bang" approach to process mapping. In this case, the work is divided among the primary participants, and all are expected to perform their process mapping simultaneously. This can be a good approach if the organization begins its process mapping prior to EHR vendor selection.

Some CDOs prefer to use a more phased approach for mapping its processes. Phasing can be done in a variety of ways. Some CDOs prefer to identify the processes that seem most in need of improvement and address those first, very aware of the old adage surrounding computers: garbage-in/garbage-out. Fixing broken processes first provides an immediate payback for the effort. It also improves the chances of getting the EHR implementation more right the first time around.

Other CDOs prefer to approach mapping processes in a logical sequence, often as performed for the care delivery event and then for non-care delivery processes. Table 4.3a and Table 4.3b are listed essentially in such an order.

Another phasing strategy is to address the "easier" processes to be mapped first. "Easier" processes usually are those that are more visible. This strategy can be helpful where the CDO is relying on their internal staff to perform the mapping and/or stakeholders are new to process mapping.

Finally, a few bold CDOs have decided to tackle the most complex processes first, especially where they are performing process mapping prior to selection and using it to assist in requirements specification.

Process Inventory Database

The Process Inventory can be used as a basis for the workflow and process management project plan, and to create a database containing pertinent information about the project. Table 4.4 provides the data that may be contained in a Process Inventory Database.

Table 4.4   Contents of Process Inventory Database

• Process Name
• Primary Process Participant (Process Owner): Job Title, Department
• Other Participants: Job Titles, Departments, and Roles: • Supplier • Customer
• Other Stakeholders
• Connects from Process(es)
• Connects to Process(es)
• I.S. Application
• Prioritization Category • Critical component comprising the EHR and HIT • Necessary contributor to EHR and HIT • Desirable process associated with EHR and HIT
• Current Process • Deputy lead process analyst: Name, Contact Information • Date current mapping to be initiated • Date current mapping actually initiated • Date current mapping validated • Validation participants: Name, Department, Contact Information

Table 4.4 (continued)   Contents of Process Inventory Database

• Forms and reports collected • Date current mapping to be completed • Date current mapping actually completed: documentation supplied to lead process analyst

• Current Process Analysis
  • EHR and HIT functional specifications identified
  • EHR and HIT goals refinement
  • Baseline data collected
  • Opportunities for improvement prior to EHR and HIT
  • Opportunities for improvement with EHR and HIT

• Process Redesign
  • Deputy lead process analyst: Name, Contact Information
  • Date redesign to be initiated
  • Date redesign actually initiated
  • Date redesign validated
  • Validation participants: Name, Department, Contact Information
  • Date redesign to be completed
  • Date redesign actually completed: documentation supplied to lead process analyst
  • Date redesign to be implemented
  • Testing requirements
  • Date redesign to be trained
  • Date redesign actually trained
  • Date redesign actually implemented
  • Improvement monitoring events schedule

Source: Copyright © Margret\A Consulting, LLC. With permission.

Key Points

■ Mapping current processes can seem like a never-ending task if not organized in a manner that defines the end state. A **Process Inventory** provides a checklist of processes needing to be mapped, and a means for stakeholders to view their progress toward completion.

■ To aid in the development of a complete list of unique processes for the Process Inventory, a **Process Inventory Worksheet** may be used. This usually includes identifying the participants in a process and its boundaries. Once all processes are listed, every connection point should be visible as a step toward achieving **process interoperability**.

- Tip: Unique processes do not necessarily begin and end within one organizational unit. Cross-departmental processes must be understood and coordinated.
- A process inventory can be maintained in a **Process Inventory Database** that also contributes to the **Workflow and Process Management Project Plan**.

References

Benson, T., 2010. *Principles of Health Interoperability: HL7 and SNOMED*, Health Informatics Series, London: Springer-Verlag, 25–26.

HL7, 2007 (Feb. 7). *Coming to Terms: Scoping Interoperability for Health Care.* Ann Arbor, MI: Health Level Seven, 13,15, 18–19, 27.

Lehmann, C.F., n.d. *Using Portfolio Management for Continuous Process Improvement— A BP Methods Management Guide.* Version 1.0. Boston: BPMethods Press, xix.

NC-DENR, 2006. Worksheet 1: Business Process Inventory. North Carolina Department of Environment and Natural Resources. Available at: http://www.enr.state.nc.us/its/pdf/DENR%COOP%20Worksheet%201.doc

Reardan, J., 2010. "A Practical Framework for Business Process Modeling." Process1st Consulting, LLC. Available at www.Process1st.com

UN/CEFACT and OASIS, 2001. *Business Process Analysis Worksheets and Guidelines.* Geneva: United Nations Centre for Trade Facilitation and Electronic Business and Boston: Organization for the Advancement of Structured Information Standards, 27 and 39.

Chapter 5

Step 3: Select Tools and Train Team

Training increases skill and competence and teaches employees the "how" of a job. Education increases their insights and understanding and teaches the "why."

—Michael Hammer and James Champy
Reengineering the Corporation: A Manifesto for Business Revolution

The third step in workflow and process management for improvement with EHR and HIT is to select the tool or tools to use for annotating processes and then train those who will be performing the process mapping on using the tool(s). If the workflow and process management steps have been followed in sequence so far, the stakeholders to the various workflows and processes to be mapped should appreciate the value of process mapping and be ready to gain skills and competence in its performance.

Workflow and Process Mapping Tool Selection

In Chapter 2 it was alluded to that the systems flowchart was the most popular form of workflow and process mapping tool, although there are other tools and structures in which workflows and processes can be annotated. The purpose and context of workflow and process management has some bearing on the selection of tools.

It can be helpful to think about the characteristics of the workflows and processes being mapped in order to begin the tool selection process. These characteristics reflect the "payload" of the workflows and processes—what are they carrying, what is their primary focus. Figure 5.1 suggests a hierarchy of payloads—from focusing at the macro level on what has typically been referred to

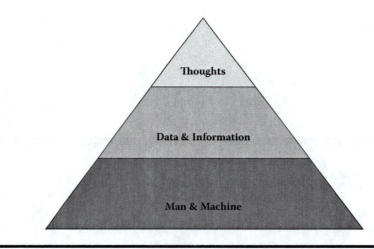

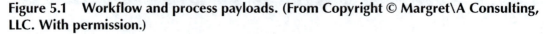

Figure 5.1 Workflow and process payloads. (From Copyright © Margret\A Consulting, LLC. With permission.)

as "man and materials" (movement of people and products), to an "information payload" (where data are processed into information), and ultimately to a micro level of "thoughts" reflecting decision making and ideally generating knowledge. Going from bottom to top, greater precision is required, and the workflow and processes become increasingly less visible.

As a result of the payload of the workflows and processes being mapped to redesign work in an environment where EHR and HIT are being added, the systems flowchart probably makes the most sense because it was designed for the purpose of documenting the flow of information.

However, sometimes the context in which workflow and process mapping occurs requires compromises in tool selection or the use of several tools. For example, it was noted in Chapter 2 that a list structure of the steps in a process could be used to document workflows and processes, although the list structure was not as conducive to documenting decision making. Understanding the decision-making process and thought flow in health care is vital—and yet, physicians who are among those who make the most decisions based on thinking about patient information will often not want to "fool around with" the symbols inherent in the systems flowchart or other structured tools. In these cases, some modification of a single list may be appropriate, the list may be used as a draft for someone else to translate into a more symbolic tool, or a process analyst may need to work with physicians to document their thought flows as they describe them.

In addition to tools that are used to document current and redesigned workflows and processes, other tools may be used to assist a process analyst in interviewing those reluctant to map their own workflows and processes. For example, mind mapping tools may assist in collecting thought flows, and then may be translated into a systems flowchart for more structured analysis. Likewise, a flowchart may have been used to map a process by a process analyst; but in order to convey the information to an end user not comfortable with the symbols used in a flowchart, a use case may be generated.

There will most likely be additional tools needed to collect baseline data (described in Chapter 7). As current workflow and process maps are analyzed, root cause analysis tools of various types, including statistical analysis tools, may need to be used. These tools are discussed in Chapter 9.

Workflow and Process Mapping Tools

Despite that the systems flowchart is the most commonly used workflow and process mapping tool for an EHR and HIT context, there are other tools that some process analysts or other stakeholders may be familiar with and want to consider using. These include the process diagram, flow process chart, and swim-lane process chart. In addition, the essential use case and mind mapping tools are newer, more software-oriented tools that can be useful for aiding the mapping of workflows and processes at the thought-flow level.

The ***process diagram*** is a tool most commonly used to illustrate the flow of people and paperwork. It uses a series of four symbols, each representing a specific type of occurrence. The operation symbol can be modified to show refinements, especially as related to information processes (Graham 2004). When using the process diagram in the context of preparing for EHR and HIT, the traditional meaning of the symbols may be modified to reflect a greater focus on information and automation, as identified in Figure 5.2.

Figure 5.3 provides an example of a process diagram, illustrating the current steps in processing a prescription refill beginning with the patient calling the

Symbol	Traditional Meaning	Modification for Data and Information Flow Mapping
○	Operation: object is arranged or prepared for another step, assembled or disassembled or intentionally changed	Non-information based operation
●	Do operation: a physical change occurs	Data are processed into information
⊙	Origination: Creation of a record	New record created
⊘	Add/Alter: Addition or change of information	Data are added, changed, or deleted
⇨	Transportation	Transmission
▢	Inspection	Control or decision point
▽	Storage/delay	Storage
D	Delay	Delay

Figure 5.2   Process diagram symbols. (From Copyright © Margret\A Consulting, LLC. With permission.)

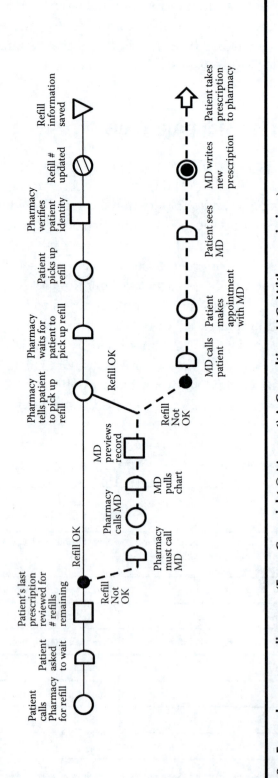

Figure 5.3   Example process diagram. (From Copyright © Margret\A Consulting, LLC. With permission.)

pharmacy for a refill and ending with either the refill information saved in the pharmacy after the patient has picked up the refill or the patient taking a new prescription to the pharmacy. (Processing a new prescription is different from processing a refill, and hence is a separate process.) The process diagram is excellent for clearly describing workflows and for highlighting delays. Some users of the process diagram will annotate the delays with the average time of the delay as well as the caption describing the delay. The process diagram can illustrate decision points and associated branches, typically by following a convention of using a dotted line to identify an alternative path. The process diagram does not provide a lot of room for describing each step in the process, and often requires placement of the captions to be alternated above and below the symbols. In Figure 5.2, two of the inspection symbols are used to illustrate a decision; however, the inspection symbol does not require branching, such as illustrated by the "Pharmacy verifies patient identity" step.

The ***flow process chart*** is the combination of a list detailing the sequences of steps in the process and the process diagram symbols, with additional analysis elements (Amatayakul 2010). This tool is illustrated in Figure 5.4.

Flow Process Chart												
Process: ☐ Present ☐ Proposed ☐ Person ☐ Material								**Analysis (✓):**				**Performed by:** **Date:**

Operation	Transportation	Inspection	Delay	Storage	Distance in feet	Quantity	Time					
								Why is it done this way?				
								Why is it done by this person?				
								Why is it done at this time?				
								Why is it done at this location?				
								Why is it done – is it necessary?				
								Details of Present/Proposed Process:				**Notes**
O	⇨	☐	D	▽				1.				
O	⇨	☐	D	▽				2.				
O	⇨	☐	D	▽				3.				
O	⇨	☐	D	▽				4.				
O	⇨	☐	D	▽				5.				
O	⇨	☐	D	▽				6.				
O	⇨	☐	D	▽				7.				
O	⇨	☐	D	▽				8.				
O	⇨	☐	D	▽				9.				
O	⇨	☐	D	▽				10.				
Totals:									Present		Proposed	
O								**Summary:**	No	Time	No	Time
								Operations				
	⇨							Transportations				
		☐						Inspections				
			D					Delays				
				▽				Storages				
								Totals:				

Figure 5.4 Flow process chart. (From Copyright © Margret\A Consulting, LLC. With permission.)

Table 5.1   Illustrating Decisions on a List

```
1. .........?
   If A.........
   Then 2.........?
        If Y, Then.........do Pink 1, then Pink 2, then Orange
        If N, Then.........do Yellow, then Orange
   If B.........
   Then 3.........?
        If <1, Then.........do Yellow, then Orange
        If >, Then.........do Blue, then Orange
        If = 1, Then.........do Green, which ends the process
```

Some process analysts like the flow process chart because it is a good way for those who are uncomfortable with using symbols to document a process while the analyst returns to highlight the applicable symbols. As previously described, however, lists are very difficult to use in illustrating branches associated with decisions. Table 5.1 illustrates how this may be done by indentions in a list, and the need to be very careful—especially where there is a complex set of decisions to be made that end up with multiple layers of indention.

One of the biggest benefits of the flow process chart, however, is that it enables capturing baseline data as part of the tool. Typically there is a place to record distance, quantity, and time. Although specific conventions should be established so as to ensure consistency in recording them, these dimensions can be invaluable as part of the analysis and redesign effort. Case Study 5.1 is an extension of Case Study 2.2 on redesigning a patient room for a new hospital. Case Study 5.1 considers nurse travel time in the new hospital utilizing the flow process chart. Case Study 5.2 illustrates how downstream time savings should make up for additional data entry in an EHR.

Case Study 5.1: Nurse Travel Time in a New Hospital

In planning to select input devices for use by nurses as a hospital plans to move to a new facility, consideration is given to using wireless-on-wheels (WOW) devices or tablets that nurses think they could carry in a sling to give them hands-free capability. To help them make their decision, the nurses were urged to evaluate the distance they traveled over the course of a day in the old hospital using the existing WOWs, which included a bar code reader and medication tray. They should then compare this to the traveling time in the new facility where they would be required to return to a medication-dispensing cabinet for each medication to be administered to a patient. It was recommended that they conduct this comparison while documenting the steps in their processes and annotating how frequently each step was performed and how long it took. It was also suggested that after they documented their current processes, they then try carrying the tablets in slings and going back to the medication-dispensing cabinet for each medication while still in the old hospital to see how that process might be different, even though the layout of the nursing units in the new hospital was quite different. The flow process chart tool was supplied to them with some training on its use for documenting their current process.

Current processes varied by nursing unit, because each unit was not configured in exactly the same way and different types of patients were assigned different units. However, virtually all nurses documented frequent trips to the medication-dispensing cabinet—literally charting miles of walking per week, despite that they had WOWs with medication trays. When asked about this, they described the fact that they often did not use the WOWs at the point of care, again citing how heavy they were to push. Rather, at times medications were to be given for each patient that they had jotted down on a piece of scratch paper they carried in their pocket, they went to the medication-dispensing cabinet, retrieved the applicable medications, stopped at the WOW to log in that they had administered the medication to the patient, and then went to the patient's room to actually administer the medication. While such a process defeats the goals of the "medication five rights" (ISMP 1999), it is not surprising to find such workarounds (Phillips and Berner 2004; Mills et al. 2006; Koppel et al. 2008). As a result of the workaround, however, it was unlikely that travel times could potentially be longer in the new hospital using only the tablet on the sling and having to constantly return to the medication-dispensing cabinet. Nurses who conducted the tablet/sling pilot test, however, reported that the tablets "got heavy very fast" and tended to shift around on their person—potentially knocking over items as they bent over or sat in and got out of a chair. Because it had been learned that WOWs were not readily able to be pushed into the new hospital's patient rooms, the nurses were now struggling with what choices they could make.

Case Study 5.2: Downstream Time Savings Saves the Day

A physician was complaining about the new e-prescribing system the clinic had acquired. He was convinced that it was taking him at least several minutes longer to enter a prescription on the computer than to scribble a prescription on his prescription pad. He actually did a mini time study for himself: keeping track on a tally sheet every other day of the time he started and ended entering each prescription in the computer. At the end of his "study," he tallied the time and found it came to an average of thirty minutes per day. He determined that in thirty minutes he could see three additional patients, earn from $150 to $300 more per day, and was preparing to stop using the e-prescribing system.

Luckily, a process analyst had been engaged by the practice administrator to help streamline back-office work. The analyst was recruited to work briefly with this physician, creating a "before-and-after" flow process chart. It illustrated that more data elements were required to be entered into the e-prescribing system and showed that the process of writing the prescription took longer. However, the physician was shown that the overall number of steps were fewer when downstream parts of the process were included. He was asked if he had also tracked the number of calls he got from pharmacists because they could not read his handwriting, the drug prescribed was not on the patient's formulary, the patient was allergic to the drug, or he had failed to document other pertinent information, such as the dose, route of administration, or number of refills. He was also asked if he had reviewed his charts recently to determine that every drug prescribed was on a single, active medication list and, if not, had he determined how long he spent scanning through notes to compile such a list for any given patient.

Agreeing that he had not considered these—and potentially other factors—he actually decided to stop e-prescribing for a week and tally the number of pharmacist calls and the amount of time each call consumed as a result. Despite the facts that he was now more cognizant of what support he had been missing in the manual environment, and that every prescription did not generate a call from a pharmacist, the average call consumed close to six minutes and there was an average of five calls per day that could have been eliminated through the use of e-prescribing. While the results were a "wash" in terms of time, the physician appreciated the "scientific process" used to generate the findings, and he also noted other potential patient safety improvements.

Similar findings to those in Case Study 5.2 have been found repeatedly in other studies. For example, one study conducted at Case Western Reserve found that the average time spent on patient-specific work outside the examination room accounted for approximately 40 percent of a physician's day (Gottschalk and Flocke 2005). A study conducted by the Medical Group Management Association (MGMA) in 2010 reported that for medical practices that have implemented an EHR report, after five years, the average operating margin for the practices was 10 percent higher than it was during the first year of EHR use.

The ***swim-lane process chart*** is another workflow and process mapping tool often used to illustrate processes where there are many tasks performed simultaneously, or where there are many hand-offs from one department to another. The tool literally gets its name from a swimming pool with a lane (i.e., set of steps) for each swimmer (i.e., different person, department, or system). Swim-lane process charts often, although not always, use the same symbols as the systems flowchart. Some swim-lane developers utilize only rectangles, while others use the same symbols as the process diagram and flow process chart. As illustrated in Figure 5.5, special symbols may also be added. In this case, a clock illustrates the passage of time, or what might be considered a delay in the process diagram or flow process chart.

The ***systems flowchart***, as previously noted, is the most widely used tool for mapping workflows and processes associated with information systems implementations. There are three basic symbols. An oval signifies the boundary, or termination, points where a process begins and ends. There may be multiple starting and ending points. For example, a current prescription refill process in a clinic may begin with a call from a patient, a call from the pharmacy, or a fax from the pharmacy. For a patient encounter in an emergency department

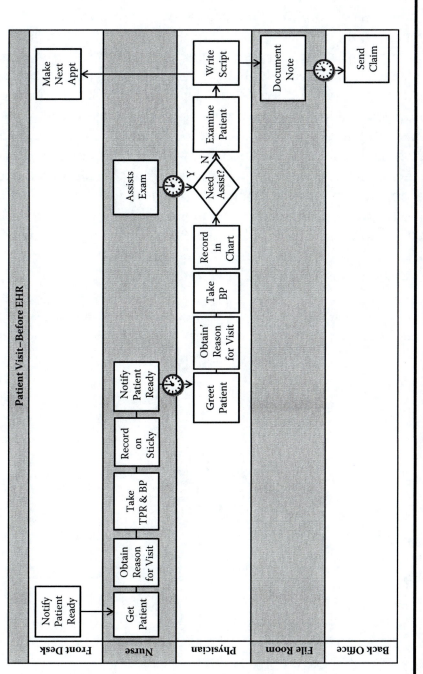

Figure 5.5 Swim-lane process chart. (From Copyright © Margret\A Consulting, LLC. With permission.)

of a hospital, the process may end with an admission to the hospital or a discharge to home. A rectangle denotes an operation. These are the specific tasks in the process with the exception of decision-making tasks. Operations are typically performed by persons, such as a clerk, nurse, physician, lab tech, etc. However, operations may be performed by an information system. For example, if depicting the process of ordering a laboratory test in the EHR, there will be an exchange of data from the EHR to the laboratory information system (LIS).

In a systems flowchart, a diamond is the symbol used to depict the decision-making task. A special symbol is used because one of the primary purposes of information systems is to provide decision support; hence it is important to highlight the decision making in every process to be automated. The diamond symbol enables one branch to *go to* it and two or three branches to *come from* it. Every decision must have at least two branches—or it would not be a decision! However, if there are more than three potential paths that result from a decision, process mappers have the choice of either using a circle from which more branches can be shown, or if there are even more branches than realistically fit on the flowchart, a decision table may be referenced. Figure 5.6a illustrates the decision making previously shown in the list structure in Table 5.1. Figure 5.6b illustrates the same decision making as shown in Table 5.1 and Figure 5.6a, but in a decision table.

Systems flowcharts have a great deal of flexibility. There are many special symbols that can be used to enhance their illustration capabilities, if desired.

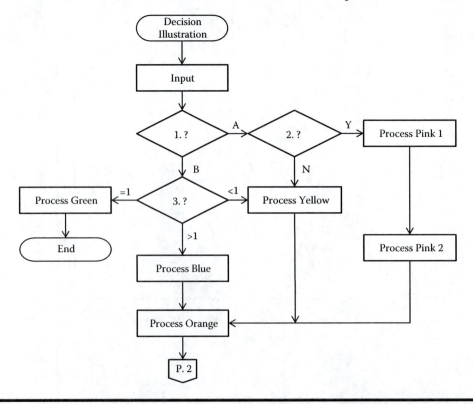

Figure 5.6a Systems flowchart illustrating decisions. (From Copyright © Margret\A Consulting, LLC. With permission.)

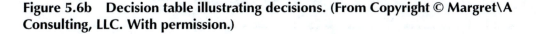

		Condition Alternatives					
Conditions	1.	A	A	A	B	B	B
	2.		Y	N			
	3.				<1	>1	=1
		Action Entries					
Actions	2.	X					
	Pink(s)		X				
	Yellow			X	X		
	Blue					X	
	Green						X
	Orange		X			X	
	End						X

Figure 5.6b   Decision table illustrating decisions. (From Copyright © Margret\A Consulting, LLC. With permission.)

However, it is not necessary to use any other symbols to be equally effective. Despite the flexibility inherent in systems flowcharts, they are a very standard annotation process that virtually all information technologists understand. In fact, the symbols and conventions for using them are standardized as an International Organization for Standardization (ISO), ISO 5807:1985. Chapter 6 provides much more information on use of the systems flowchart.

The systems flowcharts displayed throughout this book were created in Microsoft PowerPoint. Microsoft and other vendors have specific diagramming software that can be used—for any of the commonly used workflow and process mapping annotation tools. However, if process mapping is going to be performed by those actually performing the process, it can be very convenient to give everyone a pad of square sticky notes and have them record each step they perform on a separate note in the pad. Once the steps are identified, the sticky notes can be put on a wall, flipchart, or other large piece of paper. (One clinic used examining room table paper, which is huge and can be posted on a wall as well as rolled up for storage.) To illustrate the basic symbols, a sticky note placed horizontally can denote an operation; and when tilted at an angle can denote a decision. Lines to connect the notes can be drawn on the paper (preferably in pencil so that changes can be made if necessary). If variation among persons performing work is suspected, each person can be given a different-colored sticky note pad. As each person posts his or her steps, those with variations can post only those notes illustrating the variation.

Mind mapping has been mentioned as a tool that may aid in documenting primarily mental processes. Whether the knowledge worker directly uses this tool, or it is used by a process analyst who is interviewing the knowledge worker, mind mapping allows diagramming thoughts that may appear to be random; or at least occurring in no particular sequence. For example, in Case Study 1.2 in which an endocrinologist was attempting to find an alternative drug for a diabetic patient with a urinary tract infection who was unresponsive

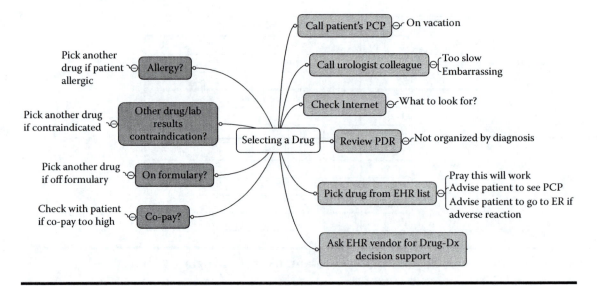

Figure 5.7   Mind mapping tool. (From Copyright © Margret\A Consulting, LLC. With permission.)

to the initial drug prescribed by the primary care provider, the endocrinologist was observed thinking about going to the Internet, then to a paperback *Physician Desk Reference*, and then to the list of available drugs in the EHR itself to select the appropriate drug. The mental processes could have occurred in any sequence, and not all of the thoughts were visible to the process analyst, because the endocrinologist acknowledged also thinking about contacting a urologist colleague or the patient's primary care provider.

Figure 5.7 illustrates the mind map that may have been drawn by the endocrinologist or the process analyst in Case Study 1.2. Although this map was drawn using special mind mapping software, many mind maps are drawn freehand. In fact, the Web has many examples of additional uses for mind mapping—often drawn freehand, such as for developing S.M.A.R.T. goals (Reed 2004), taking notes (mindtools.com), and brainstorming, which can be especially useful for redesigning workflows and processes (Druce 2009). They are simple to use, generally starting with identifying the topic in the middle of a blank page and then literally writing down in narrative or even simple drawings or symbols whatever comes to mind. When using software, what has been documented can then be moved around to show relationships. Color or highlighting can be added. For example, in Figure 5.7, the three thoughts the process analyst identified are placed in the center on the right and highlighted with thick lines. Thoughts further identified by the endocrinologist related specifically to the given patient are also placed on the right above and below the "visible" thoughts, more or less in the sequence considered. Later, the endocrinologist identified that, of course, there were also standard considerations always given to selecting any drug for any patient, such as patient allergies, contraindications, formulary benefits, and cost (of co-pay). These were placed on the left side of the mind map in shaded boxes and in the sequence typically considered (Passuello 2007).

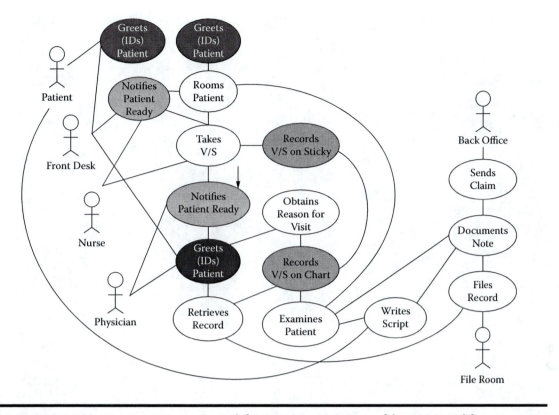

Figure 5.8   UML use case. (From Copyright © Margret\A Consulting, LLC. With permission.)

Use case is a tool originally developed as an object-oriented (OO) software modeling technique that would help developers understand customer requirements (Wiegers 1997). It is currently used in several forms. One form, often called the Unified Modeling Language (UML) use case, uses graphic notations—where stick figures denote "actors" and bubbles denote operations. Instead of illustrating sequence of workflow, however, the **UML use case** illustrates relationships among operations, particularly at the level of the data being processed. The intent is to build "objects" of data processes that can be reused in software when they occur in multiple locations. Figure 5.8 illustrates a UML use case. In this example, there are three potential candidates for creating objects: "Greets (IDs) patient," "Notifies patient ready," and "Records V/S on sticky/on chart."

In addition to the stick figure and bubble notation, UML use cases may also be drawn using other, preexisting standard notations, especially those used for data modeling. **Data modeling** is a process of identifying the operations performed on data as they move within and between systems. Data modeling depicts dataflow, which was introduced in Chapter 2. Tools commonly used for data modeling include the dataflow diagram (DFD) and the entity-relationship diagram (ERD) (Stiern 1999). This is a level of detail that is generally not included in workflow and process management, but rather software development.

When the federal government first began to develop the concept of the Nationwide Health Information Network, a series of **harmonized use cases**

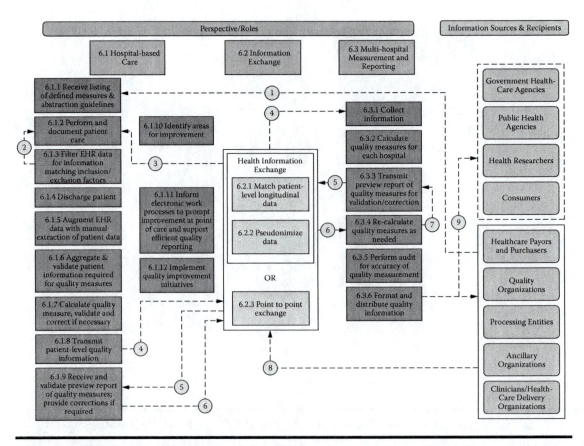

Figure 5.9   Harmonized use case for the Nationwide Health Information Network. (From U.S. Department of Health and Human Services, Office of the National Coordinator for Health Information Technology, Quality Detailed Use Case, June 18th, 2007. http:// healthit.hhs.gov/portal/server.pt?open=512&objID=1202&&PageID=15677&mode=2 &in_hi_userid=10732&cached=true)

were developed over the period from 2007 to 2009 to depict the typical work-flow and processes associated with functions that the Network would provide. "Harmonized" refers to the fact that multiple workflows and processes were reviewed and a composite was drawn that reflected the most common work-flows and processes. This could serve as a standard approach for the Network. Figure 5.9 provides an example of one of these use cases. Boxes are used to illustrate operations. They are organized by the actors, denoted at the top of the process columns, in this case from left to right a hospital ("hospital-based care"), the Nationwide Health Information Network ("information exchange"), a vendor (who would collect, format, audit, and distribute "multi-hospital measurement and reporting"), and "information sources and recipients." The workflow in the sce-nario is identified through numbers in the circles. For example, the first workflow begins with healthcare payers and purchasers defining the quality measurement specifications hospitals are to report.

Essential use case is yet another form of use case that can be used very successfully for various aspects of workflow and process management. It

Table 5.2　Essential Use Case

Primary Care Physician Use of EHR for Patient Visit	
User Intent	*System Response*
1. Physician signs on	Verifies permission to access system
	Provides list of patients
2. Selects patient	Opens patient file to dashboard displaying demographics, problem list, medication list, medication allergy list, preventive screening reminders, and most recent lab results
3. Reviews medication list with patient	
4. Adds over-the-counter (OTC) use of aspirin	Includes OTC aspirin on medication list
5. Checks off that antibiotic use complete	Marks antibiotic use complete
6. Selects tab to document patient's medical history	Pops-up box that patient is overdue for seasonal influenza vaccination
7. Asks patient about whether a flu shot was obtained this season	
8. Tasks nurse to administer flu shot at end of visit	Sends alert to nurse dashboard to give flu shot to this patient at end of visit

Source: Copyright © Margret\A Consulting, LLC. With permission.

focuses on describing the interactions between an information system and the user. Such essential use cases are often referred to as **scenarios** because they depict the story of a given process (Constantine and Lockwood 1999). The graphic notations in the UML form of use case or other data modeling tools are often distracting to users not comfortable with workflow and process mapping tools. As a result of the desire to have a more effective means of communicating directly with end users, the essential use case was conceived. Most commonly this is rendered as a table where one side identifies each step in a process that a user would perform, and the other side identifies how the information system would react (Ambler 2008). An example is provided in Table 5.2. The language should be brief and to the point, not including any technical language. For example, "Physician signs on" is something the user understands, in comparison to "user authenticates self to system," which is how a software developer might write this step. The essential use case is generally written at a high level, describing business (clinical) rules (Cockburn 2000).

Although essential use cases are excellent ways to get users engaged in workflow and process mapping and to capture their thought flows, the fact that the system response component is included makes the tool most useful for educating end users about the EHR and HIT, helping them specify functional requirements, and—after the technology is acquired, in contributing to the redesign of processes and training (Bredemeyer 2006). For example, Case Study 1.1 on workflow for preventive screening suggested that physicians were not happy with their system when preventive screening reminders were displayed (only) at the start of the patient visit workflow. It is also known that physicians do not care very much for pop-ups that require immediate action unless the action to which the pop-up is responding represents a high level of potential harm to the patient. Pop-ups interrupt thought flow and become annoying. In Table 5.2 it appears that the physician wanted to move to the patient's medical history-taking after checking on the medications. Instead, the physician chose to ask the patient about the flu shot and tasked the nurse to give the patient a flu shot. What is not as easily illustrated in the essential use case, as with other list structures, are the choices the user has when a decision point is encountered (Constantine and Lockwood 2001). For example, was there a way to decline action and perhaps request the pop-up to be viewed later, or would the reminder be lost until the next visit?

Selecting the Right Tool(s) and Following Tool Conventions

Because a number of different types of tools exist for workflow and process mapping, a question may arise as to how to choose among them. A safe bet is the systems flowchart. However, other tools may have their place, especially for unique circumstances. For instance, most work in health care is performed sequentially; but where a particular process does have simultaneous operations or hand-offs among departments, the swim lane may be chosen. Even in this case, however, the systems flowchart symbology and conventions can be overlaid on the swim-lane chart. As previously mentioned, any tool that utilizes a list structure may be easier for clinicians, and especially physicians to use or at least review.

The CDO undertaking workflow and process mapping may wish to require that all maps ultimately utilize a single tool type, but may allow drafts to be created using any tool anyone wishes. If workflow and process mapping is not performed before an EHR or HIT vendor is chosen, the vendor may have a preference for the tool they will use to help the CDO. On the other hand, many EHR and HIT vendors provide very little, if any, support for workflow and process management, so the CDO is often left to make a decision on its own.

Whatever tool or tools the CDO decides to use, it is helpful to follow some conventions so that the tools can be shared among all stakeholders. Examples of such conventions are provided in Table 5.3.

Table 5.3   Example of Workflow and Process Mapping Conventions

1. Adopt standard metadata. Supply a template to ensure all pertinent data about the workflow and process map are captured and maintained. At a minimum, every map should contain:

   a. Process name

   b. Process version

   c. Process date

   d. Process owner (person who created the map) name, title, department, and contact information

   Optional information may include:

   e. Process stakeholders' names, titles, departments, and contact information

   f. Reference materials that are attached or hyperlinked, including associated forms, reports, decision tables, protocols or guidelines, and other information that elaborates upon or further explains components of the process map

   g. Associated data maps

2. Adopt a single mapping format, such as a specific commercial software utility, generic software (e.g., word processing, spreadsheet, or presentation software), or paper based. This facilitates sharing across stakeholders.

3. Develop a project charter (see Chapter 3) that includes the process inventory, project plan, and other components associated with managing the workflow and process mapping project. Utilize a file-sharing system to manage large workflow and process management projects.

4. Adopt annotation conventions within a map (Glandon 2007), such as:

   a. Standard orientation (i.e., portrait or landscape)

   b. Standard font and symbol size

   c. Means to illustrate variation (e.g., color, grayscale, numeric designation, separate maps, or subsidiary documentation associated with a "harmonized" map)

   d. Means to reference attachments (e.g., special symbol, call-out, or footnote)

   e. Whether and how to add comments to a map

   f. Internal consistency (flow will be from top to bottom and left to right; all "yes" branches from a decision symbol will flow to the right, and all "no" branches will flow to the bottom [or other desired convention])

   g. Use of on-page and off-page connector symbols and their designations (use capital letters for on-page connectors and numbers for off-page connectors)

   h. Use of special symbols (not permitted or permitted; and if permitted, which symbols)

   i. Rules associated with connector lines (e.g., straight lines vs. curved lines, solid lines vs. dotted lines, lines with arrows or lines without arrows, no diagonal lines, do not cross lines)

continued

Table 5.3 (continued)   Example of Workflow and Process Mapping Conventions

j. Ensure that in annotating the who, does, what mappers:

  i. Reference positions and not persons' names for "who"

  ii. Specify credentials of person where it makes a difference (e.g., "nurse" could be NP, RN, LPN, CMA, and others)

  iii. Use action verbs for "does"

  iv. State clearly the "what" as an object

  v. Use generic rather than brand names (e.g., if the object is an automated medication-dispensing cabinet, use "Meds Cabinet" or other phrase rather than Pyxis).

k. Utilize a glossary of short phrases, terms, and abbreviations to aid consistency of expression. The Agency for Healthcare Quality and Research (AHRQ) provides a list of short phrases from a specific CDO. As an example, "bathe patient" should be used to describe any bathing, washing, or cleaning of patient.

Source: Copyright © Margret\A Consulting, LLC. With permission.

Level of Detail

Unfortunately, there is no standard definition of levels of detail to document for workflows and processes (Ko et al. 2009). In Six Sigma, five levels of charting are described (between 0 and 4), where a level 0 flowchart represents the least amount of detail and usually contains one or two steps, and a level 4 flowchart represents the most amount of detail and can include hundreds of steps.

In general, it is recommended that the ultimate map of a workflow/process is one that supplies the information needed for the reason mapping is being performed. Soliman (1998) relates cost of mapping to its effectiveness: The cost spent to map a process should be no more than necessary to identify non-value-added steps. When individuals new to workflow and process mapping first start their documentation, they tend to map at a very high level. Whether it is necessary to get more detailed depends on how the map will be used. Table 5.4 provides descriptions of three levels of detail that may be helpful for CDOs mapping workflows and processes associated with EHR and HIT.

Training the Workforce to Perform Workflow and Process Mapping

The first step in preparing to train the workforce to perform workflow and process mapping is to decide on the method or combination of methods to apply (Damelio 2011). These are summarized in Table 5.5.

Once the method of workflow and process mapping is determined (and it may be necessary to do some combination of methods), who should be trained will become clearer. Obviously, the self-generated mapping method requires the most

Table 5.4 Workflow and Process Mapping Level of Detail

Macro Level
• Small number of steps describing a workflow and process from the most general view possible. Sometimes called the "30,000-foot" view.
• Suitable for executive management to learn about the scope of a project.
• Unlikely to lend itself to identifying opportunities for improvement.
• May be suitable for a "harmonized" map drawn from more detailed maps.
• Provides the framework for further detail, especially for those new to workflow and process mapping.

Middle Level (also called mini or midi)
• Depicts a level of detail that should enable identification of inefficiencies in visible (i.e., non-mental) workflows and processes. This is sometimes called the "10,000-foot" view.
• Often the level used for initial redesign of workflows and processes associated with use of information technology.
• A greater level of detail may result in focusing on work methods (a style or personal preference) rather than workflows and processes.

Micro Level
• At this level every task, however minor, is represented. This is the view "on the ground."
• Micro-level workflow and process maps are generally needed for mapping mentally performed processes.
• Caution should be applied that this level of detail remains at the process level and not the data level, which would then be dataflow mapping.
• Caution should also be applied because requiring this level of detail may result in users thinking they need to map absolutely every application of a given process. For example, a primary care physician may be asked to map the process of interviewing the patient. This may include asking about the reason for visit, illustrating what happens when there are multiple reasons, seeking information about the history of present illness—what are the symptoms, when did they start, etc. However, a physician who feels the need to map the interview process for every type of condition (e.g., diabetes, hypertension, influenza, headache) he or she treats is unrealistic and unnecessary. At most, this process may be broken down into visits for new patients and established patients, single and multiple reasons for visit, acute care and chronic care follow-up, annual history and physical exam, urgent care, etc.

people to be trained and the observation method the least number. The interview method may require a small amount of training that may be more educational than skill building, and be more oriented toward purpose than process. Alternatively, the interview method may be performed where those interviewed have no training, which can make them somewhat defensive, less than cooperative or forthcoming, and curious about what is next. Self-generated training

Table 5.5   Workflow and Process Mapping Methods

Methods	*Attributes*
Self-generated	This method requires individuals who actually perform the workflows and processes to map these themselves. If properly trained and given the time, this generally delivers the most complete and accurate maps. A significant level of coaching, however, may be required to get to the level of training to achieve such results. In addition, there is still time required to compare the maps and determine if they can be harmonized. Where many people perform the same process, it is feasible for a few representative individuals to be chosen to perform the mapping and share with others to post variations.
Interviewed	This is probably the most common method, as it generally is also the most expeditious. A fully trained process analyst can capture both what can be observed and what is performed mentally. Interviewing representative individuals where there are many performing the same process can help determine the level of variation and how many individuals must be interviewed to achieve the full picture. The process analyst, however, must be non-biased and ensure that no assumptions are made about processes.
Group facilitated	This is a commonly performed method where the number of individuals performing the process is small, or it has been identified that there are a limited number of variations performed by many. For example, there may be little variation on a given nursing unit in a CDO, but there may be great variations across all the nursing units. Group facilitated sessions can help identify variations immediately so there is less need for keeping the map posted a period of time for this purpose. The group can also begin the validation process by checking on each other's interpretations of what happens. Where a group includes both supervisors and direct workforce members, however, caution must be applied that workers do not defer to their supervisors or are reluctant to reveal workarounds.
Observation (or Shadowing)	Some CDOs use this method as a way to achieve process mapping without having to remove the workforce from their daily activities. A highly skilled process analyst can achieve good results by making observations only, but the maps will rarely be as complete or at the level of detail desired to ultimately analyze and redesign mentally performed processes that are characteristic of the processes associated with EHR and HIT. Often, observation and interview are combined.

Source: Copyright © Margret\A Consulting, LLC. With permission.

requires the most training and must be performed in advance of the mapping. Training of mappers who will map their own workflows and processes can be performed in a classroom setting to reduce cost and ensure consistency, or in online sessions. Sometimes it is necessary to provide general training to a large group and then focused training at specific locations. The group-facilitated method may include just-in-time training performed at the start of the facilitated session.

When determining who needs to be trained, it must also be recognized that different individuals will play different roles. It has been emphasized that all stakeholders need to be involved—at least in being able to provide input. Before individual mappers are trained, it may be appropriate to also train supervisors in their specific role as coach, supplier of resources, and one of the types of beneficiaries of improved processes (as are all stakeholders). Special attention should be placed on assuring that supervisors will enable complete "as-is" maps to be documented before attempting to redesign them. They need to understand the importance of engaging all members of their team in the process of analyzing and redesigning workflows. Above all else, supervisors must recognize that the purpose of process mapping is to seek opportunities for improvement (with or without automation), not to penalize workers who are not performing a current procedure as written.

Consultants, auditors, and technology vendors may also need training on the CDO's conventions and methods for process mapping. Each of these may have personal preferences for mapping, especially when they are external to the organization. This is not to suggest that their methods are wrong or their methods cannot be adopted by the CDO, but if the CDO has decided to undertake a formal workflow and process management program using specific tools, then external stakeholders bringing different methods to the organization can be confusing and potentially disruptive. At a minimum, the CDO with a formal program in place would want to consider this in selecting external support. If the best service supplier uses a different approach, a frank discussion about the ability to harmonize approaches is needed.

Who performs the training is another consideration. In general, the lead process analyst provides some or all of the training. For a large CDO, it may be necessary to train several deputy process analysts who will perform the interviewing, facilitation, or observation; or serve as train-the-trainers who will train all who will be self-generating process maps. Deputy process analysts should be given released time from (part of) their daily duties to provide process mapping services. Ideally, physicians who also serve as an EHR physician champion or the medical director of information systems/chief medical informatics officer should be trained in process mapping so that they may help their peers. In a small CDO without a formal process analyst, a consultant may be necessary to provide training; or an individual with a keen interest or characteristics typically associated with a process analyst may be able to self-learn through available reference material.

Training should generally be performed in close proximity to when mapping is expected to occur. For a CDO with many processes to be mapped in association with initiating EHR, it is very likely that training will require considerable follow-up. An effective way to train mappers for such a project is to provide initial training, have them draft one map, and then have them return to a classroom environment (in-person or online) to share their maps, learn how to improve them, and learn next steps.

A final step in training should ensure appreciation for the work effort and celebration of accomplishments. Health care as an industry is not well-attuned to the importance of feedback and observance of what the workforce has achieved. Workflow and process mapping is different work than most who will be involved are accustomed to and it can be stressful when the return on a major investment, such as EHR and HIT, is riding on the results of the workflow and process mapping activities.

Key Points

- Workflow and process mapping may be performed using a variety of **tools**, although the **systems flowchart** is the most commonly used tool when adopting information systems. Other tools, however, may be used in a complementary manner to support the development of a systems flowchart, enhance or embellish upon a part of a systems flowchart, and to get to the level of detail required for **mentally performed processes**.
- Workflow and process mapping in support of EHR and HIT adoption must focus on the **information payload**. It is insufficient to map only the flow of people or things through a hospital or a clinic. How information is captured, processed, used, and fed back into the system to generate knowledge are vital components of healthcare improvement.
- In order to most effectively and efficiently map many processes as part of the overall EHR and HIT adoption project, certain **conventions** should be followed; and **mapping methods** identified.
- Once a tool or tools are selected and methods for mapping are identified, all stakeholders must be trained with respect to their roles. **Training** must include **acknowledgment** of the contribution of the mappers to the overall purpose of the activity.

References

AHRQ. A Toolkit for Redesign in Health Care, Appendix B. Definitions. Agency for Healthcare Quality and Research. Available at: http://www.ahrq.gov/qual/toolkit/tkappb.htm

Amatayakul, M., (2010). *Electronic Health Records: Transforming Your Medical Practice, Second Edition*. Englewood, CO: Medical Group Management Association, p. 87.

Ambler, S.W., 2008. *The Object Primer 3rd* edition: Agile Model Driven Development with UML 2. Cambridge: Cambridge University Press, 139–175.

Bredemeyer, D. 2006. Functional Requirements and Use Cases, Bredemeyer Consulting, www.bredemeyer.com/use_cases.htm

Cockburn, Alistair, 2000. *Writing Effective Use Cases*. Reading, MA: Addison-Wesley Professional.

Damelio, R., 2011. *The Basics of Process Mapping, 2nd edition*. New York: Productivity Press, 145–147.

Druce, L., 2009 (Feb. 4). Q&A with Mind Mapping Guru Tony Buzan. Knowledge Board. Available at: http://www.knowledgeboard.com/item/2980

Glandon, T., 2007. Flowcharting Tips for Manual and Computer-based Systems, University of Texas at El Paso. Available at: http://docs.google.com/viewer?a=v&q =cache:izr1ap2spGAJ:accounting.utep.edu/tglandon/acct3320/flowcharts/ Flowcharting%2520Conventions.ppt+flowcharting+conventions&hl- =en&gl=us&pid=bl&srcid=ADGEESj7g6qLiVCUyYbHW0ilTigZBNbQ 5L2MyqghdSh6hAQwLbZIiVtIDi16CXzHdTX7yk7YJJbHgUgOdE- 1keV6fjq3Ojbz7AxDKSao-JMnKgOviGh_lM_iq8pw4FHHGCbnc8Lg- bW21&sig=AHIEtbRbXONhPgiy_sEejiFB3EHO9DPf8A

Gottschalk, A. and S.A. Flocke, 2005 (Nov./Dec.). "Time Spent in Face-to-Face Patient Care and Work Outside of the Examination Room." *Annals of Family Medicine*, 3(6): 488–493.

Graham, B.B., 2004. Detail Process Charting: Speaking the Language of Process. Hoboken, NJ: John Wiley & Sons, 1–5.

Hammer, M. and J. Champy, 2001. *Reengineering the Corporation: A Manifesto for Business Revolution*. New York: Harper-Collins Publishers, Inc., 76.

International Organization for Standardization, 1985. ISO 5807:1985 Information Processing — Documentation Symbols and Conventions for Data, Program, and System Flowcharts, Program Network Charts, and System Resources Charts.

ISMP, 1999 (April 7). The "Five Rights." ISMP Medication Safety Alert. Institute for Safe Medication Practices. Available at: http://www.ismp.org/Newsletters/acutecare/ articles/19990497.asp

Ko, R.K.L. et al., 2009. "Business Process Management (BPM) Standards: A Survey." *Business Process Management Journal*, 15(5): 744–491.

Koppel, R. et al. (2008 July/August). Workarounds to Barcode Medication Administration Systems: Their Occurrences, Causes, and Threats to Patient Safety. *Journal of the American Medical Informatics Association* 15(4):408-423

Constantine, L.L. and L.A.D. Lockwood, 1999. "Task Modeling with Essential Use Cases." *Software for Use: A Practical Guide to the Models and Methods of Usage-Centered Design*. Reading, MA: Addison-Wesley Professional.

Constantine, L.L. and L.A.D. Lockwood, 2001. "Structure and Style in Use Cases for User Interface Design." *Object-Modeling and User Interface Design*. Reading, MA: Addison-Wesley.

MGMA, 2010 (Oct. 25). *Electronic Health Records Impacts on Revenue, Costs, and Staffing: 2010 Report Based on 2009 Data*. Medical Group Management Association. Press Release Available at: http://www.mgma.com/press/default. aspx?id=39824

ONC, 2007 (June 18). Quality Detailed Use Case. U.S. Department of Health and Human Services, Office of the National Coordinator for Health Information Technology. Available at: http://healthit.hhs.gov/portal/server.pt?open=512&objID= 1202&&PageID=15677&mode=2&in_hi_userid=10732&cached=true

Passuello, L., 2007. "What is Mind Mapping? (and How to Get Started Immediately)."*The Very Best of Litemind: 2 Years of Mind Explorations*. Available at: http://litemind. com/what-is-mind-mapping?

Phillips, MT and ES Berner (Fall 2004). Beating the system—pitfalls of bar code medica- tion administration. *Journal of Healthcare Information Management* 18(4):16–18.

Reed, W., 2004 (Feb. 16). "Use Mind Mapping with Templates to Develop 'SMART' Goals." Innovation Tools. Available at: http://www.innovationtools.com/Articles/ ArticleDetails.asp?a=124

Soliman, R., 1998. "Optimum Level of Process Mapping and Least Cost Business Process Re-engineering." *International Journal of Operations and Production Management*, 18(9/10): 810–816.

Stiern, K., 1999. Comparison of Diagramming Methods. Available at: http://www.umsl.edu/~sauterv/analysis/dfd/DiagrammingMethods.html

Wiegers, K.E. 1997. Listening to the Customer's Voice, Process Impact. Available at: www.processimpact.com/articles/usecase.html

Chapter 6

Step 4: Map Current Workflows and Processes

Employees who feel capable of solving problems, do.

—Patrick L. Townsend and Joan E. Gebhardt

This chapter provides detailed information on mapping current workflows and processes. Because those who actually perform the work should perform the mapping to the extent possible, the chapter begins with practical tips on "documenting while doing." Those who perform the work that will be changed by an electronic health record (EHR) or other health information technology (HIT) are in the best position to describe the actual work, will gain an appreciation of the need for EHR, and are more able to anticipate better ways to perform work with HIT. The primary purpose of the chapter, then, is to give detailed instruction on current workflow and process mapping techniques. The key components of a workflow and process map are discussed in detail: boundaries, operations, decisions, and flow. Incorporation of special symbols, annotations, subsidiary documents, and tips on reaching the right level of mapping are also supplied throughout the chapter.

Documenting While Doing

Irrespective of who performs the process mapping (see Chapter 2) or the method used (see Chapter 5), those who actually perform the work and who will be the users of new technology must be engaged in workflow and process mapping in some way. Such engagement is part of change management. In fact, although rarely the case, mapping current processes should be considered part of the training time necessary to learn the new HIT or EHR—because, in fact, it is!

Mapping current processes helps overcome resistance to change. It demonstrates the efficiencies, safety, and security of computer systems. It helps those who will be new users anticipate change and feel they are part of creating the change. No one wants change thrust upon them; and most everyone genuinely wants to be successful with new technology. By participating in the change, healthcare workers are in a better position to recognize where workarounds have had to be created, where there is duplication of effort, how patient safety risks occur, etc. They can apply these insights to recommending better workflows and processes with EHR and other HIT, and they are more likely to adapt more easily to the new technology because they have been a part of the overall process of defining requirements and redesigning workflows and processes.

Ideally, a process analyst has trained end users or a team of super-mappers to work with end users, in mapping their workflows and processes. If the care delivery organization (CDO) has opted to use an interview or observational method where end users are not performing the mapping directly, they still need to understand what is being done and why, and they need to fully participate in responding to interview questions or revealing their thought processes. In other words, they need to feel a part of process mapping. Yet, even the time it takes to be interviewed or observed requires time away from performing required work, and can be a distraction in the busy and complex environment of health care. So this extra time must be both minimized and resourced, such as by the following:

- **Recording on sticky notes** while performing the job is one way to minimize the time required to document workflows and processes. Chapter 5 suggested keeping a pad of sticky notes in a pocket and writing down every step being performed. Later, time can be set aside to post the sticky notes to a wall or large piece of paper.
- **Dictating into a digital voice recorder or wireless speech recognition system** is a similar way to document while doing. Digital voice recorders can be purchased as pens, watches, ID badges, or key fobs. There are also dictation "apps" for smart phones, some of which are free (France 2010). A CDO may already have a wireless speech dictation system (Anderson 2009) used by physicians or even by nurses installing intravenous lines, and this can be used by process mappers to send notes to a process analyst. If cost is a factor where the CDO cannot anticipate future use of these devices, a small number can be purchased and their use rotated until all current workflows and processes are documented.
- **Timeouts** are yet another way to minimize documentation time that also avoids the distraction of having to pause and write on a sticky note or dictate. Much like The Joint Commission's (2010) Universal Protocol for Preventing Wrong Site, Wrong Procedure, and Wrong Person Surgery that has been adopted for other procedures as well (Govern 2011), this timeout should be taken at a nurse's station or other location away from the patient. Steps in a process just performed can be documented in a log or journal—again available for later transcription into a flow process chart or systems flowchart by a process analyst. Although a paper journal can be kept, encouraging new users

of computers to type these into a computer log begins to acquaint them with the computer and keyboarding. It enables others to quickly review a log for a process they also perform and identify variations. Case Study 6.1 describes an interesting example of documenting ambulatory care processes where one of the physicians had set up a mini-EHR on a spreadsheet for tracking follow-up needed for chronically ill patients.

Case Study 6.1: Mini-EHR Serves a Dual Purpose

A physician at a federally qualified health center (FQHC) believed chronically ill patients were not being followed up on a timely basis. In addition, key information needed about recent lab results and current medications were often not readily available. The physician decided to create a mini-EHR (often called a registry) to track patients with diabetes and heart disease. It was nothing more than a spreadsheet that could perform limited database functions. A form was designed for physicians and nurses to document the desired data while seeing the patient, which would be keyed in by clerical staff during off-hours. As lab results were received, they were also entered by staff. Lists of patients to be called for follow-up could be generated easily. In preparation for the next visit, the form used to record key data could be generated with previous data already recorded. As a result, documentation of notes could be shortened to only information not recorded on the forms. By a simple addition of a few fields on the form, both nurses and physicians could also document key process elements that could be translated into a systems flowchart by clinic administrative staff.

Whether dictating or using a log to document steps in a process, a template should be followed where the worker records in sequence what operation is being performed or decision being made. The documentation can then be translated into a flow process chart or systems flowchart by a process analyst. Caution must be applied, however, to ensure that the process being documented is one specified on the organization's Process Inventory (see Chapter 4). This ensures that the process conforms to the boundaries pre-established by the organization and makes it easier for a worker to limit the effort applied to documenting the process. Table 6.1 provides a sample template.

Table 6.1 Sample Template for Dictating Process Steps

1. State name, credential, process being documented, and date.
2. State first operation.
3. State "next," then the next operation or decision. If a decision, state choices thought about.
4. Turn recorder off at any point where it is inconvenient to continue. If entire process has been dictated, state name of process and "end."
5. To continue dictating the same process, return to Step 3 and continue.

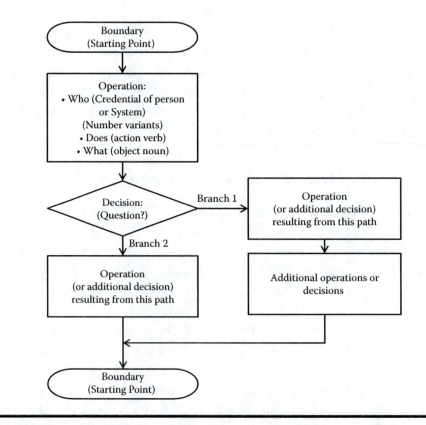

Figure 6.1 Basic components of a systems flowchart for process mapping. (From Copyright © Margret\A Consulting, LLC. With permission.)

Documenting Current Processes

This chapter adopts the systems flowchart to illustrate mapping current processes. As previously noted, this is the most widely used tool to map workflows and processes, even where lists, sticky notes, or dictation may be used initially to capture the steps. The basic components of the systems flowchart include boundaries, operations, decisions, and flow. Figure 6.1 reviews the basic components of a systems flowchart used for process mapping.

Documenting Boundaries

The CDO's Process Inventory should identify the boundaries of each of the workflows and processes to be mapped. These should be given to process mappers as the boundaries for what they are expected to document. The boundary (sometimes called terminator) symbol is an oval. It should be used to clearly state the beginning and ending of the process. A good check to make is that no flowchart or part of a flowchart starts or stops with a symbol other than the boundary symbol.

The designation of a boundary is not the title of the flowchart, name of the process, or name of the department in which (part of) the process occurs. Rather, the boundaries should identify what causes the process to start and end.

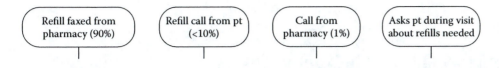

Current Prescription Renewal Process (Medical Assistant View)

Refill faxed from pharmacy (90%) Refill call from pt (<10%) Call from pharmacy (1%) Asks pt during visit about refills needed

Figure 6.2 Multiple boundaries. (From Copyright © Margret\A Consulting, LLC. With permission.)

For example, in a clinic, a "Registration" process may start with "patient arrives" and end with "nurse takes patient to exam room." There may be several beginnings and/or endings within a given process. For example, the "Prescription Renewal" process may begin with a call from a patient, a call from a pharmacy, a fax from a pharmacy, or even a patient visit. At some point, the steps may converge, but then diverge depending on the source of the renewal request. Figure 6.2 illustrates multiple boundaries as in the beginning and ending parts of a prescription renewal process.

Because not every CDO compiles a Process Inventory, it may be necessary for each mapper to be extra vigilant about the start and end of the process being mapped. Communicating regularly with all mappers and sharing maps helps overcome duplication of effort or gaps.

Whether or not there is a Process Inventory that guides the scope of the processes to be mapped, there may be processes that expand or shrink as the mapping occurs—for very good reason.

A process may expand when there are more stakeholders than initially anticipated, when a certain other stakeholder and a subsidiary process are critical to the primary process being mapped, or when the process includes hand-offs to different departments and there are reasons to elaborate on the operations and decisions performed in these departments. For example, a hospital may identify that the medication administration recording process begins with receiving a medication administration record (MAR) form from the pharmacy information system and ends with documenting the date and time of medication administration. However, the process mappers who are primarily nurses may want to emphasize the pharmacy's role in stocking the medication-dispensing systems that are part of the medication administration recording process.

A process may shrink when it is found to be too large to map all at one time. For example, a hospital may identify that the medication management process begins with an order for a medication and ends with administration of the medication to the patient. As mappers get started, however, they may find that due to very different professionals performing the key tasks as well as the fact that there are actually steps to be taken before an order is placed and after a medication is administered that are part of medication management, this process may need to be divided into several processes.

If there is a formal workflow and process management program with a Process Inventory being maintained by the lead process analyst, changes to boundaries should be discussed, if not approved, by the lead analyst, and the Process Inventory should be updated when there is any change to the process scope.

Documenting Current Operations

Documenting current operations are the fundamental steps in a process. However, workers may need to be reminded that for purposes of documenting workflows and processes associated with implementing HIT and EHR, the focus must be on information (or when workers wished they had information that they did not have, or they did not take time to find—as is often the case in health care).

In process mapping, an operation is the method or practice by which actions are performed. When considering operations on information, workers should document *who, does, what.*

"Who" is the person documenting the operation as he or she performs it (or the person being observed or interviewed). However, instead of recording the person's name on the map, the credential and/or title should be documented, such as MD, RN, LPN, PharmD, charge nurse, etc. The reason for this is that credentials are very important in health care. Degrees, licensures, and certifications make a difference in what a person is allowed to do. Case Study 6.2 illustrates how credentials made a difference in a clinic considering moving to a triage process for approving prescription renewals.

Case Study 6.2: Credentials Make a Difference

A clinic was implementing an e-prescribing (e-Rx) system prior to, but in anticipation of, an EHR. The administrator of the clinic along with the nurses documented the current process, which included every physician's nurse performing the renewal process for that physician, resulting in a significant number of variations, many physician-specific rules about what prescriptions could renewed and when, and the realization that it was often taking as many as two or three days for the clinic to call back the pharmacy with a decision. As they approached redesign of the process, they decided it would streamline things immensely if they used a triage system, where nurses would take turns managing the process for the day. Engaging a set of different nurses would allow for coverage of personal time off (PTO) needs and keep nurses current on the process. What they did not consider, however, was that the physician-specific rules about renewals were based on the credential of the "nurse," who may actually have been a medical assistant (MA), certified medical assistant (CMA), licensed practical nurse (LPN), or registered nurse (RN). This failure in redesign came about for several reasons. First, they simply recorded "nurse" for anyone who was performing the process. Second, the administrator had just previously worked in one state that had much more liberal rules about who could approve a prescription renewal than the state in which this clinic existed. And finally, they had not consulted

Table 6.2 Action Verbs

Add	Dictate	Instruct	Remind	Task
Alert	Document	Label	Report	Tell
Assign	Draw	Leave blank	Review	Throw away
Calculate	Estimate	Locate	Rotate	Time
Chart	Explain	Match	Select	Time out
Check	Fill in	Note	Show	Transcribe
Code	Find	Order	Sign	Verify
Compare	Give	Point out	Size	View
Copy	Highlight	Read	Supply	Write down
Cross out	Identify	Recall	Take	*and many others*
Deduce	Index	Recognize	Tag	

with the physicians who were aware of these differences, and hence their "rules" were not just personal preferences but compliance with regulation.

In addition to "who" being a person, it is also possible for the "who" to be a computer system. For example, if a laboratory information system (LIS) sends an EHR a lab result, the "who" in this process is the LIS.

"Does" represents the action taken by the person or system. The action may be observable or not observable (i.e., a mental process). When mapping processes performed with information, the actions documented will largely surround use of information. However, as information is used to take care of patients, there will certainly be some operations that address an action associated with the patient, a medical device, or other person taking care of the patient.

"Does" is an action verb. Short but precise verbs should be used. For example, "note" or "record" is shorter than "write down" or "document." The shorter the word, the easier it is to record within a flowchart symbol. Examples of verbs commonly found in systems flowcharting for healthcare workflow and process mapping are listed in Table 6.2.

"What" is the object of the "does" action. Whereas "does" is a verb, "what" is a noun. However, sometimes what is done may be implied by the action and the context of the map, such that no explicit statement of "what" is needed. For example, "Take temperature" may very likely be interpreted as "Take temperature of patient." Wherever such an implication is not clear, however, it is always best to clarify.

Sometimes, "what" may better be described by "where" or "to whom," or may require both "what" and "to whom." For example, "Charge nurse gives medication to staff nurse" includes who (charge nurse), does (gives), what (medication) but also adds to whom (staff nurse). This elaboration may be necessary if there are feasible alternatives, such as "Charge nurse gives medication to physician" or "Charge nurse gives medication to patient." (Note that this is a fairly long phrase.

Some CDOs provide process mappers with a list of acceptable abbreviations, such as "med" for "medication." Whatever abbreviations are used should be documented in a reference list or be easily interpretable by all who will be reviewing the process map in the future.)

Documenting Variations in Operations

In many cases, CDOs want to illustrate the degree of variability in a process, especially in current processes. This may be done in a variety of ways, often depending on the nature of the variation:

■ **Assign number** to each variation if essentially the same task is being performed in a different way by different people. Case Study 6.3 describes the scenario of a critical access hospital with only five nurses, but considerable variation in how each nurse performs various operations.

Case Study 6.3: Process Variation

A critical access hospital (those with twenty-five beds or less and with a special Medicare reimbursement plan) had five nurses taking care of an average 1.5 patients per day. The hospital was beginning its quest to implement an EHR and had begun with mapping all clinical processes. Figure 6.3a provides part of the process map initially drawn by the charge nurse at the hospital. If each of the five nurses performed an operation slightly differently, there were then five statements of who (by number) did what. If there were only three variations (two nurses performing the operation in the same way as one or two others), then each of the three variants were identified by number. In this example, "OR" was used to emphasize that there were different nurses performing the step differently, not different steps in the specific operation. (Even if there are few people performing the task with variations, do not record names. This can suggest that one or more people are to blame for doing something different, and mapping processes is not about assigning blame. If the situation needs immediate correction—as was true in this case, the observation should be made that there is variation and that the CDO needs to standardize processes for patient safety, quality, productivity, etc. Agree on what the practice should be and help each person perform the process accordingly.)

■ **Decision symbols** can be used to describe variations that appear to depend on different factors. Sometimes such variation actually does result from different factors, in which case the variation is actually a decision; in other cases, the variation is caused by differences in training, location, longevity of workers performing the task, or even simply habit, as was the

Medication Administration

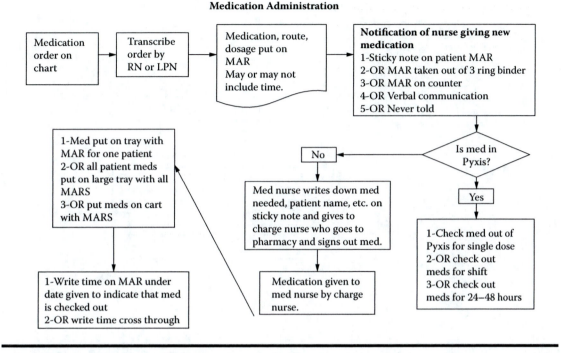

Figure 6.3a Illustration of variation by numbering. (From Copyright © Margret\A Consulting, LLC. With permission.)

case described in Case Study 6.3. The result still should be standardization on a best practice, which may occur before implementation of HIT or EHR, or may need to wait until HIT or EHR can support the standard practice. Figure 6.3b illustrates the same task as in Figure 6.3a, but with causality explained via a decision symbol. Two things should be observed in this process map: (1) there is no specific reason for the variation, and hence the mapping as illustrated in Figure 6.3a should suffice; and (2) the process map has been redrawn following more of the systems flowcharting conventions—as discussed throughout this chapter.

■ **Color-coding symbols** may be used to illustrate variation. Using different-colored sticky notes for persons to record how they perform a task differently is very effective during the initial stages of drafting a process map. While it is feasible to fill flowchart shapes with different colors, having multiple operations symbols with essentially the same task only performed with a color-coded variation can be somewhat confusing, especially if converted to a black and white map—which is generally the norm. However, if different people perform a similar but slightly different task, and it is desirable to highlight where there is a risk or to indicate where there are different areas where an EHR is needed to overcome the variation, color coding or shading can be effective to highlight these. For example, the operation with the five variations in Figure 6.3a could have been highlighted as an area of risk to be addressed immediately.

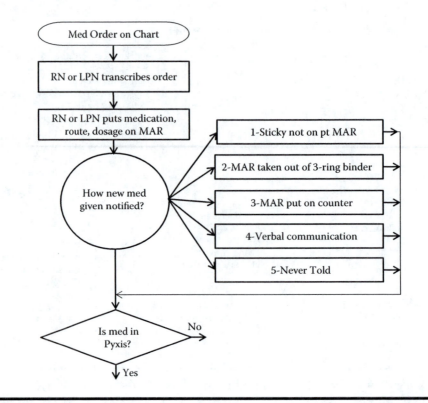

Figure 6.3b Illustration of variation by decision symbol. (From Copyright © Margret\A Consulting, LLC. With permission.)

Documenting Appropriate Operational Detail

Many new mappers have difficulty documenting the appropriate level of detail in their early attempts at process mapping. A good way to think about how much detail is to reflect upon whether or not the specific task to be included on the map is something that can be automated. If it can be automated, the level of detail should fully explain what action is taken with each type of information. If the task cannot be automated, the task probably only needs to be documented at a high level of detail. The following Case Studies 6.4 and 6.5, both of which are real-life, regularly repeated examples, illustrate detail-leveling issues and potential solutions.

Case Study 6.4: Too Little Detail

Staff members in a small clinic were mapping prescription renewal calls to the clinic. The resultant map is illustrated in Figure 6.4. The map as initially drawn only identified that a CMA received faxes from the pharmacy, reviewed the chart, and either gave it to the physician to approve or approved the renewal as is, ultimately calling the pharmacy. Recognizing that this is not a sufficient level of detail, a professional process analyst began asking the following questions: Did the CMA need to request the chart from the file room? How long did it take to receive the request? What is the CMA looking for in the chart? What criteria are

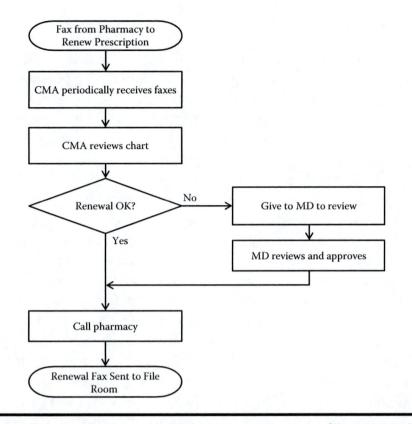

Figure 6.4   Too little detail. (From Copyright © Margret\A Consulting, LLC. With permission.)

being applied to approve or to not approve a renewal? When given to the physician, is the renewal always approved as it appears on the map? What happens if the renewal is not approved? Is it always black and white (approved or not approved), or are there other choices, such as approving a limited supply of the medication? Is there any documentation made in the chart that such a request was approved and when, and for how many pills if the approval is only for a limited supply? What action is taken to ensure that the patient returns for a visit to provide a full supply?

When a map lacks specificity such as this, asking the mapper questions and having the mapper add the necessary documentation helps make clear the level of detail. It may also be necessary to remind the person that whatever they do is fine for purposes of mapping workflows in preparation for HIT or EHR. While not going into too much detail, it can be helpful to explain that some of the steps can be aided by the computer. Caution must be applied, however, in not making the person think that his or her job is at risk. Being careful about what is said is needed to help overcome such concerns. For example, the request for further detail may be stated as follows: "When we get an EHR, we want to make sure that all the information you need to make the decision to renew a prescription or not will actually be in the computer. Therefore, please write down all the information you need."

Case Study 6.5: Too Much Detail

A large clinic was preparing for its EHR implementation. In mapping a workflow associated with having the patient supply a urine sample to be tested in its own lab, the map drawn described documenting that the physician left the room to find the nurse to take the patient to the rest room; that, en route, instructions for supplying the sample were given; that the nurse waited for the patient to receive the sample and to accompany the patient back to the exam room; and that the nurse took the sample to the in-house lab area and handed it to the lab technician. Such a map would be too detailed for a process that will largely not be automated. In fact, the only task that could be automated in this workflow is the physician sending a task via the EHR to the nurse's workstation to request that the patient be taken for a urinalysis. Sometimes just reminding new process mappers that, for example, "you can't automate going to the bathroom," helps them get the point with humor (that probably only works in a healthcare environment).

The level of detail needs to enable the CDO to differentiate between EHR products, ensure the right data are collected, and anticipate and guide workflow redesign—which will include changes in how clinicians process information mentally. Caution should be applied in avoiding over-documenting processes associated with information. Healthcare workers are very aware of the extreme variability in patients. For example, a drug given to one patient may work very effectively; when given to another patient with the same condition, the patient may have an adverse reaction; and yet another patient may have no reaction—including not finding any benefit from the drug at all. This does not mean that a map is needed for every condition, drug, or patient to be encountered. This is completely not feasible; is not necessary. It is possible to document at a very acceptable level of detail categories of processes. If desired, it may be suggested that a particular process could be mapped for chronic-care patients versus acute-care patients, or medical versus surgical patients, etc. Once such categories are identified and mapping ensues, however, most will come to the realization that either the differences lie in the decision points to be incorporated in a single map or there really is not the degree of difference in how information is used that would warrant such level of detail. However, it is true that in almost every process mapping activity in CDOs, there will be at least one if not many workers who have difficulty with the level of detail—too much or too little—until they actually start mapping their processes.

Documenting Decision Making

While workflow and process mapping is often not easy at first, mapping operations tends to be easier than mapping decision making. This is generally the case because decision making is a mental process, not able to be seen by others, and often something that is so "second nature" to the worker performing the mental process that the thinking is often not recognized as part of the process. Also, decisions tend to be made in a somewhat random order. New mappers are often hesitant to string a series of decision symbols together because they may not know in what order they will always be considered. Reassuring new mappers that, while workflow is important and there probably is a logical workflow to the decision making, the important aspect of documenting current decision making is to identify the decisions that need to be made, their sources of information, and the choices or alternatives they reveal.

Decision making is vital to health care. While decision making will always remain the responsibility of the healthcare worker applying his or her professional judgment, it is also the part of the healthcare process that can benefit the most from computers that can tirelessly process data, not forget data, do not get distracted, and are able to jog the worker's memory. Hale (2008) observes that "a physician who reads all day long for six weeks will already be a century behind."

Computers are, however, dumb machines and must be programmed correctly to process the data that humans feed them and from which humans expect answers, guidance, reminders, alerts, etc. Computers are only as good as their programmers; and programmers are only as good as their understanding of the processes to be mapped.

For example, if there is no instruction in the computer software to alert a physician that a drug being ordered is contraindicated for patients over sixty-five years of age (Scott and Cupp 2007), there is no way that the computer can intuit such information and provide an alert without being programmed to do so—and without being kept up-to-date. There are companies that specialize in designing such evidence-based guidance software (Hagland 2010; Elsevier n.d.) and keeping it current by supplying daily, weekly, or monthly updates from the literature, the Daily Med, and other resources (Mountain 2011). E-prescribing and EHR technology vary in their utilization of such software services, but all include at least basic-level support.

While critical alerts are valued by clinicians, if the computer has been programmed to provide every physician with an alert about every potential medication contraindication known, the physician will acquire the deadly disease of alert fatigue—the only cure for which seems to be avoidance of alerts altogether (Lee et al. 2010). The best alerts are those that are specific to the patient, relevant and important, accurate, directed to the right person, and require urgent action (Van der Sijs et al. 2006; Karsh 2009). Ideally, their computer programming should enable a CDO to be able to set the sensitivity of alerts to the type of recipient and nature of alert (Paterno et al. 2009). For example, specialists may not need alerts in their specialty, but would need alerts related to medications used to treat conditions outside their specialty. House staff (new physicians in training) may need more alerts than attending physicians who have been in practice for some time; although some attending physicians will tell you it is difficult to keep current. Alerting should be applied to situations that are dangerous.

Clinical Decision Support

Alerting is provided by systems referred to as clinical decision support and most often associated with medication contraindications. However, decision support is more than alerting, and more than about medication safety.

In addition to alerts about medications, clinical decision support systems provide alerts for duplicate studies and therapy, cost of drugs and diagnostic studies, and patient preferences and needs (the child is scared of Nurse Fierce, or the patient needs an interpreter or signer). Clinical decision support also includes reminders—about preventive services coming due, to take a timeout before a surgical procedure commences, and to follow up with chronically ill patients. Access to reference information, such as in conducting a differential diagnosis or invoking an infobutton that links to knowledge sources based on patient parameters, such as to read more about a recent addition to the Beers List, are forms of clinical decision support. Templates, order sets, and pathways and protocols are also forms of clinical decision support that provide context-sensitive guidance for documenting, ordering common sets of tasks, and checking that all steps in a procedure have been taken or all considerations have been made with respect to an important decision. Maintaining the problem list, managing the medication list, and generating a clinical summary (i.e., the continuity of care record [CCR] or continuity of care document [CCD] as required by the federal incentive program for making meaningful use of EHR technology) are forms of clinical decision support.

In addition to *clinical* decision support, other decision support tools designed for CDOs are available to aid productivity, such as by being able to manage patient wait times, direct tasks to various members of the clinical team, and reduce unnecessary calls from pharmacies. Workflow tools aid in organizing scanned images of documents such as from old records or patient-supplied documents. They aid in capturing information for medical forms, such as back-to-work documents, camp physicals, etc.; and for supplying information to patients and capturing signatures, such as supplying the notice of privacy practices, an authorization for release of information, or a Medicare advance beneficiary notice. There are informed consent "forms" that are mini-educational programs that walk a patient through a surgical procedure and then capture the patient's consent for the procedure. Decision support tools also aid in revenue generation through guiding accurate and complete diagnostic, procedural, and professional service coding, formulary checking and other eligibility verification, determining claim status from a health plan, and managing electronic remittances.

Finally, clinical decision support can be directed not only to the workers in the CDO, but to patients—such as having them complete a context-sensitive medical history assessment based on patient gender, age, and other factors; or a history of present illness assessment that asks questions only about the patient's reason for seeking health care. Direct monitoring of patient vital signs with applicable alerts and reminders are forms of clinical decision support directed to patients and their caregivers (Berner 2009).

Use knowledge of the various forms of decision support to help train process mappers. Recognizing the potentiality for such use of a computer can help new mappers reflect upon the decisions they make today so they can better document how and when decisions are made. This will aid in evaluating HIT and EHR products for the type of decision support desired, during implementation to anticipate changes in workflows and processes, and after adoption to optimize use of the systems and achieve their greatest value.

Documenting Decisions in a Process Map

So, how are decisions captured in a workflow and process map? The basic decision symbol is the diamond and it typically reflects a question. Much as for the operation symbol, insert a minimum number of words to convey the question. Inserting a question mark makes it clear to the reader that it is a question, and also helps new mappers remember that decision making reflects questions. Table 6.3 suggests some short questions that are common in healthcare process mapping, although there may be many others reflecting specific types of decisions.

In addition to the decision symbol itself, there must be at least two flow lines coming from the symbol reflecting at least two choices in answer to the question within the symbol. The question being asked is placed in the symbol and the choices of answers are placed as labels to the flow lines extending from the symbol. Compare Figures 6.5a, 6.5b, and 6.5c for their effectiveness in conveying the intended information. The decision in Figure 6.5a is clearly incomplete, as discussed above. Referencing whether a (renewal) protocol has been met, as

Table 6.3 Decision Questions

Allergic?	Final?	Reason for visit?
Approve?	How?	Right body part?
Available?	How many?	Right dose?
Complete?	Known?	Right information?
Condition?	Level of pain?	Right patient?
Covered (*by insurer*)?	Match?	Right route?
Contraindicated?	Normal/within normal limits?	Right specimen?
Diagnosis?	On formulary?	Right time?
Exception?	Preliminary?	When?
Evidence based?	Ready?	Where?

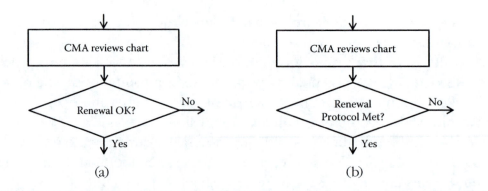

Figure 6.5 **(a) Incomplete decision. (b) Decision from a reference. (From Copyright ©
Margret\A Consulting, LLC. With permission.)**

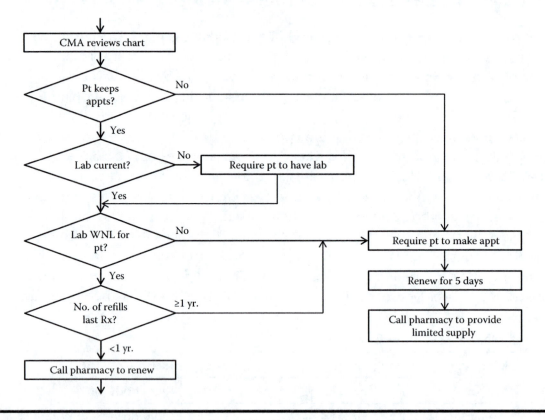

Figure 6.5c **Decision flow. (From Copyright © Margret\A Consulting, LLC. With
permission.)**

in Figure 6.5b, is an effective way to convey more complete information. The
protocol should be attached to the process map. If the protocol is not lengthy or
there will be subsequent parts of the process to be illustrated based on different
outcomes of the protocol review, the map illustrated in Figure 6.5c can be most
effective. The map in Figure 6.5c clearly illustrates that there is a sequence to following the protocol and identifies that there are different operations that result
from each point in the protocol where the answer is "no."

Rule Number		1.	2.	3.	4.	5.	6.	7.		
	Condition Alternatives									
Conditions	1. Appt kept?	Y	Y	Y	Y	Y	Y	N		
	2. Lab current?	Y	Y	Y	N	N	N			
	3. Lab WNL for pt?	Y	Y	N	Y	Y	N			
	3. No. of refills last Rx?	<1 yr.	≥1 yr.		<1 yr.	≥1 yr.				
	Action Entries									
Actions	Require pt to have lab				X	X	X			
	Require pt to make appt		X	X		X	X	X		
	Renew for 5 days		X	X		X	X	X		
	Call pharmacy to provide limited supply		X	X		X	X	X		
	Call pharmacy to renew	X			X					

Figure 6.5d   Decision table. (From Copyright © Margret\A Consulting, LLC. With permission.)

If there are more than two answers, choices, alternatives, or other forms of paths from a question being asked, consider one of the following:

■ Are there simply three or a few more distinct paths directly from this question? In this case, add a third branch to the diamond symbol or use a circle with a few branches, such as illustrated in Figure 6.3b.
■ Is the question too broad, such that there are actually multiple decisions following in a sequence? In this case, illustrate each decision separately, such as illustrated in Figure 6.5c.
■ Are the decision choices too many or not easy to plot sequentially on a map? A decision table supports sequencing of many choices, such as illustrated in Figure 6.5d.

Annotating Frequency of Decision Making, Operations, and Boundaries

Some new mappers struggle with the sequence of decisions. This may reflect the fact that decisions appear to be made randomly. However, as decisions are mapped out, either in a sequence of decision symbols or on a decision table, a logical sequence usually emerges. The sequence of decision making is almost always relevant, that is, it is rare that there is no dependency among choices. However, in mapping current processes, it is important to document what is actually happening. To reflect that there is variation or apparent randomness in decision-making, it is recommended that one of two forms of documentation be used:

- **Annotation symbol** can be used to document that the sequence of a set of operations or decisions varies or is random for no apparent reason. The annotation symbol is illustrated in Figure 6.6 (see "Special Symbols"). This symbol can actually be used anywhere in the systems flowchart where you want to add a comment. The dotted line can be drawn to one symbol in the main flow of the map, or it can be used to put brackets around several symbols in sequence.

- **Record percent of time or instances of events** in the applicable symbols. For example, if there are four sources of prescription renewal requests such as shown in Figure 6.2, then adding the percent to each boundary symbol (as shown) can be useful information. In some clinics, calls from patients may comprise 90 percent of all such calls with the remainder spread over the other four starting points. In other clinics, perhaps if e-Rx has already been initiated, the number of calls from patients may be very low, even less than 1 percent (<1%). If an operation or decision is performed in exactly the same manner every time it is performed, but half of the time it is performed prior to another step and half of the time at the position documented—again for no reason that would be otherwise mapped—the percentages can be shown in the decision symbol. Likewise, if one-third of the time an RN performs an operation and two-thirds of the time an LPN performs the same operation, these differences in frequency can be illustrated using percentages.

The extent to which frequency is documented in a workflow and process map may vary with the CDO's desired level of detail, and with what is being documented. It is often desirable to illustrate frequency where it can be anticipated a workaround step or undesired step can be eliminated or significantly reduced with HIT or EHR. Judgment should be applied as to where such additional information will be helpful.

Note that variation and frequency have different meanings. Variation means a step or a decision is performed by different people, has different actions, and/or focuses on different objects, or different decisions are made. Frequency refers to how often or what percent of the time a variation occurs.

Documenting Flow

The conventional way to document the sequence of steps and decisions being performed in a process is to connect the symbols with arrows, from top to bottom. For enhanced readability of decision making, document the paths from a

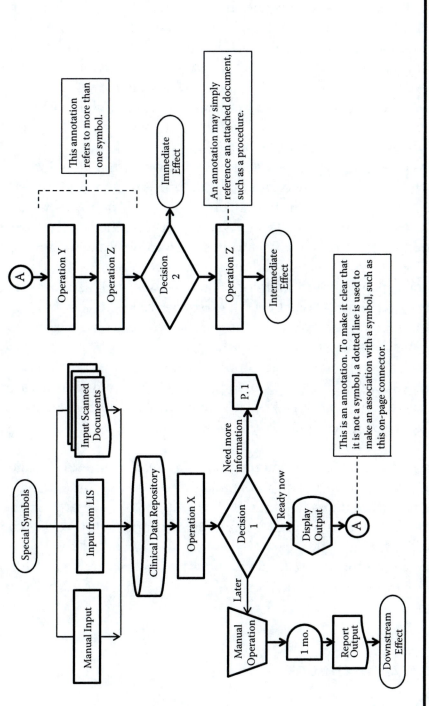

Figure 6.6   Special symbols. (From Copyright © Margret\A Consulting, LLC. With permission.)

decision point such that all of one kind of an answer flows down and the other answer choice flows from left to right. For example, all "yes" answers may go down and all "no" answers go to the right. If the choices are not yes and no, then frequently the advice is to illustrate the most common or frequent path to follow from top to bottom, and the less common path from left to right.

Another convention is that all arrows should go to a symbol rather than a line. However, if there are two or more flows that go to a single symbol, it may not be feasible to keep this convention. Figure 6.5c is an example where two paths (where the lab results are not within normal limits and the number of refills for the last prescription exceeded one year's worth) both end up going to one operation (require patient to make an appointment).

For those following the typical conventions of flowcharting, flow lines should never be drawn at an angle. If necessary, an elbow connector can be used. See also Figure 6.3b where the flow from the five variations of notification go back to the question of whether the medication is in Pyxis (the medication-dispensing cabinet). Not only is the elbow connector illustrated in Figure 6.3b, but the flow, by necessity, must go from right to left rather than left to right.

The flow from one symbol should not branch to two symbols unless there is a decision symbol that explains what choice exists between the two symbols. This is a common mistake of new mappers and can be corrected by always asking what causes a flow to separate.

A final consideration in flow relates not to the content but to the recording process. Often, a flowchart will become long and will not fully fit from top to bottom on a single page. Two types of connector symbols are available, both illustrated in Figure 6.6 (see "Special Symbols"):

- **On-page connector** for continuing a flowchart within the same page is a small circle. This enables you to potentially draw two or three components of a flowchart in columns, without having to draw a long line from the bottom of one section to the top of another. Each connection point should be labeled with a capital letter (e.g., A goes to A, B to B, etc.)
- **Off-page connector** for continuing a flowchart to another page is depicted using the Chevron symbol. Each connection point should be label with the page number.

Flowcharting Conventions

A number of commonly applied conventions are described in this chapter. They help make mapping easier to perform, and certainly make maps easier to read. However, mappers should understand that is not always feasible to follow the conventions precisely. Some divergence from convention may be necessary (Morgenstern 2009).

Special Symbols

The basic flowchart symbols of oval boundaries, rectangle operations, diamond decisions, flow lines, and connectors are all the symbols needed to fully map all current and redesigned processes. However, a variety of special symbols are available to depict special types of operations, should process mappers get the desire to be "fancy" or believe a special shape may help highlight the nature of a particular type of operation. Edraw Soft 6.0, for example, to emphasize where a largely automated process continues to depend on paper may benefit from highlighting documents, manual input, and manual operations.

A database symbol is frequently used to highlight that data are going into a database where the data may be specially processed. Three types of databases are used in health care (although each is depicted with the same "database" symbol). It may be desirable to illustrate how data flow in relation to each type of database, which includes:

- **Application database** refers to the database within a single application that manages data related just to the specific application. For example, a Registration/Admission-Discharge-Transfer (R/ADT) System in a hospital will collect demographic data about the patients; their admission and discharge dates; and when in the hospital, their bed location. This database may be used to generate a variety of patient lists, feed other applications with patient identifying information, etc.
- **Clinical data repository (CDR)** refers to a special type of relational database that has been optimized for online transaction processing (OLTP). Sometimes it is called a transactional database. A transaction in this case is any action taken on data being collected about providing patients' healthcare services. For example, entering a new patient's name is a transaction. Retrieving a patient's last lab result is a transaction. Documenting a patient's blood pressure is a transaction. Ordering a medication for a patient is a transaction. The unique aspect of the CDR is that it serves to put data from many application databases into one place where the data can be operated upon together. So whereas a computerized provider order entry (CPOE) system will be able to compare an ordered drug against other drugs the patient is taking, it alone cannot compare an ordered drug against the existence of lab results, such as a liver function study to determine if the drug being ordered may be contraindicated for a patient with poor liver function. This type of process can more easily be performed where data from the CPOE system and the LIS have both been put into a CDR and can be processed together. The Healthcare Information Management and Systems Society (HIMSS Analytics, Q2 2011) reports that approximately 46 percent of hospitals have such a repository to help integrate their data.

■ **Clinical data warehouse (CDW)** refers to a special type of, often hierarchical or multi-dimensional, database that has been optimized for online analytical processing (OLAP). In this case, a *copy* of all or a subset of the data collected from application databases and/or a CDR are put into this special type of database for the purpose of performing sophisticated analytical processes on the data, such as data mining. So where the CDR works on data for each patient at a time, the CDW works on data from very many patients at a time (Laszlo 2006). The reason that such different databases exist is due to their inherent processing capabilities. A separate warehouse eliminates the contention for resources that results when analytical processing is confounded with operational processes (White 2005). No user taking care of patients is willing to wait literally minutes for a screen to load or data to be retrieved. The disadvantage of having two separate types of database structures is that the CDR which is most desirable for data-to-day use, such as in an EHR, often does not enable the easy generation of reports and degrades system performance when analysis is being performed. However, it must also be recognized that a CDO with a small population of data would likely not be able to produce analyses that are valid. It is only the very large CDO, integrated delivery network, or health plan that typically uses a CDW. The Healthcare Information and Management Systems Society (HIMSS Analytics, Q2 2011) reports that only about 1 percent of hospitals have such a warehouse to perform data analysis.

Special symbols are illustrated in Figure 6.6. Note that this figure includes not only several commonly used special symbols, but also the annotation symbol and the on- and off-page connectors (Heeb 2011). It might be observed that once so many different symbols are added, the flowchart can become somewhat cluttered in appearance. For a "cleaner," easier-to-read workflow and process map, it may be desirable to limit the use of special symbols to those absolutely necessary.

Flowcharting Software Support

One additional point to be made about using systems flowcharts for workflow and process mapping relates to using flowcharting software. Whether using presentation or spreadsheet software, or software designed specifically for flowcharting—and there are many such products on the market—there are several key features to look for in selecting such software, and certainly to learn how to use. The following are a few key features from some of the popular flowcharting utilities and packages (reference to which implies no endorsement by the author or publisher):

■ *Alignment of symbols and dynamic flow lines.* This feature is available even in simple presentation or spreadsheet software (e.g., Microsoft Office 2010) as well as specific flowcharting software (e.g., FlowBreeze 2.5, SmartDraw®

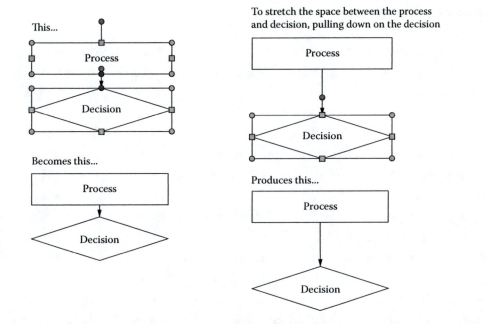

Figure 6.7   Alignment of symbols and dynamic flow lines.

VP, Visio 2010). It is immensely helpful to be able "attach" a flow line to the two symbols to be connected and enable the flow line to adjust as one of the symbols is moved, perhaps to make an insertion. Users should grab a flow line from the Shape toolkit and place it on the location where the grab boxes are on the symbol. When the circle at the start of the flow line turns red, it is attached. Likewise, when the bottom of the arrow is moved to grab a box on the next symbol, the circle at the end of the flow line will turn red. Figure 6.7 illustrates what this looks like and how the flow line lengthens as it is moved lower. (The dark circles represent red circles; the white boxes on the corners and centers of each side of the symbol are the grab boxes.) Specialized flowcharting software has many additional flow line features, such as automatically adding a flow line from a previous symbol and reminding the user to add a flow line if the newest-placed symbol is not aligned with the previously placed symbol.

■ *Symbol size and font size.* This is a common feature of specialized flowcharting software that is extremely helpful in enforcing uniformity in symbol sizes and ensuring that text fits within the symbol.

■ *Text-to-symbol wizards.* Many of the specialized flowcharting software enable a user to enter text and have it automatically convert to the right symbol. For example, text that does not include a question mark would automatically be put into a rectangle, and text with a question mark would be put into a diamond.

■ *Hyperlink capability and collaboration tools.* These tools help link documents to the flowcharts and enable sharing of all components of the current maps with others for validation, redesign, and other uses.

Subsidiary Documents

As current workflow and process maps are developed, it is recommended that all forms, reports, protocols, practice guidelines, decision tables, procedures, physical layouts, job descriptions, and other documentation associated with the operations and decision making be collected.

Order forms will serve as a basis for template development for a CPOE system. A paper-based medication administration record (MAR) form used today will highlight the basic set of data currently recorded to ensure that this minimum data set is also available when this process is automated. Reports generated—and needed—today will provide a checklist for what reports will be needed in the future.

Protocols, practice guidelines, and decision tables can serve as the guidance for decision making, such as illustrated in Figure 6.5b. Comparing the current process with the current procedure can be useful to highlight where workarounds have been created—either by default or by necessity. Such a comparison lends insights that help ensure that the HIT being acquired and implemented will address the needs that caused these workarounds to be created in the first place.

Physical layouts may need to be changed based on how new technology is implemented. Capturing the current layouts during current process mapping helps in not having to take the time to do this during HIT implementation. Job descriptions of persons currently performing the process may need to be reviewed in light of both credential review for potential job changes with automation and in light of tasks that may be eliminated, enhanced, or changed in the future.

It is very likely that as subsidiary documents are collected, several different versions of forms and even procedures and job descriptions will be found to be in use. If during the current mapping it is agreed that only the latest version will be used going forward, it is acceptable to add only this document to the collection. However, if agreeing on which version is desirable will take considerable time, it is probably best to collect all versions currently used. It may be that different data are collected that is useful information for redesigning the process.

Process Mapping Template

A final consideration in mapping current workflows and processes is to develop a standard template onto which all process maps should be recorded. For small CDOs, this may simply include that each map should contain the name of the process, the name of the person who drafted the map, and the date the map was drafted.

For larger CDOs or large projects, such as for EHR, it may be desirable to establish a formal template, such as illustrated in Table 6.4.

Table 6.4 Template for Workflow and Process Maps

1. Name of Process
2. Primary Author(s)
3. Date
4. Department(s)
5. Version
6. Link From Process(es)
7. Link To Process(es)
8. Stakeholders Engaged
9. Glossary of Terms Unique to Map
10. Abbreviations Unique to Map
11. List of Attachments
12. Baseline Data Collection (see Chapter 7)
13. Certification of Validation (see Chapter 8)
14. Analysis for Redesign (see Chapter 9)

Key Points

■ Mapping current workflows and processes requires **thinking about processes** outside of the context of a specific job or department, at the **level of detail** necessary to achieve the intended purposes of process mapping, and incorporating **processes performed mentally** that are often **taken for granted**. The **symbols** and **software tools** that support flowcharting are new to new mappers and must be learned. Mapping current workflows and processes, then, is not necessarily an easy task.

■ To make current workflow and process mapping more efficient and effective, a variety of strategies can be deployed. **Documenting while doing** ensures accuracy and helps instill a sense of ownership for the impending change in the people involved in the mapping activity. Mastering the basic symbols and gaining an understanding of the level of detail needed to achieve value from a map requires guidance and support. **Guidance** and **support** may come from a professional process analyst, can be aided by all stakeholders working together, and must be supported by executive leadership on down to each and every supervisor who is responsible for resourcing the project.

■ Clinicians can be aided in their mapping by anticipating how HIT and especially EHR achieve **data integration** from multiple **application databases** into a **clinical data repository** and especially provides **clinical decision support**, as well as contributes to the generation of new knowledge by contributing to a **clinical data warehouse** that supports sophisticated analytics.

■ Establishing **conventions** and careful **annotation** and **collection of subsidiary documents** may initially seem burdensome and unnecessary, but actually make the project easier to perform and much easier to use in redesign and other later uses.

References

Anderson, H.J., 2009 (April 1). "Nurses Replace Clipboards with Headsets to Document Their Work." *Health Data Management*, 17(4): 2.

Berner, E.S., 2009 (June). Clinical Decision Support Systems: State of the Art, Agency for Healthcare. Research and Quality. Available at: http://healthit.ahrq.gov/portal/server.pt/gateway/PTARGS_0_1248_874024_0_0_18/09-0069-EF.pdf

Edraw Soft, 6.0. Standard Flowchart Symbols and Their Usage. Available at: http://www.edrawsoft.com/flowchart-symbols.php

Elsevier, n.d. "Elsevier Clinical Decision Support: Impacting the Cost and Quality of Healthcare." White Paper. Available at: http://www.clinicaldecisionsupport.com/fullpanel/uploads/files/elsevier-clinical-decision-support-impacting-the-cost-and-quality-wp-4web-00001-00001.pdf

France, J., 2010 (July 28). "Talk to Text with Two Free iPhone Dication Apps." CNET.com Reviews. Available at: http://reviews.cnet.com/8301-19512_7-20012021-233.html

Govern, P., 2011 (Mar. 31). "'Timeout Protocol' Helps Keep Procedures on Track." *Reporter*, Vanderbilt University Medical Center's Weekly Newspaper. Available at: http://www.mc.vanderbilt.edu/reporter/index.html?ID=10463

Hagland, M., 2010 (July 6). "Evidence-Based Order Sets and CPOE: One Clinician Discusses His Organization's Transition to CPOE." *riversideMD.net*. Available at: https://www.riversidemd.net/news/hci070610.cfm

Hale, P.L., 2008. *Electronic Prescribing for the Medical Practice: Everything You Wanted to Know But Were Afraid to Ask*, Chapter 1. Chicago: HIMSS, Available at: http://www.himss.org/content/files/EPrescribing_Hale_Chapter_1.pdf

Heeb, N., 2011. Flowchart Symbols Defined: Flowchart Symbols and Their Meanings, How to Create Flowcharts in Excel Series — BreezeTree Software. Available at: http://www.breezetree.com/article-excel-flowchart-shapes.htm

HIMSS Analytics, 2011 (Q2). US EMR Adoption Model. Available at: http://www.himssanalytics.org/hc_providers/emr_adoption.asp

Karsh, B., 2009 (June). "Clinical Practice Improvement and Redesign: How Change in Workflow Can Be Supported by Clinical Decision Support." Agency for Healthcare Quality and Research. Available at: http://healthit.ahrq.gov/images/jun09cdsworkflow/09_0054_ef.html

Laszlo, G., 2006. Clinical Data Repository (CRR) 1l1, The Laszlo Letter, available at: http://laszloletter.typepad.com/the/laszlo_letter/2006/07/clinical_data?r.html

Lee, E.K. et al., 2010. "Improving Patient Safety through Medical Alert Management: An Automated Decision Tool to Reduce Alert Fatigue." *AMIA 2010 Symposium Proceedings*, 417–421.

Morgenstern, D., 2009. *Essentials of Clinical Workflow Analysis*, CPOE University, A CSC Clinical Excellence Service Offering. Available at: http://www.masstech.org/ehealth/CPOE%20University/WFACSC%20.pdf

Mountain, D., 2011 (Mar. 15). "Order Sets and Evidence—Thomson Reuters and Zynx Partnership." *Meaningful Discussions*. Thomson Reuters Community.

Paterno, M.D. et al., 2009 (January/February). "Tiering Drug-Drug Interaction Alerts by Severity Increases Compliance Rates." *Journal of the American Medical Informatics Association*, 16(1): 40–46.

Scott, G.N. and M. Cupp, 2007. "Preventing Adverse Drug Events in the Elderly: The Role of the Beers List." *Pharmacist's Letter* #230907: 10–12.

The Joint Commission, 2010. "Facts about the Universal Protocol for Preventing Wrong Site, Wrong Procedure, and Wrong Person Surgery." Available at: http://www.jointcommission.org/assets/1/18/Universal%20Protocol%201%204%20111.PDF

Townsend, P.L. and J.E. Gebhardt, 2006. *Leadership in Action: Complete Quality Process*. Singapore: Pearson Power.

Van der Sijs, H. et al., 2006 (Mar/Apr). "Overriding of Drug Safety Alerts in Computerized Physician Order Entry." *Journal of the American Medical Informatics Association*, 13(2): 138–147.

White, C., 2005 (July 18). "The Smart Business Intelligence Framework." *BI Research and Intelligent Solutions*. Available at: http://www.b-eye-network.com/view/1182

Chapter 7

Step 5: Obtain Baseline Data

You can't manage what you don't measure.

—Old saying, source uncertain

It is interesting that this quote (or another, "You can't manage what you *can't* measure") is often associated with the management guru Peter Drucker or the statistician and philosopher W. Edwards Deming, when its source remains obscure. It is known, however, that Deming observed that:

> …the most important figures that one needs for management are unknown or unknowable, but successful management must nevertheless take account of them. (*Out of the Crisis*, 1982)

While seemingly these two sayings/quotes are contradictory, they really are not; and they are especially not contradictory in health care. In fact, the dilemma in health care is to improve the use of data for quality improvement and at the same time improve health care in the absence of data that are either very difficult or impossible to measure.

This chapter discusses the need to measure and manage performance in the context of workflow and process management. It encourages the use of and describes ways to collect baseline data—where feasible or in surrogate form—in order to determine whether goals for health information technology (HIT) and electronic health records (EHR) have been met. While it is the expectation that the data collected will be a good approximation of reality, it is not the intent of this chapter to provide instruction or necessarily promote the use of the most sophisticated quantitative methods, statistical analysis, or empirical research. Rather, it is hoped that a pragmatic approach to data collection and benefits realization can be achieved with only reasonable incremental effort in which results provide payback in the form of better utilization of HIT and EHR.

Purposes and Uses of Baseline Data Collection in Workflow and Process Management

Care delivery organizations (CDOs) are urged to establish goals for their HIT and EHR projects; and for any activity they undertake to make improvements, be it for quality, patient safety, revenue generation, employee satisfaction, or myriad other factors.

Chapter 3 introduced the topic of goal setting, the purposes of goal setting for EHR and HIT, and writing S.M.A.R.T. (Specific, Measurable, Achievable, Realistic, and Time-based) goals. That chapter reminded us that from our early childhood readings of *Alice in Wonderland*, having directions in life is important. Fitzhugh Dodson (interestingly a child psychologist) has observed, "Without goals, and plans to reach them, you are like a ship that has set sail with no destination." In good economic times or bad and with or without monetary incentives, no one can afford to make the investment required of HIT and EHR and not want to realize some benefits.

However, benefits do not just happen when new technology is adopted. Benefits evolve over time as people learn to use the technology (Thorp 2003). There also must be expectations set about what benefits are desired. André Godin (in *Thought*, 1950) notes, "The quality of expectations determines the quality of our action." A good part of expectation setting is to have clear goals that all stakeholders have contributed to and have bought into as their own. And there must be effort expended to measure benefits and manage the environment—to celebrate successes and support course correction where necessary—in order to continuously see results.

Setting expectations and defining goals requires an understanding of the current state of affairs ("before data"), **S**pecific **M**etrics, a **R**ealistic picture of what it takes to **A**chieve those goals, and **T**imelines, or milestones, at which to measure benefits ("after data")—that is, S.M.A.R.T. goals and data collection. Benefits realization is a process that can and must be managed, just like any other business process.

Types of Benefits Studies

Baseline data collection has several purposes. It is ultimately intended to help an organization determine if it is meeting its goals. This is often referred to as a benefits realization study or, in the case of financial goals, a return-on-investment (ROI) analysis. However, baseline data collection can also be used for cost/benefit analysis and in a performance-based request for proposal.

Benefits realization study is one conducted some period of time after an intervention occurs that is believed to contribute factors that will help achieve improvement. It should be explicitly structured around the organization's original goals for the intervention. Figure 7.1 supplies an example of a form that can be used to track benefits realization.

Goal	Action	Source of Data	HIT	Metrics	Baseline	Goal	Rationale/ Obstacles	Results Q1	Results Q2
Prevent over- or underdosing	Check for single, daily, cumulative overdosing	DKB SPL	CPOE	Dosing errors	53/year	Dosing errors = 0 in one year	Requires 100% use of CPOE	Dosing errors = 8	Dosing errors = 7
Sign verbal orders (VO) within 4 hours and all by D/C of patient	Notify MD on login to sign VO	CPOE	Login screen	Number of charts with VO signed	80% of charts with at least one VO upon D/C of patient	5% of charts with VO on D/C in 6 months; no VO on D/C in 1 year	Joint Commission requirement	65% charts with VO	60% charts with VO

Figure 7.1 Benefits realization study. (From Copyright © Margret\A Consulting, LLC. With permission.)

On the form there are two examples. The first relates to a patient safety goal of preventing over- or under-dosing. While "prevent" or "eliminate" are often actions that are difficult, if not impossible, to achieve, the organization that proposed this goal did so with the expectation that within one year of using tools within a computerized provider order entry (CPOE) system, they would achieve their goal. Baseline data were collected showing that fifty-three such errors had occurred in the previous year. After implementing their CPOE system with a drug knowledge base (DKB) and structured product label (SPL) information available to (all) ordering providers, they found that after the first quarter they had reduced such errors to eight and showed another slight improvement by the end of the second quarter.

Figure 7.1 also includes an example that may seem trivial in light of the first goal on the list, but verbal orders (VOs) often result in wasted time for many staff members throughout a CDO and, more importantly, pose significant risk for error. The Joint Commission (2010) has long addressed the requirement for timely authentication of VOs. The hospital conducting this benefits realization study therefore wanted to significantly improve in this area and established a goal, with (very aggressive) milestones, that via the login screen to the CPOE system providing verbal order reminders, VOs would be signed within forty-eight hours, and all verbal orders would be signed by the time the patient was discharged (D/C). The health information management department supplied baseline data that 80 percent of all charts had at least one unsigned VO upon their discharge review of all charts.

Return-on-investment analysis is similar to a benefits realization study, in that it is performed after an intervention occurs. However, its focus is on financial benefits. Figure 7.2 supplies a tool similar to that in Figure 7.1, but illustrates cost savings. What is unique about the information in Figure 7.2 is that it is seeking cost savings from clinical quality and patient safety goals. Most cost savings are expected to be derived from reducing paper chart costs, avoidance of paper chart storage, reduced transcription expense, or increased revenue from better

Intervention	Means of Benefit	Baseline	Goal	Savings*
Lab charge display	*Reduces overall lab test costs*	700,000 *displays*	5% ↓	$1M
Duplicate drug warning	*Prevents overdose*	100,000 *warnings*	30% 30% X	**
Drug–drug interaction	*Prevents ADEs*	27 *ADE*	95% ↓	$160,000
Shift summary	*Reduces medical management errors*	120 *MME*	80% ↓	$500,000

* Based on annual average additional hospital costs to manage ADE, including extended LOS, additional testing and therapeutic measures. Cost does not include detrimental effect to patient or liability hospital may incur.
** Reduction in total ADEs captured elsewhere in table.

Figure 7.2 Return on investment. (From Copyright © Margret\A Consulting, LLC. With permission.)

coding, collections, more favorable contracting, or increased number of patients. In Figure 7.2, costs savings are derived from the average cost to manage adverse drug events (ADEs), but excluding the more occasional cost of a malpractice claim or the unknown and unable-to-be-estimated detrimental effect to the patient.

An ROI analysis may use the data such as from a tool like that shown in Figure 7.2 to calculate a financial expression of return, such as payback period, internal rate of return, or net present value. **Payback period** is the amount of time it takes for the investment to pay for itself from the financial benefits. For example, if an investment of $100,000 is made and savings accrue at the rate of $35,000 per year, the payback period would be close to three years. CDOs often look at this from the perspective of whether they have enough capital resources over the period of time to make the investment. The **internal rate of return** (IRR) is the interest rate at which the present value of the project cash inflows equals the initial investment. In other words, it considers the time value of money, suggesting that if the $100,000 were invested elsewhere, it would earn money at some rate. An investment is considered acceptable if its IRR is greater than the cost of capital. Net present value (NPV) is similar to the IRR because it also considers the time value of money, but is expressed as the amount one could earn after a period of time. NPV is more typically used to describe long-term capital investments. When interest rates are low, neither the IRR nor NPV are as useful as the payback period in helping differentiate among investments. Furthermore, many EHRs are acquired on a subscription-type basis and so the bulk of the cash outflow occurs over time.

Cost/benefit analysis is similar to an ROI analysis in that it looks at financial data, but it differs in that it utilizes baseline data to make projections. In fact, the idea behind the cost/benefit analysis is to determine the feasibility of an investment and then to use it in comparing actual results against projections.

Performance-based request for proposal (RFP) can be an important use for baseline data. For example, when approaching the marketplace for HIT or EHR, the CDO may describe that it wants to reduce transcription costs by 85 percent. The result should be that vendors who rely heavily on dictation for documentation in the EHR would be rejected. Performance-based RFPs are not very common in health care because many CDOs do not take the time to map out their workflows and processes or set financially related goals far enough in advance of their selection process (World Bank Institute 2009).

Risks and Benefits of Baseline Data Collection

Data collection is not necessarily easy, especially for HIT and EHR projects where there are many confounding variables and aspirations for quality improvement that require more risk analysis than investment analysis. For example, who is to say that it was new technology or the people making another change that made the difference in improving scores on Medicare's Hospital Compare? HIT and EHR are highly complex. Was it the upgrade to the laboratory information system that made lab results more accessible, a Web portal that delivered results to the ordering provider, the EHR that embedded the lab results into a dashboard, all of the above, or something else that caused a reduction in duplicate lab testing? Finally, what is the cost savings to a hospital when the patient does not have to be readmitted; or to the physician who takes the extra time to educate diabetic patients so their disease is better controlled?

In fact, answers to these questions are generally very difficult to determine, controversial, and vary with the researcher and context of research (Baldwin 2011). This is especially true when collecting data for ROI studies. RAND Corp. studies suggesting the potential for $81 billion annual savings from EHR (Taylor et al. 2005; Hillestad et al. 2005) were influential in the federal government establishing goals and later incentives for EHR adoption. ROI has been found for some physician practices, as reported in a recent study conducted by the Medical Group Management Association (MGMA 2011) indicating that "total medical revenue goes up with the EHR." Hospitals have found cost savings, with anecdotal evidence primarily from hospitals that have studied returns extensively (HIMSS Analytics 2011). The Healthcare Financial Management Association (HFMA 2010) suggests that there is inconsistent evidence of savings from a traditional ROI standpoint, although it acknowledges that there are both tangible and intangible benefits from reductions in length of stay, gains in staffing efficiency, improved adherence to medication protocols, easier regulatory reporting, simplified physician referrals, and increased capture of allowable billable expenses.

Part of the issue in achieving ROI from HIT and EHR is that while not intentionally keeping people sick to generate revenue, the more CDOs keep people well, the less revenue is generated under the present U.S. healthcare reimbursement system. The result is that ROI has to come from other sources to make up the difference. It is really only at the macro-economic level that keeping people well may have an impact, and yet Sidorov (2006) notes, "On the macro-economic level, we are [only] moving chairs around on the deck of the Titanic." Still, he and many others believe that the EHR is an insufficient yet necessary ingredient to alter medical practice.

Another part of the issue in achieving ROI is that perceptions without facts can become self-fulfilling prophecies. There has been much written about loss of productivity by clinicians when implementing an EHR. So much so that most assume this to be true and will only "bite the bullet" to acquire or use EHR because of incentives, for competitive posturing, or because they are employed by a CDO that requires them to use the technology. In an office setting, not only do providers themselves often refuse to change their documentation practices with EHR to achieve better productivity for themselves, but they condone—at least by inaction—poor workflows and processes in the rest of the office. They often seek to purchase a product that looks "familiar" as opposed to one that might actually make a difference.

Willingness to manage workflows and processes in light of new technology and collect data about the results go hand-in-hand to produce better benefits (Nelson, 2011).

Interestingly, a recent survey of physicians' perceptions of EHR surrounding ROI reveals that the primary goal for EHR in physician practices not yet using an EHR is increased revenue, but that once an EHR is implemented, the primary goal seems to shift to reporting and tracking healthcare outcomes. (Otter-Nickerson 2011). This finding does not suggest that CDOs should not push to get an ROI, but it does suggest that ROI may occur in a downstream, sometimes unrecognizable way.

Indeed, the purpose of making public healthcare quality reports is to encourage patients to make selections about the providers they use based on quality. Increasing the number of patients a CDO treats because they will receive better care should be the goal for increasing revenue.

Admonishments, then, from Deming to "take account" of what is happening and from Godin to set expectations whether or not you can precisely measure benefits, are vitally important to realize value from HIT and EHR investments.

Metrics for Benefits Data

To be able to collect data and use them in benefits realization studies, the nature of the data to be collected and the metrics that will allow data to be consistently collected must be determined. The nature of data needed to help define goals and evaluate benefits from improvement in workflow and processes using HIT and EHR is described in Table 7.1.

The ease and accuracy with which data may be collected must also be considered in light of the nature of the data. Virtually all types of data can be measured using one or more of the generic metrics identified in Table 7.2.

CDOs must wrap specificity around these generic metrics. Once this is done, the metrics can be categorized as applying to processes or outcomes and related to financial/administrative or clinical quality/patient safety goals. Examples are provided in Table 7.3.

Table 7.1 Nature of Data

Quantitative (i.e., measurable) or qualitative (i.e., an anecdote)
Quantitative data may be objective (i.e., observed and verifiable) or subjective (i.e., an expression of personal preference or perception)
About the quantity performed (which is quantifiable) or the quality of the performance (which may or may not be quantifiable)
Performance data may be focused on process (i.e., how many times was the process performed correctly) or outcomes (i.e., how many times was the process a success—if success can be defined)

Table 7.2 Examples of Generic Metrics

	Quantifiable	*Not Quantifiable*
Objective data	• Counts • Tallies • Seconds, minutes, hours, days • Revenues • Expenses • Miles	• Anecdotes • Surrogate measures • Extrapolations
Subjective data	• Ratings • Rankings	• Anecdotes • Perceptions

Source: Copyright © Margret\A Consulting, LLC. With permission.

Quantifiable measures of objective data are relatively easy to define and for which to institute collection processes. For example, a hospital may want to count the number of requests for chart pulls before and after EHR has been implemented. A physician office may tally the number of calls from patients requesting prescription refills before and after e-prescribing has been instituted. A hospital receiving complaints about a system being slow may want to use a stopwatch to measure time while clinicians are using the EHR to determine the number of seconds it takes for screens to move or invoke an action. After applicable technology upgrades, they can remeasure to determine improvement. Physicians may want to review their monthly revenue reports before and after using an EHR to determine the impact of coding support. A nursing home may want to examine its annual chart supply expenses before and after implementing an EHR. Nurses in a hospital may wear pedometers to determine the number of miles they walk each day before and after using an EHR at the point of care.

Metrics to define quality of care are more difficult to define and measure. It is for this reason that many of the measures to assess quality of care that have been instituted to date focus on process. For example, the number of patients given prophylactic heparin according to clinical guidelines is a process measure. Alternatively, the number of patients with pressure ulcers is generally considered an outcome measure, where the process of turning the patient and other measures to prevent the ulcers should have been taken.

Sometimes measures relating to quality processes and outcomes may be borderline subjective. For example, number of unnecessary repeat tests has been a significant focus of those implementing robust clinical decision support tools in EHRs in order to reduce what is perceived as unnecessary cost or over-utilization of laboratory testing. However, the measure depends on the definition of unnecessary. This will vary considerably by test type, environment of care, provider practices, and patient population (Van Walraven and Raymond 2003). Without a very specific definition that is kept up-to-date with relevant clinical evidence, this measure is not only subjective but could also lead to unintended consequences

Table 7.3   Examples of Specific Metrics Relating to HIT and EHR

	Process Data	*Outcome Data*
Financial/ administrative Objective data	• Number of patients seen • Number of lines typed • Number of hours worked • Number of patients seen without charts	• Value of lost charges recovered • Revenue earned from improved coding • Number of patients with "acceptable" wait time • Reduced transcription expense • Elimination of two clerical positions
Financial/ administrative Subjective data	• Number of unnecessary repeat tests • Perceived amount of time to write a prescription • Perceived reduction in duplicate data entry	• User satisfaction with EHR scores above 95% • Number of patient complaints about EHR
Clinical quality/ patient safety Objective data	• Number of calls from pharmacy about wrong drug • Number of times patients given drug at wrong time • Number of times patients given the wrong drug • Number of patients at risk for pressure ulcers • Number of patients given prophylactic heparin according to clinical guidelines	• Number of patients with adverse drug events • Number of patients with adverse drug reactions • Number of patients with improved D5 results • Number of patients with pressure ulcers • Number of wrong site procedures • Number of patients with potential nosocomial infections • Number of 30-day re-admissions
Clinical quality/ patient safety Subjective data	• Perceived number of near misses • *Anecdote about an alert that kept a clinician from doing the wrong thing or aided in doing the right thing*	• *Patients comply better with their treatment regimen* • *Patients are more informed about their illness*

Source: Copyright © Margret\A Consulting, LLC. Reprinted with permission.

(Groopman and Hartzband 2009). For example, it has recently been found that women who test positive for the human papillomavirus (HPV) should be tested twice within an interval of one to three months, or risk unnecessary treatment (Gyllensten et al. 2011).

The ability to accurately capture data has a lot to do with whether data used to describe benefits from HIT and EHR workflow and process changes are objective or subjective. Case Study 7.1 provides an example relating to the time it takes to perform a nurse assessment in a hospital.

Case Study 7.1: Why Does it Take Twice as Long to Document?

A hospital was preparing to implement electronic templates for conducting a nursing admission assessment. Prior to this, it conducted baseline data collection. Nurses were asked to document the time they started an assessment and the time they ended the assessment on each assessment they conducted, and the difference was calculated. Nurses were instructed that if they were interrupted during the assessment process, they should record the intervening times and these would be deducted from the overall assessment time. On average, the hospital found that it took approximately an hour and eleven different forms to conduct a nursing admission assessment.

Because the hospital saw that some of the data to be recorded on the assessment could be prepopulated from other sources and redundancy in documenting on multiple forms would be eliminated, it told nurses that they believed it should ultimately take half as much time to document the nursing admission assessment.

As the templates were being implemented, nurses started to complain that the time it took to document on the computer was much longer—reportedly twice as long. Supervisors attributed this to the learning curve and tried to be supportive. However, complaints continued to persist for a long period of time. It was then decided to do another time study, based on metadata available in the computer system (i.e., time stamps that recorded when the system was accessed). Results, however, were next to impossible to retrieve because often nurses had more than one patient record open at a time, and frequently left records open while doing other things. So, a process analyst was tasked with shadowing nurses and recording times. The workflow and process map drawn originally for the process was used as a data collection tool (illustrated in Figure 7.3).

Several interesting observations resulted in the need for both process redesign and reconsideration of the amount of data to be collected. Indeed, it was taking considerably longer to document the nursing assessment.

One reason appeared to be that nurses now were multi-tasking much more than previously because they could see other tasks arriving in their in-box. Instead of getting more work done, however, less work was actually being accomplished. Frequently when work was left to do another task, the previous work had to be reviewed before further work could proceed. The intervening time often included wasted time in moving to a different location and getting additional interruptions. In the paper environment, when a nurse was observed to be in the room with the patient, others tended to leave the nurse alone until he or she became available at the nursing station.

A second reason for the added time was that the templates required much more complete data collection. Previously, nurses used their professional judgment in deciding what questions to ask. In addition, they made some

	Number of Occurrences	Exceptions			
Pt Admitted to Bed					
RN receives admit orders	///	2 at 7:00 AM, 1 at 8:30 AM			
	/				
Urgency? No	//				
Yes / RN IDs pt	///				
RN explains assmt	///				
RN begins assmt	//	Family present; postpones 30 minutes			

	Patient 1	Min.	Patient 2	Min.	Patient 3	Min.
Data exists? — Yes → RN asks to verify	/////-/////-///	13				
No						
RN asks, records, con'ts	/////-/////-/////-/////-//	36				
Data observable? — Yes → RN asks to confirm	///	2				
No						
RN asks, records, cont's	/////-/////-/////-/////-/////- /////-/////-/////-////	38				
Task appears? — Yes → RN interrupts assmt for task	///	4				
		10				
No		12				
RN con'ts assmt	/////-/////-/////-/////	16				
RN Adm Assmt Completed		131				

Figure 7.3   Workflow and process map data collection tool. (From Copyright © Margret\A Consulting, LLC. With permission.)

observations and documented these without asking specific questions. The computer, however, prompted them to respond to every question, so they felt compelled to ask a question even if they could have more quickly documented only an observation. In addition, where data had prepopulated, they also felt the need to ask the patient to verify the answer. Finally, a side-by-side comparison of what data were required in the automated process in comparison to the manual process revealed that a fair amount of additional data was being required. A form such as that illustrated in Figure 7.4 was used to conduct a full analysis of the data elements in the assessment.

The results of the nursing admission assessment study were discussed with nurses and their supervisors. It was agreed that some of the additional data were actually useful, but not all—in which case it was agreed to remove such data from the assessment or delegate its collection to another person. It was agreed that while some observations could result in accurate data, this was sometimes risky. The practice was not always acceptable in the paper world, and would not always be acceptable in the electronic world. However, nurses were left to apply professional judgment in these cases. As a result of the finding that none of the

Nurse Admission Assessment Data Model			
Standard	*Today's Practice*	*EHR Assessment*	*Local Decision*
Patient name	Patient name		Yes (patient name collected by registrar)
Date of birth	Age		Yes (age derived from date of birth)
Gender	Gender		Yes (gender collected by registrar)
		Meal time preference	No (delegate to dietary department)
Presenting problem	Chief complaint		Yes (presenting problem collected by registrar)
	Pet (name and type)		Add (optional)
Current medications	Current medications		Yes (from SureScripts) plus validation and additional entries
Blood pressure	Blood pressure	Blood pressure	Yes

Figure 7.4   Data on documentation analysis. (From Copyright © Margret\A Consulting, LLC. With permission.)

prepopulated data were ever changed by the nurse doing the assessment, it was agreed that those questions did not need to be asked again unless—again in the professional judgment of the nurse—it was believed that there was an error. In addition, nurses were reassured by supervisors that they did not need to respond immediately to every task that appeared in their in-boxes. It was decided to try having the computer triage these with urgent requests appearing as a pop-up and all others staying on the in-box that would be hidden from view during the assessment-taking process.

Three months following the changes that were made, nurses felt the assessment was taking less time. To be certain, the observer returned and found that the time it took them to do their documentation of the admission assessment was reduced to about forty minutes on average. The nurses felt the additional ten minutes from the original goal of only thirty minutes was acceptable in that the additional data elements would contribute to improved quality of care and potentially some downstream time savings.

Case Study 7.1 deals with capturing time, which can be time-consuming to collect accurately, but is still easier to collect than other data related to benefits often cited for EHR and other HIT. For example, collecting data about improving diagnosis with an EHR might be extremely difficult—both to quantify and to collect. A diagnosis may be made at a clinic visit or during a hospitalization. Even if the physician is somewhat uncertain about the diagnosis, there will generally be some conservative treatment or referral made to another provider. The patient may then never return to the clinic or hospital for any number of reasons, including getting better, being regularly seen by another provider for the first and presumably correct diagnosis, or being re-diagnosed (whether correctly or not) and treated elsewhere. To collect such data would require following up with every patient in a manner that would require a very sensitive discussion and still not result in very accurate information. If the patient did return and it was recognized that the first diagnosis was not correct, such occurrence could be documented as a misdiagnosis; but it would be impossible to determine if that is only one patient out of many who were misdiagnosed or that the one patient was the only patient misdiagnosed.

Finally, all the numbers in the world may not be as powerful as a few anecdotes that really get someone's adrenaline going. Case Study 7.2 provides an illustration of a dismayed physician whose process error convinced him to acquire an EHR.

Case Study 7.2: Dismayed Physician Resolves to Acquire EHR

A physician was regularly seeing an elderly patient every three months for a diabetes checkup. He always asked if she was staying on her diet and feeling well, and he observed she was maintaining her weight and looking healthy. He believed her condition was well-controlled. He actually enjoyed the conversations he had with the patient, as she was quite a philosopher, had a sharp mind, and a ready wit. On one visit, the physician reviewed the paper record to check the last HgA1C result and found, to his great dismay, that he had not ordered such a lab test for over nine months. Based on that one instance where he felt he let down his patient, he resolved immediately to get an EHR. He did not feel the need to collect baseline data on how many patients had the HgA1C test performed regularly.

Strategies for Conducting Benefits Realization Studies

The benefits realization studies (or ROI analyses) described so far in this chapter assume "before" and- "after" data collection. There are, however, other approaches that can be used to assess benefits, including benchmarking, surveys, anecdotal evidence, and surrogate data.

Before and after studies are theoretically the best approach for benefits realization studies because they not only supply data to demonstrate the impact of a change, but also enable comparisons based on a relatively stable set of environmental factors. In other words, the same people using paper records will use EHRs. The patient population is unlikely to suddenly become much sicker or have significant health improvements. The physical environment, both within the CDO and its surrounding community, is usually the same unless EHR is implemented at the time of a move to a new facility or there has recently been a natural disaster. It is noted that such factors—in theory—should enable an apples-to-apples comparison that would attribute change to the one intervention of HIT or EHR.

Unfortunately, theory rarely equates to reality; and in health care there are many factors that cause change almost continuously. In fact, some suggest that there is no reason to do baseline data collection or benefits realization studies because too much changes, there are too many confounding variables, and HIT and EHR are virtually becoming necessities anyway. Samuel O. Thier, MD, president of the Institute of Medicine when the first patient record study was commissioned in the mid-1980s, is quoted as saying that EHR has become much like indoor plumbing—no one would consider building a building without such. However, Dr. Thier was also a firm believer in setting goals and earning an ROI. For Dr. Thier and many others, it is important to make the right choices and ensure that the necessary investment is used wisely.

To be realistic, however, many CDOs still do not do baseline data collection in preparing to acquire HIT or EHR. Some, however, find they would like to better understand their ROI from such acquisitions, or at least understand whether they are making optimal use of HIT or EHR.

Benchmarking studies, then, enable an organization to collect only "after" data to be compared with benchmark data. Benchmark data may come from an industry source, a survey the CDO conducts of like organizations, or other sources. The federal government collects considerable data in the National Information Center on Health Services Research and Health Care Technology that may provide suitable data for specific focus areas. Many hospitals and clinics regularly contribute data on Core Measures for Medicare and The Joint Commission, or on the National Committee for Quality Assurance (NCQA) Healthcare Effectiveness Data and Information Set (HEDIS). These data may be sent to a vendor that can provide analysis of the data and anonymous benchmarking.

An advantage of doing benchmarking studies is that "before" data do not need to be collected. Another is that of comparing actual data to industry norms. For example, if the goals set forth in the CDO represented in Figure 7.1 are unrealistic with respect to industry norms, benchmark data would help "level set" their goals. In fact, benchmarking can be performed even when a before-and-after study is conducted. The disadvantages of attempting to do benchmark studies include, first, the unavailability of benchmark data; and second, the data's comparability. There are not a lot of benchmark studies about HIT and EHR implementation. Most of the data about benefits is anecdotal. For example, Clinfowiki (2011) includes a wiki on "EMR Benefits and ROI Categories." The preface to the wiki provides the following caveat:

> The following EMR-related benefits have been identified within various health care organizations. Before one assumes that just because some other organization was able to realize a specific benefit they will be able to achieve the same

thing, one must ensure that they have the same EMR features and functions available AND the clinicians will use them at their organization.

Surveys to supply benchmark data that a CDO collects may overcome some of the issues expressed in the caveat above. Surveys, however, present issues of intellectual property, comparability even when it appears an organization is comparable, and cost and time to conduct them.

Anecdotal evidence without "before" or "after" data refers to information collected by a CDO from the literature, conferences attended, personal experiences, etc., to use in making a business case for an investment in HIT or EHR or to use in strengthening a mandate to use the technology after acquired. Anecdotal evidence should not be discounted out of hand as being unscientific and therefore unworthy of use. Just as the anecdote relayed in Case Study 7.2 was actually an antidote for the situation, stories are quite credible among health professionals. Health professionals often learn in a "see-one, do-one" mode. As a result—and somewhat unfortunately—while healthcare professionals want (and should have) scientific evidence before leaving their conservative posture, one story about how long it took to regain productivity after an EHR implementation can become gospel truth forever. Sadly, it may require an anecdote of how an EHR saved a life or had another significantly positive impact to be the antidote for use of the technology.

Surrogate data are yet another form of data that may be an option for some baseline data collection to be used in benefits realization. Surrogate data are data used in place of other data that suggest the impact of an intervention. For example, if a clinic implements an EHR and wants to gauge physician adoption, surrogate data may be the rate at which dictation decreases where dictation of notes prior to acquiring the EHR was the norm. Such data are easier to capture than asking physicians to tally their use or probably a more accurate estimate than to use computer login data—where the computer could have been logged on and never used. There may not be a lot of examples of surrogate data to measure impact of an improved workflow and process, but where they exist they can be very useful.

Data Collection Tools

There are a variety of data collection tools that may be used to capture baseline data, varying by the type of data to be collected (World Bank Institute 2009). These are summarized in Table 7.4.

Tallying and counting samples of work are probably the most popular and easiest tools to use for determining the volume of activity. Figure 7.3 is an example of a simple tally process documented on a spreadsheet containing the systems flowchart workflow and process map. Instead of recording data on such

Table 7.4 Data Collection Tools

Type of Data to be Collected	Data Collection Tools
Volume	Tally
	Count
Time	Diary
	Log
	Stopwatch
Distance	Pedometer
Process	Observation
	Interview
Perceptions	Survey
Outcomes	Record review

Source: Copyright © Margret\A Consulting, LLC. With permission.

a spreadsheet, volumes of work and/or time to accomplish work can be documented directly within the symbols of the flowchart. For example, Figure 6.2 in Chapter 6 identifies the percent of prescription renewal requests that come from each source within the symbols representing the sources (i.e., boundary symbols in this case). If a goal is to reduce the volume of calls from pharmacies for renewal requests, the "before" data as shown in Figure 6.2, which is the "as-is" map, can be compared with the "after" data on a "to-be" map. It was also noted in Chapter 5 that the flow process chart is explicitly designed to show distance in feet, quantity, and time (see Figure 5.4). This could be modified to show other quantitative data, such as number of errors in a process, if desired.

A **diary or logbook** can be used to capture time. Chapter 6 discussed documenting while doing, and Case Study 7.1 illustrated this in describing how nurses collected baseline data in the paper environment by documenting directly on their assessments the time they started and ended and any intervening interruptions. Other examples of documenting baseline data while doing a process include an emergency department receptionist recording entry and exit (to the emergency treatment area) times for each patient. A clinic telephone receptionist could record hash marks on a plain pad of paper every time a pharmacist calls. CDOs can count the number of chart requisition slips or calls to the file room to determine how many charts are pulled per day.

Pedometers can be used to capture distance traveled. Such studies are often used in CDOs where workers spend a considerable amount of time walking to and from patients, and especially where such walking introduces a fatigue factor. Fatigue—due to many factors—in both nurses and physicians has been attributed to patient safety issues (Mullins 2010; ACOG 2008).

Record review techniques are often required for clinical quality outcomes measurement. Not only is it more difficult to establish metrics for quality measurement, but often quality measurement does not lend itself to simple collection tools such as tallying or time studies. Health records often need to be audited and quality data abstracted therefrom. For example, even collecting data about the number of unsigned verbal orders (as in Figure 7.1) requires someone to review the contents of the charts. Record reviews are also necessary for outcomes associated with revenues and expenses, where the general ledger, accounts receivable, and other sources of such data require inspection and application of various formulas.

Surveys, interviews, and observations can be constructed and used to collect baseline data. Surveys and sometimes interviews tend to be used for more subjective types of data, such as patient perceptions or user satisfaction. However, if constructed properly, they can yield useful information. Case Study 7.3 describes a survey conducted to capture patient perspectives on the use of a new EHR in a clinic.

Case Study 7.3: Patient Perspective Survey

A clinic wanted to understand what patients' perspectives were on its new EHR. However, it had previously conducted a survey on satisfaction in general and thought it would be good to use the same "before" data to determine if other factors might have been influenced by use of the EHR. In addition, the clinic did not want to over-emphasize the EHR as a major change, believing that a few questions as part of a larger survey would be looked upon more as one of several improvement factors the clinic had instituted since its last survey. In reviewing the previous survey, it was noted that one of the questions asked if staff were friendly. Looking at the results, the clinic felt this appeared to be rather subjective. It decided, therefore, to reframe this question and ask a series of more objective questions, such as whether staff members always introduced themselves when entering a room, always addressed the patient by name, etc. Patients' responses may not be completely accurate if memory fails them about a particular part of their visit, but the clinic felt the greater objectivity of the data would reveal better results.

For process improvement, observations and sometimes interviews may be more effective than surveys. For example, observation can help determine whether all steps in a process are always performed. Whatever data collection tools are used, applying them consistently—or recognizing when a change has been made, such as in Case Study 7.3—is very important.

Sampling Methodology

As noted at the start of this chapter, it is desirable to collect good quality data, yet demanding highly scientific approaches will very likely result in data not being collected at all, except in the most academic of organizations. Most people understand that to get good results, a sufficiently large sample must be taken. The randomness of the sample and the reliability and validity of the data collection tools are other factors that influence how well one can rely on the results of any measure (Golafshani 2003).

Reliability is the extent to which results are consistent over time and an accurate representation of the population being studied. A simple way to determine if your data collection process is reliable is to have more than one person perform the data collection process and consider how close they are in getting the same results. While it is conceivable that they can be off by one or two tallies or counts as a matter of human error, a wide difference suggests that something is wrong. While such a discrepancy may be due to one person not being adequately trained or conscientious about collecting the data, it is also possible that the instructions are not clear or the process entails so much variability that it is difficult to know what to tally. For instance, in measuring patient wait time in a very busy emergency department where patients have the opportunity to walk around—perhaps to the restroom, a vending machine area, or cafeteria—it may be difficult to get an accurate count by simply noting each person's entry and exit time. The degree to which a data collection process can be made simple will improve the reliability of the data being collected. For instance, it may be necessary to have the emergency department receptionist annotate the time the patient first arrived, but the nurse annotate the time the patient actually was taken to the exam room in the emergency department.

Validity determines whether the collection process truly measures what it is intended to measure. There may be several considerations here.

The first consideration is whether the collection instrument relates to the topic being evaluated. This is often referred to as **content validity**. For example, in Case Study 7.3, the clinic wanted to understand patients' perspectives on its use of EHR, but then asked a variety of other questions about patient satisfaction with the clinic visit, such as the friendliness of the staff. One might question whether these other questions relate to use of EHR. This does not mean that the data collection process should not be performed; it simply means that without further evidence, the conclusions that might be drawn from the data may not be as accurate as desired. The staff seemed to recognize this because they explicitly chose not to ask only about use of the EHR.

A second consideration relates to the data collection tool's ability to measure nonobservable traits, or constructs. This is called **construct validity**. Again, the Case Study 7.3 should demonstrate construct validity because it is a perception survey. Measuring the construct validity of the data collection tool might have to be performed by drawing inferences or using other subjective data collection. For instance, if a comment section is added to the survey and only positive comments are made about the EHR, one could infer that the patients were aware of the use of EHR and probably responded to the survey questions about the EHR truthfully. If no comments were made, it is conceivable that the patients did not think anything was unusual or different, and one might conclude that if most responses to the survey are the same, there is no negative impact from the EHR. Clinic staff might also want to be trained in watching patients as they leave the examining room the first time they are seen with the EHR. If they are asking questions about the EHR, even in a positive way, this may suggest that there are some concerns. If they are rejoicing that the clinic finally arrived at the information age, one could probably conclude that the patients were happy about the EHR. Some clinics have even taken the step to have a nurse accompany the patient out of the exam room during this period of time and ask questions such as, "How was your visit today?" This can help both to determine impact as well as to be able to immediately respond to any questions or concerns. **External validity** is the extent to which the findings can be generalized to other people or groups. For example, if this clinic has quite a diverse population of patients—different age groups, ethnic backgrounds, languages spoken, case mix, etc.—it might be useful to ask patients to record such distinguishing data or use a coding system to reflect these differences. It is also very likely that differences in physician behavior with the EHR cause different experiences, so capturing which physician the patient saw could be very important.

Sample size is influenced by the CDO's degree of confidence they want to achieve in the data collection process. **Confidence interval**, also called margin of error, is the interval between which the likelihood of same answers will exist. So if the tolerable margin of error is 4 percentage points and 47 percent of those surveyed answered the same way, the CDO can be "sure" that the data reflect between 43 percent (47 − 4) and 51 percent (47 + 4) of the relevant population. The **confidence level** describes the surety with which the results reflect the population within the scope of the confidence interval. The wider the interval a CDO accepts, the more certain it can be that the population of answers would be within that range. Most researchers use a confidence level of 95 percent. Finally, the sample taken must be **random** in order to rely on the confidence interval and confidence level. Randomness removes bias from the sampling. Random number generators exist to assist in selecting a truly random sample. For CDOs conducting benefits realization studies, it is important to consider the population and take samples from all applicable segments. For example, sampling the workforce with respect to workflows and processes that will be impacted by HIT and EHR should include those working every shift, in every affected department, and with every patient type.

To determine the sample size needed in order to achieve a specific confidence interval (e.g., 3, 4) and a specific confidence level (e.g., 95 percent, 99 percent), statistical methodology can be applied. Fortunately, there are a number of companies that provide sample-size calculators on the Web. Table 7.5 shows the results for a clinic with a patient population of 5,000.

Table 7.5   Sample Sizes

Confidence Level	95%	95%	99%
Confidence Interval	3	4	3
Population	5,000	5,000	5,000
Sample size calculated	880	536	1,350

Note: Sample size calculator used from Creative Research Systems at www.surveysystem.com/sscalc.htm.

Communications Surrounding Baseline Data Collection and Benefits Realization Studies

Whether or not a CDO applies such statistical methodology to determine appropriate sample size or takes a formal approach to evaluating reliability and validity, the results of any data collection process should be "eyeballed" to get a feeling for whether the results make sense.

Different types of data collection may require different considerations. One phenomenon to watch out for in evaluating satisfaction with the use of EHRs is "cognitive dissonance." This is a discomfort caused by holding conflicting ideas simultaneously. For instance, it is frequently found that physicians' perceptions of time to chart a patient note is one of increased time, yet they will simultaneously report they were able to see more patients or leave earlier at the end of the day. One reason for this result is that many tasks are now being performed on the computer, "charting" a note only being one of them. Hence, the perception relates to the total time spent looking at results, tasking a nurse, writing a prescription, and charting the note (Keshavjee et al. 2001).

There may also be a negative Hawthorne effect. The Hawthorne effect is a form of reaction where those being studied in some way improve or modify their behavior simply because they are being studied. It is conceivable that those who are resistant to an EHR may—even unconsciously—modify their behavior negatively to match their interest in having the EHR removed or for them to be excused from using it. Chapter 11 covers change management in depth, but suffice it to say that EHR implementation requires considerable change management.

One other caveat must be made when measuring and managing quality improvement in health care. Quality measurement is quite a new process and one that is very complex. Furthermore, it has been found that quality data often correlates to EHR sophistication (HIMSS Analytics 2006). There are increasing concerns that quality metrics that are not evidence based and regularly kept up-to-date with new evidence can be potentially dangerous to patients. Groopman and Hartzband (2009) observe that "human beings are not uniform in their biology; that diseases with many effects on multiple organs, like diabetes, act differently in different people. Medicine is an imperfect science and its study is imperfect." Tonelli (2006), writing in the *Virtual Mentor: The American Medical Association Journal of Ethics*, calls for flexibility in applying evidence from clinical trials. Rigid adherence to required guidelines is not only bad for patients, but is also counterproductive when applied to knowledge workers.

Lee et al. (2010), Paterno et al. (2009), and Van der Sijs et al. (2006) were cited in Chapter 6 as finding that the key to compliance with clinical decision support intended to contribute to quality improvement is flexibility in the design of technology. Alert management in general, tiering alerts by severity, and being able to override alerts when professional judgment calls for such are essential for effective use of clinical decision support. All these methodologies recognize how knowledge workers work—and should work. Likewise, communications about improvement, sanctions, education, and other strategies to improve quality of care must be carefully considered in light of how to achieve the most value from knowledge workers.

Key Points

■ Baseline data collection has many uses, including setting **goals** and **expectations**, issuing **performance-based requests for proposal**, determining the **cost/benefit** or feasibility of making an investment, and conducting **benefits realization** studies including **return-on-investment** analysis.

■ Baseline data collection is not necessarily easy, especially in health care where there are many **confounding variables** and **complexities**. However, it is commonly agreed that assuring that benefits are achieved from a planned intervention, such as acquiring HIT and EHR, requires an understanding of the difference **"before" and "after"** the intervention. There are strategies to **benchmark** "after" data with industry or survey data—and while such a comparison can be helpful in determining whether goals and outcomes are consistent with industry expectations, benchmarking does not describe the effect of a specific intervention in a specific environment.

■ Collection of baseline data requires defining **metrics** and utilizing appropriate **data collection tools**. CDOs should attempt to get the most **valid** and **reliable** data they can using a realistic, but **random sample size** so that the process of collecting baseline data is not so burdensome that it will not be done.

References

ACOG, 2008 (Feb. 1). ACOG Addresses Physician Fatigue and Patient Safety. *Obstetrics & Gynecology*, Committee Opinion #398.

Baldwin, G., 2011 (June 1). "The $80 Billion Question." *Health Data Management Magazine*. Available at: http://www.healthdatamanagement.com/issues/19_6/health-care-electronic-health-records-42538-1.html

Clinfowiki, 2011. EMR Benefits and Return on Investment Categories. Available from http://www.informatics-review.com/wiki/index.php/EMR_Benefits_and_Return_on_Investment Categories

Creative Research Systems, 2010. Sample Size Calculator. Available at: http://www.surveysystem.com/sscalc.htm

Golafshani, N., 2003 (December). "Understanding Reliability and Validity in Qualitative Research." *The Qualitative Report,* 8(4): 597–607.

Groopman, J. and P. Hartzband, 2009 (April 8). "Why 'Quality' Care is Dangerous." *The Wall Street Journal.* Available at: http://online.wsj.com/article/SB12391487625199185.html

Gyllensten, U. et al., 2011 (August 23). "Short-time Repeat High-Risk HPV Testing by Self-Sampling for Screening of Cervical Cancer. *British Journal of Cancer,* 105: 694–697.

HFMA, 2010 (Feb. 16). "ROI on EMR: Elusive — or Illusive?" Available at: http://www.hfma.org/Communities/Forums/CFO/ROI-on-EMR — Elusive-%e2%80%93-or-Illusive-/

Hillestad, R. et al., 2005. "Can Electronic Medical Record Systems Transform Health Care? Potential Benefits, Savings, And Costs." *Health Affairs,* 24(5): 1103–1117.

HIMSS Analytics, 2006. EMR Sophistication Correlates to Hospital Quality Data. HIMSS Analytics White Paper.

HIMSS Analytics, 2011. Sentara Healthcare. Stage 7 Award Case Study. Available at: http://www.himssanalytics.org/hc_providers/stage7casestudies_Sentara.asp

Joint Commission, The, 2010. *Comprehensive Accreditation Manual for Hospitals.* Oakbrook Terrace, IL: RC 02.03.07.

Keshavjee, K. et al., 2001. "Measuring the Success of Electronic Medical Record Implementation Using Electronic and Survey Data." *Proceedings of the American Medical Informatics Association Symposium,* 309–313.

Lee, E.K. et al., 2010. "Improving Patient Safety through Medical Alert Management: An Automated Decision Tool to Reduce Alert Fatigue." *AMIA 2010 Symposium Proceedings,* 417–421.

MGMA, 2011. Electronic Health Records: Status, Needs and Lessons: 2011 Report Based on 2010 Data. Englewood, CO: Medical Group Management Association.

Mullins, K.J., 2010 (May 11). "Nursing Fatigue Threatens Patients." *Digital Journal.* Available at http://digitaljournal.com/print/article/291857

National Information Center on Health Services Research and Health Care Technology, http://www.nlm.nih.gov/hsrinfo/datasites.html

Nelson, R. 2011 (March). "Why the Return on Investment in an EHR is Poor." *MedPage Today.* Available at: www.MedPageToday.com

Otter-Nickerson, B., 2011 (Aug. 11). "Vendor Survey Shows that Physicians' Perception of EHR is Often Defined by Previous Usage." *EMR Daily News.* Available at: http://emrdailynews.com/2011/08/11/vendor-survey-shows-that-physicians%E2%80%99-perception-of-ehr-is-often-defined-by-previous-usage/

Paterno, M.D. et al., 2009 (January/February). "Tiering Drug-Drug Interaction Alerts by Severity Increases Compliance Rates." *Journal of the American Medical Informatics Association,* 16(1): 40–46.

Sidorov, J. 2006 (July/Aug). "It Ain't Necessarily So: The Electronic Health Record and the Unlikely Prospect of Reducing Health Care Costs." *Health Affairs,* 25(4): 1079–1085.

Taylor, R. et al., 2005 (Sept/Oct). "Promoting Health Information Technology: Is There a Case for More-Aggressive Government Action?" *Health Affairs,* 24(5): 1234–1245.

Thorp, J., 2003. *The Information Paradox.* Revised. Fujitsu. Available at: http://www.businessweek.com/adsections/dmr/parabene.htm

Tonelli, M., 2006 (February). "Evidence-Based Medicine and Clinical Expertise." *Virtual Mentor American Medical Association Journal of Ethics*, 8(2): 71–74.

Van der Sijs, H. et al., 2006 (Mar/Apr). "Overriding of Drug Safety Alerts in Computerized Physician Order Entry." *Journal of the American Medical Informatics Association,* 13(2): 138–147.

Van Walraven, C. and M. Raymond, 2003. "Population-Based Study of Repeat Laboratory Testing." *Clinical Chemistry*, 49(12): 1997–2005.

World Bank Institute, 2009 (May 11). Monitoring & Evaluation for Results. Washington, DC. Handouts available at: http://web.worldbank.org/WBSITE/EXTERNAL/WBI /0,,contentMDK:22064992~pagePK:209023~piPK:335094~theSitePK:213799,00.html

Chapter 8

Step 6: Validate Workflow and Process Maps

Trust, but verify.

—Phrase made famous by President Ronald Reagan

This chapter describes steps to take to ensure that workflow and process maps are complete, easy to understand, encompass variations, have connection points that link to applicable other processes, and enable a care delivery organization (CDO) to finalize the documentation of an "as-is" workflow and process map.

Need for Validation

The purpose of validating current, or "as-is," workflow and process maps is to ensure that they can be used for their intended purpose. If a map is incomplete, not drawn at the appropriate level of detail, or does not fully describe variations—it essentially is only then a picture of a static procedure document. In fact, a good way to evaluate a current map is to get a sense that it is "alive." A current map should clearly identify all the "warts" and workarounds that exist in the way work is performed today. This is because these warts and workarounds reveal the very aspects of workflows and processes that need help, and often where technology can provide the most help.

To achieve accurate reflections of living, breathing workflows and processes, workers—whether performing the mapping themselves or being shadowed by someone who documents the map—must understand that the purpose of workflow and process mapping is ultimately to help them. Redesign of workflows and processes should streamline work, ideally make work easier, or at least provide the satisfaction that a job is well done.

Too often, however, workers are fearful of being blamed for the issues that arise from creating workarounds. Or they may feel that the technology is being introduced only to "squeeze one more ounce of work" out of them. Many healthcare professionals feel inadequate when faced with new technology and are convinced they will lose their jobs. Interestingly, when computerized provider order entry (CPOE) systems were first becoming popular in hospitals, the "buzz" at a convention of clinical pharmacists was loss of jobs. As it turns out, the emphasis on all aspects of patient safety in hospitals has only created new jobs for pharmacists. (*American Journal of Health Systems Pharmacists* 2003)

Nursing jobs are already severely in demand, and many new opportunities for nurses, such as in nursing informatics (Hebda and Czar 2009), have been created as a result of the increasing use of technology (as well as the aging population and other factors). In fact, insufficient staffing is raising the stress level of nurses and driving many to leave the profession, creating even more job openings. In 2011 the Association of Colleges of Nursing identified that the U.S. Bureau of Labor Statistics (BLS) reported that the healthcare sector of the economy is continuing to grow, despite significant job losses in nearly all other major industries. Hospitals, long-term care facilities, and ambulatory care settings added 37,000 new jobs in March 2011 alone, the biggest monthly increase recorded by any employment sector at that time. As the largest segment of the healthcare workforce, nurses likely will be recruited to fill many of these new positions. The BLS 2011 report also confirmed that 283,000 jobs had been added in the healthcare sector within the previous year. This has been a trend for some time, and is expected to continue into the foreseeable future (American Association of Colleges of Nursing 2011).

To counteract fears and improve the value of workflow and process mapping, supervisors and all others up the leadership chain must instill in the workforce that the goal of workflow and process mapping is to make work better and to contribute to quality patient care and safety. While such leadership starts at the top, it is often found that it is the supervisor who is also fearful who may actually cause the most "damage." Supervisors need as much reassurance and support as the general workforce who will be expected to use new technology. If support for accurate process mapping is not provided, the exercise to create such maps will not be beneficial.

Collaboration

Collaboration is an essential part of validating workflow and process maps. However, sharing such maps across departments may also serve the potentially more important purpose of creating community. "Turf" issues are not uncommon in any industry (Cassidy and Guggenberger 2001), and care delivery organizations (CDOs) are no exception. Consider the example of obscure terminology between the nursing and pharmacy departments described in Case Study 8.1.

Case Study 8.1: Obscure Terminology

Nurses were in the process of adopting an electronic medication administration record (EMAR) system in a hospital. They documented their current workflows—and anticipated redesign opportunities. Their "as-is" medication administration record workflow and process map is provided in Figure 8.1a. Once the EMAR was implemented, however, it came as quite a shock that the electronic form now included drug terminology completely unfamiliar to nurses. Initially, they felt the pharmacy staff was being obscure because they did not want nurses to have so much control over the medication distribution process. The hospital's vendor urged the two groups to get together and compare their new workflow and process maps, which are provided in Figure 8.1b. Unfortunately, the fact that the nursing department's "as-is" map as well as the two separately drawn maps of the redesigned processes were drawn at a very high level and did not include some necessary detail. As a result, neither department working alone would have recognized that the source of the drug names was actually different for the two departments and this was causing the difference in terminology. Even at a fairly high level of detail, the redrawn "as-is" map in Figure 8.1c might have revealed more clues as to the impending issue with the new process. Physicians write orders for drugs using clinical drug terminology (often proprietary, or when automated, using a terminology from RxNorm) that then is translated by the pharmacy staff into drug inventory terminology (National Drug Code, NDC). Where

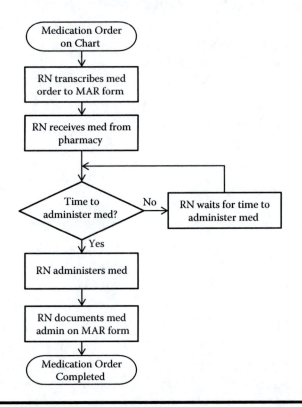

Figure 8.1a Current nursing medication administration record (MAR) workflow and process. (From Copyright © Margret\A Consulting, LLC. With permission.)

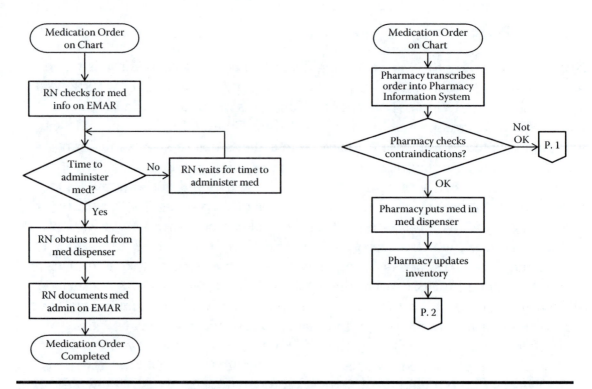

Figure 8.1b   New nursing and pharmacy workflows and processes for EMAR. (From Copyright © Margret\A Consulting, LLC. With permission.)

nurses originally created their MAR forms from physician orders, the EMAR was now coming from the pharmacy information system and contained NDC names. When this was recognized, it became evident to both groups that collaboration in understanding the current workflows and processes would have helped them get to the appropriate level of detail and better anticipate the impending change. (Some EMAR systems now are able to make the translation, transparent only to the pharmacy so that the drug names coming across the EMAR continue to use an RxNorm set of terminology.)

Workflows and processes often do not adhere to departmental boundaries (Tomatsu 2002). Collaboration is essential between departments where workflows and process boundaries are shared (or collide!), as illustrated by Case Study 8.1. Such collaboration, however, also serves to help ensure clarity and appropriate level of detail. As one department starts to ask questions about a workflow and process map of another department, it should become apparent that further clarity or detail may be necessary. It may even be necessary to consider switching from a systems flowchart tool for mapping to a swim-lane approach that may better show the hand-offs between departments, especially if there are several departments performing related work simultaneously (Damelio 2011).

Collaboration is also necessary among workers within a department—whether an entire process or only part of a process is performed therein. In fact, this should be one's "first line of defense" when validating the accuracy of an "as is" workflow and process map. If such a map is not clear to all who perform the process then it is very likely not sufficiently well drawn and will not be clear

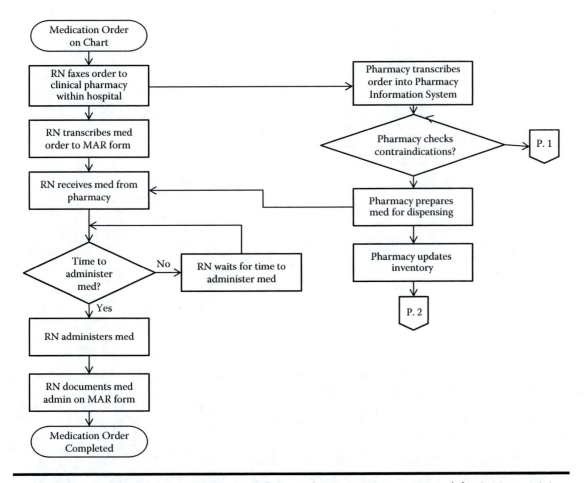

Figure 8.1c   Validated "as is" MAR workflow and process. (From Copyright © Margret\A Consulting, LLC. With permission.)

when shown to another department—the second line of defense. The power of collaboration achieves documentation of variations that either must be acknowledged as important to retain in any redesigned workflow and process or which should be standardized where feasible.

Sharing workflow and process maps can be achieved by posting maps on walls where staff frequently walk and can post a sticky note or otherwise add documentation, or in a conference room where staff can work together to improve a map. Collaboration software can also be used to share maps and have others annotate their questions, variations, or further detail.

Issues in "As-Is" Maps Are Common

Throughout the previous chapters a variety of workflow and process maps have been illustrated. In many cases they were "real" maps (or partial clips of real maps), as originally drawn in a CDO—many times with all their warts and bad habits. The map in Figure 6.3a is a good example of where following the convention of drawing a systems flowchart from top to bottom was not followed. In fact,

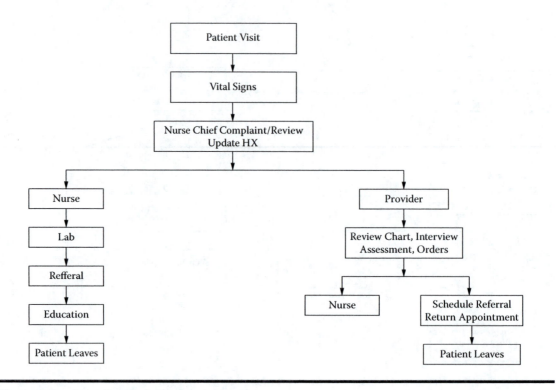

Figure 8.2   Map in need of improvement.

the full map virtually followed an S-shape! Figure 8.2 is another example of a map that has many issues.

It is not at all uncommon for maps to be drawn initially with issues of design or substance, or both. As previously noted, those who perform the work are in the best position to know it—yet they can know it so well that they may take for granted certain aspects of the work or make certain assumptions that lessen the clarity of the map for others. Two steps can be taken to help improve maps. One is to use a checklist of common issues and ways to overcome them to help remind mappers of their obligations for clarity and completeness in their mapping. The second is to recognize that, just as no one can proofread their own work, few mappers can validate their own maps and need help to do so.

Seven Deadly Sins of Workflow and Process Mapping and Their Salvations

Table 8.1 provides a checklist of common issues associated with drawing maps of current workflows and processes, and some recommendations for overcoming these issues. While this table is dubbed the "Seven Deadly Sins of Workflow and Process Mapping and Their Salvations," use it in good spirit. The purpose of this chapter is to help a CDO achieve clarity and completeness in its workflow and process mapping. Still, it must be recognized that so long as maps are clear and complete to both those who perform the process and those who do not perform the

Table 8.1 Seven Deadly Sins of Workflow and Process Mapping and Their Salvations

Sins	Salvations
1. Not enough detail or too much detail: New mappers either tend to take on too big a process with insufficient detail; or they get too detailed, often where automation will not impact a process. An irrelevant step here or there is probably not an issue, but missing steps that should be included is vitally important.	• Consider if several different types of people (e.g., physician, nurse, receptionist, biller, pharmacist) are included in the map. If so, the map may be at too high a level of detail. • Look at Figures 4.1a and 4.1b to evaluate if the map includes more than one process identified on these lists. If so, the map may be at too high a level of detail and should be subdivided. • For each operation in the map, consider how it would be automated. If an operation cannot be automated, the level of detail may be more than necessary in planning for automation. These steps should be grouped together into one: • If there are a number of steps that are on the map but are really a subsidiary process or a process clearly performed outside the scope of the main focus of the map, ensure it is mapped elsewhere and then simply reference that another process is performed and then the flow depicted continues. • As a map is reviewed, read each step out loud and think about actually performing the step. If the map does not clearly move from one step to another, there is something missing. • For each step in the map, ask "How does one get from the previous step to this one?" If the answer is clear from the map, there is no missing step.
2. Decision points are missing: This is one of the easiest "sins" to spot because of the distinctive diamond symbol. Many new mappers often forget decisions because they are so frequently not visible.	• There is almost never a map without a decision point. Review every operation and ask the following questions that should result in the addition of a decision point: • Is there more than one path to or from this operation? • Is there variation depending on the patient, location, or other factor? • Are there times it is necessary to not do an operation or to perform an operation differently? • Are there differences in data used to perform the subsequent operations? • Are data always available? If not, what happens? • Without looking at the map, think purposefully about decisions that have to be made in the process being mapped. Add these at the appropriate points. • In validating the completeness of a map, consider every point where a control or checkpoint should be. Add these as decisions at the appropriate points.

continued

Table 8.1 (continued)   Seven Deadly Sins of Workflow and Process Mapping and Their Salvations

Sins	Salvations
3. Decision flow is not clear: Many new mappers need extra practice in mapping decision making. Sometimes they use operation symbols as labels. Sometimes they only have one branch coming from a decision symbol.	• Make sure every decision symbol includes a question with at least two possible answers, or pathways. • Label every branch from a decision symbol with a unique choice (e.g., yes/no, >/=/<, normal-borderline-abnormal). • Ensure that every branch goes to either another decision symbol or an operation symbol. • If there are more than three pathways but fewer than five or six, use a circle to represent the decision. If there are more than five or six pathways, consider: • Are there really this many choices from one question, or are there really several questions in sequence? Redraw. • Using a decision table. Once the decision table is laid out, it is possible to gain clarity that may enable sequencing of multiple decisions. If not, reference the decision symbol in an operations symbol at the appropriate point in the map. If the multiple decisions result in re-entry to the map at several different points, use connector symbols annotated in the decision table to show where each pathway re-enters the flow.
4. "As is" is depicted as it is supposed to be, not as it really is: This may be one of the most difficult "sins" to pinpoint from the map itself, but can often be detected by the process used to draw the map.	• There is almost never a current map without an operation, decision point, or flow that suggests some type of workaround, redundancy, delay, rework, etc. If such cannot be observed, it is very likely that the map does not reflect reality. • If many people who perform the process were involved in mapping the process and there is no variation, the map is unlikely to reflect reality. It is rare that many people can perform a process in the exact same manner all the time.
5. Documentation within the symbol does not reflect who does what, or ask a question.	• There is precious little space in each systems flowchart symbol, but the person, the action taken, and the object that is impacted by the action must be clear. Practice describing every step using only three words: person, verb, noun. • If the entire map is performed by only one category of worker in all cases, the worker's credentials can be used in the first symbol and not repeated thereafter. This situation is relatively rare in health care. • Make sure the "doing" action is an action verb. Review the list in Table 6.2.

Table 8.1 (continued) Seven Deadly Sins of Workflow and Process Mapping and Their Salvations

Sins	*Salvations*
	• Check that there is a question mark (?) in every diamond shape. If not, it may be that the diamond shape was misused. Refer to the list in Table 6.3.
6. Flow is not clear: While making changes to a map will often disrupt the flow of the symbols temporarily, the final flow should be from top to bottom and left to right for clarity.	• Check that the map flows from top to bottom. • Where there are decision points, check that the map flows generally from left to right. • If it is necessary to have flow lines going from right to left (e.g., a third branch on a decision symbol or a pathway from a decision point returns to the main path, make sure they do not cross over another line, suggesting an alternative flow that is not intended). • If flow must carry forward to another column on the same page or a second page, use connector symbols rather than long lines. • Unless all parts of the flow are from top to bottom and left to right, make sure that all flow lines have arrows pointing in the correct direction.
7. Boundaries do not match those in the process inventory; or each process does not clearly link to the processes that occur before and after it.	• After all maps are completed, every workflow and process that will be impacted by HIT or EHR should be documented. The result should be that each map can connect to the map representing the preceding map and to the map that follows. • There may be more than one starting point and/or more than one ending point. Each point, however, must link to a preceding and following map.

Source: Copyright © Margret\A Consulting, LLC. With permission.

process but may be impacted by it in some way, there is no harm in not sticking absolutely to conventions. In general, however, the more conventions are followed, the more likely the maps become clear and complete, and hence more useful.

Taking a Validation Timeout

Validating a workflow and process map may be performed by the original author, a representative group of people who perform the process but may not have been involved in the mapping, and/or others.

Because it is sometimes difficult to tease out all the nuances of a workflow and process that a self-mapper performs, it can be helpful to step away from the documentation process for a while and then return to view the map anew. This timeout may be just a few days or a couple of weeks at most from the original mapping activity. As time passes, some of the original thought processes that occurred while performing the mapping will have gone away. This enables the person performing the mapping to look at it as if he or she was looking at the map for the first time. The advantages of having the original author do the validation include that the mapper learns tricks about mapping right the first time, and there may be parts of a process that were missed and can be added. The disadvantages, of course, include that the mapper may still be too "close" to the process to give it an effective critique, and does not have the opportunity to truly see the map from someone else's perspective.

As noted under collaboration, a group enables people to bounce thoughts off each other, but can suffer some of the same issues as a single person performing the mapping. If the number of people performing a process is large enough to have another group not originally involved in the mapping perform the validation, then the validation may not only yield a clearer and more complete map, but also engages others in the overall process leading up to acquiring and implementing HIT and EHR. They can benefit from starting to think about what the technology may mean in the future.

Finally, a truly unbiased perspective is obtained when someone not at all involved in the mapping or the performance of the process reviews the mapping product. In fact, some organizations specify the nature of a validation team, such as a process auditor, a participant in the process, an individual impacted by the process, and a programmer or systems analyst who will be responsible for the new system's configuration such that it matches the specifications in the redesigned process (EPISD n.d.). At a minimum, this tests the clarity of the map. If such a person or team is able to "talk through" the process with someone who actually performs the process and the discussion reveals precisely the steps performed, then the map obviously is clear and it is very likely that the map is also complete. Sometimes, talking through the map provides the original mapper or others familiar with the process the ability to remember something to add or even helps them recognize something that needs correction. A mere question such as "How does this go from here to there?" can suggest something is missing.

It was noted that Figure 8.2 has many issues with it. That map is a good candidate for validation. It be may helpful to consider what issues exist in the map in Figure 8.2 and compare to the summary of the issues described in Table 8.2.

Key Points

■ President Reagan used the phrase "trust, but verify" often. In fact, the transcript of Reagan signing the Intermediate-Range Nuclear Forces Treaty on December 8, 1987, with Mikhail Gorbachev, reads as follows:

> ...But the importance of this treaty transcends numbers. We have listened to the wisdom in an old Russian maxim. And I'm sure you're familiar

Table 8.2   Issues in the Map in Need of Improvement

Issues	*Correction*
1. Not enough detail	This map attempts to describe much too big a process. In fact, it covers nearly half of the processes listed in Table 4.3b, each of which should be a separate map. As a result, the map provides virtually no detail useful in identifying functional requirements for an EHR, the type of workflow and process changes needed after implementation of an EHR, or the nature of the decision making that an EHR can supply in support of quality and other improvements.
2. No decision points	Although the map has two main branches, the branches appear to suggest there are two types of patient visits: one that is a nurse-only visit, perhaps where the nurse draws blood and provides some education; and the other that involves a physician or physician extender performing a typical visit. These are really two separate processes. Within the "provider" branch there is a sub-branch with no decision symbol to provide direction.
3. Decision flow is not clear	Branches (where there should be a decision symbol) are not labeled.
4. The map is at such a high level that one cannot even determine if it has been drawn as actually performed or as intended to be performed.	
5. Documentation within the symbol does not reflect who does what, or ask a question.	Symbols containing "Nurse" and "Provider" appear to be labels for the two respective flows. However, the remaining symbols do not include who or an action verb. It is unclear if the nurse performs a lab test, or only collects a specimen. "Refferal" (which is misspelled) is not clear at all, especially as nurses generally do not make referrals, although they may be instructed by the provider to set up a referral. It appears that the "Nurse" set of steps includes broad "buckets" that may or may not be performed in a given visit. The symbols under "Provider" are somewhat clearer, although way too general. However, it appears that perhaps the provider asks the nurse to schedule a referral, although there is no decision point to clarify. Many assumptions could be made based on the informed reader's understanding of a normal patient visit, but there should be no assumptions in process mapping.
6. Flow is not completely clear	Although the majority of the flow is from top to bottom, and the decision pathways not marked as noted above, it is not clear why the "Nurse" box in the center does not connect to the leftmost "Nurse" series of boxes. The flow line should extend all the way to the left, or if not the same nurse, so specify.
7. Boundaries are incomplete	Although the first box, not shown as a boundary symbol, suggests that the flow starts with the patient visit, this is more likely the name of the process and not the fact that the patient arrives for a visit—which would be a starting point. "Patient leaves" may be appropriate as an ending symbol, but there is no ending symbol after the box in the center labeled "Nurse." This flow line should reach a conclusion.

Source: Copyright © Margret\A Consulting, LLC. With permission.

with it, Mr. General Secretary, though my pronunciation may give you difficulty. The maxim is: Dovorey no provorey—trust, but verify.

The General Secretary: You repeat that at every meeting. [Laughter]

The President: I like it. [Laughter]

This agreement contains the most stringent verification regime in history, including provisions for inspection teams actually residing in each other's territory and several other forms of onsite inspection as well. This treaty protects the interests of America's friends and allies. It also embodies another important principle: the need for glasnost, a greater openness in military programs and forces...

■ To some it may seem like a stretch to suggest that "trust, but verify" is a key ingredient in achieving **transparency** in action. However, the last sentence in the above transcript suggests that both are key contributing factors to creating an organizational **culture** that supports workflow and process mapping in an environment **without blame**. "Trust, but verify" implies that no one is perfect, but all must work together to ensure greater benefits.

■ **Validation** of workflow and process maps engages all **stakeholders**, whether involved directly in the mapping, or not. It ensures that the maps depicting the current, **"as-is"** processes are complete, true to actuality, encompassing of variations, having connection points that link to applicable other processes, and achieve their intended purpose in helping to reap benefits from new investments in HIT and EHR and other applicable interventions for quality improvement.

References

American Association of Colleges of Nursing, 2011 (July). "Nursing Shortage Fact Sheet." Available at: http://www.aacn.nche.edu/media/factsheets/nursingshortage.htm

American Journal of Health-System Pharmacists, 2003. "CPOE, Bedside Technology, and Patient Safety: A Roundtable Discussion." *American Journal of Health-System Pharmacists*, 60: 1219–1228.

Cassidy, A. and K. Guggenberger, 2001. *A Practical Guide to Information Systems Process Improvement,* Boca Raton, FL: St. Lucie Press, 106–111.

Damelio, R., 2011. *The Basics of Process Mapping*, 2nd edition, Boca Raton, FL: CRC Press, 73–92.

EPISD, n.d. "Process Mapping. El Paso Independent School District." Available at: http://www.episd.org/_departments/business_svc/what_is_proc_mps.php

Hebda, T. and P. Czar, 2009. *Handbook of Informatics for Nurses & Healthcare Professionals, 4th edition*. Upper Saddle River, NJ: Pearson Prentice Hall, Chapter 1.

Reagan Archives, 1987 (Dec. 8). Remarks on Signing the "Intermediate-Range Nuclear Forces Treaty." Available at: http://www.reagan.utexas.edu/archives/speeches/1987/120887c.htm

Tomatsu, 2002. Process Mapping Training Workshop, Deloitte Touche for Department of Health Information for Social Care, Available at: www.publications.doh.gov.uk

Chapter 9

Step 7: Identify Process Redesign Opportunities

> The way we see things is the source of the way we think and the way we act.
>
> **—Stephen Covey**
> *Author of the bestseller* The Seven Habits of Highly Effective People,
> *and co-founder of FranklinCovey, leadership institute*

Although it may seem like it has taken many steps to get to the point of redesigning workflows and processes, this step represents the culmination of all previous efforts and paints the picture for going forward. It is in this step that the design for the future state is crafted. The above quote is particularly apropos because in health care, the clinical transformation that is expected to occur with health information technology (HIT) and electronic health records (EHRs) impacts both thought processes and actions. Clinical transformation is a fundamental change in the way healthcare professionals will think and act. This chapter describes the process to take to redesign workflows and processes, key process improvement characteristics to guide the redesign effort, and approaches for validating that the new process can work. Although some changes to workflows and processes will need a root cause analysis to "get to the bottom" of an issue with respect to an improvement opportunity, which is covered in Chapter 10, this chapter discusses specific areas of HIT and EHR that are the most challenging but most important to redesign.

The Process of Redesign

Creating maps of current, or "as-is," workflows and processes entailed planning, organizing, and doing. So too, there is a process to redesign that encourages the care delivery organization (CDO) to identify a process owner, organize redesign teams, establish parameters for redesign, conduct redesign sessions to create "to-be" processes, design and document the new process, and validate the new process.

It was observed earlier in this book that organizational culture and leadership played a critical role in the overall process of managing implementation of technology and changes able to be brought about as a result. Readiness for workflow and process management was discussed as important to be assessed. Although team building was encouraged, it was also recognized that some CDOs approach current workflow and process mapping using a skilled process analyst to do the bulk of the work. Still, the importance of collaboration was stressed—both for achieving accurate current-state maps as well as to begin to develop a sense of community. CDOs were urged to engage all stakeholders to help them feel a part of the impending change.

A philosophy of collaboration is vital for mapping the "to-be" state of workflows and processes. It is now essential for stakeholders to be brought together and to contribute to the redesign of processes and workflows. As the technology being introduced focuses ever more on clinical workflows and processes and requires integration of data to support the continuum of care, information "silos" are breaking down. Likewise, people must work more as a team rather than as a hierarchy with defined roles that have significant boundary constraints. Credentials will continue to dictate specific practice limitations, but thought processes and concerns are not so restrictive. Baby Genesis, described in Case Study 2.1, died as a result of a series of mishaps across several departmental boundaries and technological snafus. The baby also died because individuals made certain assumptions and perhaps did not feel "free to" or "responsible for" checking, taking a time out to follow up on erroneous information, or even acting to implement technology in the best interests of the organization's patients. It is these factors that the federal government is looking to change in its value-based health reform initiatives. It is also these factors that make for a happier and more effective workforce. Drawing again from Stephen Covey's (2004) work,

> If you want to *have* more freedom, more latitude in your job, *be* a more responsible, a more helpful, a more contributing employee. If you want to be trusted, *be* trustworthy. If you want the secondary greatness of recognized talent, focus first on primary greatness of character.

A **process owner** was described in Chapter 4 as the person performing the bulk of a process, or the person who will ultimately be responsible for adopting a new process. Often, many people perform a process. Many people should be engaged in process redesign. But there needs to be a team leader, or quarterback, for each team. If there were process owners during the "as-is" process mapping activity, these individuals may continue to lead the redesign effort for their respective processes. If a process analyst was used to map current

Table 9.1 Process Owner Characteristics and Responsibilities

Characteristics
• Understands goals established for adoption of HIT and EHR
• Works collaboratively with all stakeholders to the process being redesigned
• Has the motivation and personal tolerance for change
• Exhibits leadership, team building, and communication skills
• Has the ability to analyze a situation, identify problems, and suggest alternatives for their resolution
• Exhibits attention to detail while seeing the big picture
• Demonstrates skill at workflow and process mapping
Responsibilities
• Guides the process redesign effort for the impacted process
• Organizes team members to contribute to the redesign effort
• Aids in overcoming barriers to improvement
• Seeks to analyze the root cause of workflow and process issues prior to redesigning the process
• Harmonizes the impacted process with others to avoid conflicts or surprises
• Documents the redesigned workflow and process
• Oversees that the redesigned workflow and process is validated
• Champions implementation of the redesigned workflow and process
• Contributes to assessing the effectiveness of the redesigned workflow and process to ensure that goals are met or modified accordingly

processes, then it is time to identify those who tend to be the most committed to making changes work in the various processes to lead process redesign teams. Process owner characteristics and responsibilities include those identified in Table 9.1.

Redesign teams should be formed to design new workflows and processes. As with the process owner, these teams may already be in place from the "as-is" process mapping activity. However, it may be appropriate to re-look at the teams and determine if the right people are represented. In Chapter 8, a validation team was described as potentially including a process auditor, a participant in the process, an individual impacted by the process, and a programmer or systems analyst who will be responsible for the new system's configuration. These types of individuals are a good place to start to build the redesign team.

Generally, a process auditor, as a person who is not aligned with the process but knows process mapping well, may or may not be included in the redesign team until such time that the redesign needs validation. Instead, the redesign team will include the process owner, of course, and several representatives of participants in the process. Ideally, these should include some of the original "as-is" mappers as well as those new to the mapping activity. Original mappers can aid in understanding the "as-is" maps where necessary and will very likely have ideas for changes. New participants lend new ideas for solutions to problems as well, and are also brought in to extend ownership in the new process to many more people. In fact, it may be a good idea to bring in a few contrarians (Mellin 2010), or others who demonstrate strong resistance to the impending change. Case Study 9.1 illustrates how a clinic utilized such an individual to turn himself and others around.

Case Study 9.1: Contrarian Contributions to Process Redesign

A clinic with about twenty physicians was planning to implement an EHR, with the strong support of most of the physician leadership and many of the staff. It was widely known, however, that Dr. Dark, who was on the board of directors, was not happy about this, and had convinced a few colleagues as well that the EHR could not be good. In planning for the EHR, the clinic diligently went through current workflow and process mapping and vendor selection. Once implementation was to begin and processes needed to be redesigned, they formed teams to do so. The president of the board of directors, Dr. Savvy, decided to ask Dr. Dark and his naysayer colleagues to participate on the teams. Dr. Savvy approached Dr. Dark by noting that the majority vote on the board had resulted in this decision and that to ensure that all of Dr. Dark's concerns were addressed, they wanted to get his participation in the design of the system. Although initially stating he did not want anything to do with it, Dr. Savvy pressed on, indicating that he felt Dr. Dark had many legitimate concerns and would truly help the clinic ensure that none of these concerns would impact their patients. He reminded Dr. Dark that when the clinic moved to digital dictation, it was Dr. Dark who contributed the best ideas for helping overcome some design issues after implementation, and that these same good ideas would be appreciated in advance of implementing the EHR. Dr. Dark finally acquiesced; and, of course, his colleagues then followed suit, agreeing to be on other teams.

It was agreed in advance that the first meeting in which Dr. Dark would participate would be a short, fifteen-minute meeting to review the current process and simply generate a list of issues to be addressed and ideas for improvement. A colleague positive to the EHR, Dr. Cool, agreed to be coached in advance about the "as-is" process and to sit next to Dr. Dark during the meeting. An external process analyst facilitated the session and was warned that Dr. Dark could be troublesome. It was agreed he would be managed so that he would be asked to state specific issues and not vent randomly. The meeting was reasonably successful, and three subsequent redesign sessions were scheduled, each for thirty minutes. The goal was set that by the end of the third meeting there would be a first draft of the redesigned process, and during the final meeting there would be opportunity to validate the redesign. The bulk of the actual mapping would take place "offline" by a sub-group. Dr. Cool volunteered to serve as an advisor to the sub-group, recognizing that he did not have time to participate at the mapping level but would be happy to contribute where he could.

Immediately after the first meeting, Dr. Dark approached Dr. Cool and asked why he, Dr. Dark, could not also participate in the sub-group. Of course, Dr. Cool was inwardly delighted but also skeptical with this turn of events and told Dr. Dark that he would identify him as a co-advisor. He suggested getting together weekly at lunchtime to hash out issues they were seeing. As Dr. Cool guided Dr. Dark to address issues by offering suggestions for changes, Dr. Dark came to see that it was not the technology but rather the underlying way the office operated and the improvements he would benefit from that would be embodied in the EHR. He even expressed surprise at some of the things the EHR would make easier for him. Dr. Dark kept pressing for more improvements. By the end of the four sessions, he "demanded" to be put on another team to be sure they benefited from his expertise. Dr. Savvy followed up and expressed appreciation for Dr. Dark's work and encouraged him to get others to partici-pate. When it came time for EHR training, Dr. Dark was one of the most pre-pared physicians in the group. While his disposition remained "testy," Dr. Dark had actually become something of a champion of the EHR, demanding that his colleagues participate in "jam" sessions just as he did to ensure optimal use. Sometime after implementation of the EHR, Dr. Dark was overhead at a medical society meeting saying that the EHR was a terrible thing although it did ensure that he always had his charts when needed, supplied good information about drugs, and helped him spend more time with his patients.

Not all CDOs may have the staff to form a lot of teams. Sometimes the staff and physicians of a critical access hospital or small physician office may all be the one team to work on process mapping. The map illustrated in Figure 6.3a was drawn by all (five) of the nurses who worked at a critical access hospital. That hospital actually had used process mapping previously to help them stream-line workflows outside the scope of HIT and EHR. Sometimes it is necessary to remind an organization—large or small—that process mapping is not just a tech-nique to implement HIT and EHR. In fact its part of the implementation process of HIT and EHR is workflow and process redesign—whether or not the vendor has delivered the product yet or provided such service.

Process customers should also be included on redesign teams. Process cus-tomers are individuals representing other processes that interface with the pri-mary process being mapped. For example, in Case Study 8.1 where nurses were surprised by the terminology generated from the pharmacy information system for their electronic medication administration record (EMAR) system, pharmacists would be customers of the EMAR process and nurses would be customers of the related pharmacy process.

A **systems analyst** should also be present during redesign team meetings. A systems analyst can guide the participants as to what changes are feasible from the system standpoint. The systems analyst will also be responsible for translating redesigned workflows and processes into the configuration of the system as applicable. The only caveat here is that the systems analyst, knowing of the responsibility to make the configuration changes, must be very comfortable with doing so or the organization risks a systems analyst saying something cannot be done when it can. Some HIT and EHR vendors who support workflow and process redesign for their customers bring their own systems analysts with them for this purpose.

Key Characteristics for Redesign

There are several important considerations in preparing to redesign workflows and processes to achieve improvements from HIT and EHR. Perhaps the most important is to appreciate the nature of the HIT and EHR, and the extent to which changes can be made in the technology in comparison to the changes that need to be made to accommodate the technology. In addition, some rules to apply in brainstorming changes, redesign opportunities, and recognizing the need for root cause analysis are key elements of redesigning workflows and processes.

Parameters for redesign must be established up-front, or redesign teams with overblown expectations can become deflated very quickly once the product is implemented. Few CDOs want to acquire HIT or EHR that dictates the changes they must make in their workflows and processes. Although it is also noted that while "few" want such direction, interestingly some CDOs believe their workflows and processes are so dysfunctional that implementing an EHR that does provide direction for change is welcome. Still, such changes should not be accepted out of hand without consideration for how they will be implemented within a given CDO. This is one of the reasons for conducting current process mapping in advance of HIT and EHR selection. The informed CDO will better be able to assess how well the technology fits their workflow and process improvement needs. For example, in the hospital described in Case Study 8.1, nurses were not only surprised by the terminology coming from the pharmacy information system to their EMAR system, but even more dismayed to find that their vendor could not change the terminology to what they were accustomed to. (Many vendors have subsequently enabled the reverse translation so that clinical expressions encoded with RxNorm in the computerized provider order entry [CPOE] system can be translated to National Drug Codes for pharmacy inventory purposes and yet retained in RxNorm form for the EMAR.)

A philosophy of change directed by the organization that is enabled by the new technology should apply in all cases, or the organization will risk both resentment of the new technology and missing opportunities to carry forward best practices of their own.

Brainstorming to generate solutions is the most frequently used approach that redesign teams use to map "to-be" workflows and processes. Brainstorming can be fun, but must be effective and produce specific results.

Participants need to be kept focused. Some CDOs find they need external facilitation for this. Some HIT and EHR vendors supply such services, either as a part of their implementation process or as an adjunct service. However the brainstorming sessions are managed, Table 9.2 provides some guidelines for brainstorming workflow and process redesign sessions (Cassidy and Guggenberger 2001).

Redesign opportunities were listed in Table 2.3 when introducing process analysis, or the act of studying a current process to identify ways to improve or change workflows and processes to take advantage of HIT and EHR. Bottlenecks, delays, inconsistent data entries, lack of information, cycle time, rework, role ambiguity, unnecessary duplication of work, and other issues were identified.

Redesign techniques are available to help identify ways to overcome these issues. Many business process reengineering references describe such techniques (Mansar and Reijers 2005). As they are used in health care, ensure that the focus of the redesign is not just speeding up processes or eliminating waste, but also ensuring quality of care, patient safety, and the other Quality Aims from the Institute of Medicine in Table 2.7 (2001). It is often very easy to find ways to eliminate duplicate steps, reduce rework, shorten cycle time, or add information, but these may actually not be ideal ways to redesign a healthcare process. Case Study 9.2 illustrates some examples of apparent duplication of data that were clinically relevant.

Case Study 9.2: Clinically Relevant Duplication

Many patients visit their physicians' offices and are asked by both the nurse that rooms them and the physician what the reason is for their visit. Some patients may wonder if the nurse and the physician communicate. This is a very common process in physician offices, as was identified in Figure 5.5 in Chapter 5, which illustrated the swim-lane process chart. This workflow and process map is provided below in Figure 9.1, with arrows labeled "1" to show the apparent duplication of information gathering. When physicians are asked about this, they note three things. First, the nurse asks the patient the reason for the visit to prepare the patient for the physician visit. Some reasons for a visit require the patient to disrobe, others to take off their shoes and socks, and others require no preparation. Second, the physician asks the patient the reason for visit because patients often request an appointment with only a vague reason; and sometimes this vague reason is different from what they tell the nurse, and still different from what they tell the physician. Third, the reason for visit as told to the nurse is often not a "billable" reason. It is for this reason that, as illustrated by the arrows labeled "3," the nurse is asked not to record the reason for visit in the chart but on a sticky note. So, for reason for visit the duplication is clinically relevant, although with better training and explanation to the patient, it is possible for this repetition to be eliminated.

Table 9.2 Brainstorming Guidelines

• Address redesign, not current processes. Use the current map as a launch pad, but do not get mired down in why something is done currently when it will change. Put changes that truly are needed today prior to HIT or EHR in a parking lot to be addressed by supervisors. However, ensure that any clinical controls that exist today are carried forward—whether or not they can be automated. Timeouts for surgical procedures and other patient safety areas (Maine General n.d.) are a good example of a step in a process that requires human intervention. Adding them to the redesign of a process will ensure they continue to be observed. There may be an automation factor that provides an alert to take a timeout or to document that a timeout was taken.
• Center the discussion on workflow and process, not people. While credentials are important (see Case Study 6.2), a focus on people can start to introduce blame and causes participants to put their guard up, which generally results in stifling ideas for improvement. However, it may be necessary at times to consider people who may be missing from the team who could lend help with the redesign. It can also be effective during brainstorming to create a competitive environment where everyone contributes ideas. To do this, a skilled facilitator should document all contributions without judgment. At this point, no idea is a bad idea. Get as many ideas out as possible. Record what is said, not what is heard, as humans always do some filtering of messages they hear and introduce bias (DeCarlo 2011). Such a competitive environment can help everyone be more creative—setting up a win-win environment. However, rewards or prizes for "best" ideas will create a win-lose environment that is not desirable (Sutton 2006).
• Focus on solutions, not problems. While finding a solution may require an investigation into problems to determine their root cause, the focus should be on solving the problem. Once a root cause is known, the focus should shift immediately to solving the underlying cause. Dwelling on the problem without finding a solution does not move the process redesign effort forward.
• Draw attention to good solutions but avoid singling out "good people." Recognizing good work by the team enables everyone to become good at generating ideas and redesigning processes. Focusing on one or a few people who are eager to share their ideas serves to suggest they are the only ones "in the know." The result will be missed opportunities from those who start to feel less valued. To overcome this, different group facilitation techniques can be used. The nominal group technique (NGT) asks each individual to generate ideas either by a round-robin discussion process or by working silently and independently during a meeting followed by discussion of each idea (CDC 2006). This "levels the playing field" and removes the potential for any ill-will to be directed at the generator of an idea not liked by the group. Some view NGT as a less-stimulating group process than other techniques because silent recording of ideas may not permit piggybacking of new ideas. However, the method is excellent where there are team members who feel they can never get their opinions voiced. The Delphi Method is even less interactive, as idea generation is performed through an anonymous voting processing. This technique can be very effective when the number of people performing a process is very large and everyone needs to feel involved, when there are different shifts and locations of people who cannot come together readily, and especially for reaching consensus on which idea is best (Straker and Rawlinson 2003). Often, a mix of the traditional open brainstorming and NGT and/or the Delphi Method may be appropriate.

Table 9.2 (continued)   Brainstorming Guidelines

• Consider the feasibility of the solutions proposed. While many good ideas for solutions may be generated, the bottom line requires the right solution to be found and fleshed out. The best solutions probably will include both automation and non-automation components. Recognize that everything cannot be automated. In fact, over-reliance on automation and not applying professional judgment is a risk in implementing EHR (NSO n.d.; Brouillard 2010). On the other hand, if automation appears to be a necessity but not deemed feasible at this time, a long hard look must be taken at both the accompanying workflow and process to compensate for this technical omission and to obtaining technology improvements in the future. Including a vendor's systems analyst in the redesign sessions should enable the vendor to address workarounds necessitated by technology in subsequent versions of the product (Gur-Arie 2010; Stout 2010).
• Be driven by the Institute of Medicine's Quality Aims (see Table 2.7) and the National Quality Forum's National Health Priorities (see Table 2.6) in every process redesign. The value of health care is measured by cost and quality. As such, every process redesign must ensure safe, effective, efficient, timely, patient-centered, and equitable healthcare processes. Quality must be improved through engaging patients and their families, improved care coordination, improved population and public health services, and ensuring adequate privacy and security protections for protected health information in EHRs and personal health information in personal health records (PHRs).

The arrows labeled "2" might be another apparent duplication. Here, the nurse takes vital signs (V/S) and blood pressure (BP), and the physician also takes blood pressure. Are both necessary? There are several potential considerations. First, this practice may be one the physician wants to retain—especially in cardiology (where sometimes three blood pressure readings are taken per visit). However, not having the nurse record the first blood pressure reading suggests there is another issue. A second consideration is that this process as depicted may be a true duplication of effort, especially if the blood pressure recorded by the nurse is believed to be accurate and normal for the patient. In this case, it appears that the physician documents this in the chart. On the other hand, if the physician felt the blood pressure was high for the patient, it would be clinically relevant to repeat it. (And this should be reflected in the process map as a decision.) In this case, however, both readings are generally documented in the chart—again suggesting that there is another issue. The third consideration then is, what other issue is driving these potential duplications? Upon querying physicians who follow this process, many say they fear the first blood pressure reading is inaccurate because the nurse is not well trained. They ask the nurse to record on a sticky note, presumably so that if the second recording is different, it can be considered the only one that is correct and gets documented. If this is the case, however, either the nurse should not bother taking the blood pressure or be better trained.

In considering how to redesign workflows and processes so they can best take advantage of HIT and EHR, the focus must be on the "information payload." What can be done to make sure all relevant data are available to enhance

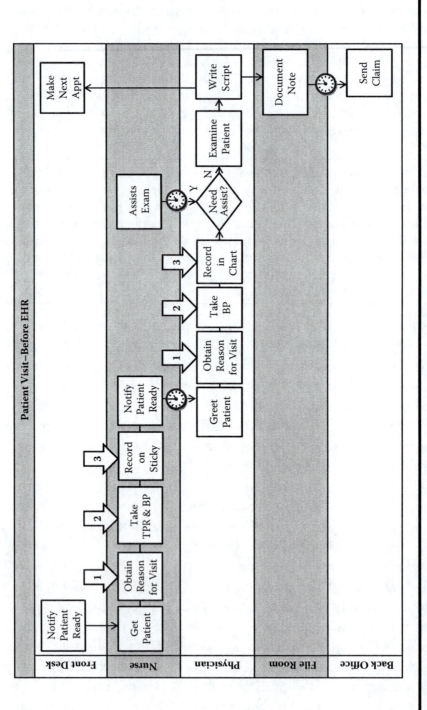

Figure 9.1 Clinically relevant duplication. (From Copyright © Margret\A Consulting, LLC. With permission.)

Table 9.3   Redesign Techniques

1. Add steps (or data).
2. Find a better way.
3. Combine steps.
4. Eliminate steps (or data).
5. Empower staff and patients.
6. Reorganize tasks and data.
7. Reuse (data).
8. Separate steps.
9. Simplify work.
10. Standardize work (and data).

decision making, to ensure decision support technology is accurate and up-to-date, to ensure follow-up on all diagnostic studies results (Casalino 2009), to afford opportunities to better listen to and educate patients, to study data to generate new knowledge, and more? The focus on the information payload helps direct the attention of those who are redesigning processes to look at HIT and EHR as a means to enable process improvement. But just as in the "as-is" process mapping, process analysis for redesign requires "looking at" thought processes performed mentally and often not readily visualized.

It can be helpful to apply the ten redesign techniques described in Table 9.3. These are listed in alphabetical order because there is no set order in which they can best be applied across all types of workflows and processes to be redesigned in health care. In addition, each redesign technique comes with both risks and rewards. If in any case the risks appear to outweigh the rewards, the considered redesign action should be avoided. However, as is usually the case, the higher the risk, the higher the reward. Health care tends to be a highly conservative industry, so only those "rewards" that can be achieved if the risks are known and can be fully mitigated should be attempted. Finally, some authors add "automation" to such a list. For purposes of redesigning workflows and processes in light of HIT and EHR utilization, automation is subsumed throughout all ten techniques described here.

- *Add steps (or data)*. While this may seem completely counterintuitive to simplifying, eliminating, and reorganizing process steps such as those discussed later, adding steps or data collection in certain limited circumstances can be an effective redesign technique. Consider where errors occur or there are rework steps. Is the cause of these a lack of action taken or data not captured earlier in the process? Look for missing data in a process that disrupts the workflow. Lab results are often not available to providers.

Previous records of patients may not be accessible when desired. Such examples are precisely why the "as-is" process map needs to identify all the "warts and workarounds" currently being performed. Any time a decision symbol asks, "Are data available?", consider the need to at least resequence steps if not add steps or data. (If no such question is asked in any of the maps being redesigned, consider the maps deficient.) Case Study 7.1 is a good example of both unnecessary data and additional data. That case study described why it was taking twice as long to perform a nursing admission assessment in the EHR, but also concluded that certain additional data collection requirements actually contributed to quality of care and patient safety, as well as downstream time savings. Adding a step to ensure a medication being administered is the right medication is a very common redesign in CDOs. An extremely important caveat here, of course, is to not add so many steps or so much information that it becomes distracting. Herbert Simon, Nobel Prize winner and one of the founding fathers of artificial intelligence, is quoted in *Computers, Communications and the Public Interest* (Greenberger 1971) as having said:

> What information consumes is rather obvious: it consumes the attention of its recipients. **Hence a wealth of information creates a poverty of attention**, and a need to allocate that attention efficiently among the overabundance of information sources that might consume it.

■ *Find a better way.* Often, looking at workarounds and quality issues will not result in adding, combining, eliminating, or even reorganizing work, but simply finding a better way to perform the same set of tasks can help immensely. For example, many hospitals have found that nurses create workarounds for using bar-code EMAR systems. Case Studies 2.2 and 5.1 described issues associated with implementing such a system in a new hospital. Obviously there were physical layout issues that would be categorized as needing reorganization (see below), but there were additional issues associated with not having access to the information needed at the bedside when administering medications. For some hospitals, the problems have been technical—the bar-code reader was not wireless and the cable was not long enough for the nurse to reach the patient's wristband comfortably. In other cases, nurses have complained that "wanding" a patient felt like they were grocery-store clerks wanding cans of beans. Sometimes taking the step of explaining to the patient why the bar-code process is performed helps put both the nurse and patient at ease. (This might also be an example of adding a step that does not take a lot of time but can be very important.) Finding ways to overcome issues associated with medication error documentation through the use of EMAR is also very important. Many nurses really do not like EMAR systems because they view the system as "big brother" watching over them. But if the system can be used to explain why the medication cannot be given on time or why a dose was adjusted, there would be fewer actions interpreted as errors and better documentation to substantiate any subsequent questions about procedures followed.

■ *Combine steps.* Combining steps may be considered when workflows and processes appear to include rework or duplication of effort because several different people are involved. As a current workflow and process is reviewed, look at how many hand-offs need to be made within the process. Also consider separate processes typically performed in sequence (hence the reason for specifying boundaries so processes can be linked together). Some of the ways that combining steps may be achieved include centralizing certain functions, creating a triage process, appointing a case manager, creating a SWAT team (e.g., Code Blue Team, Emergency Response Team), and providing dashboard functionality in an EHR. Obviously, combining too many steps into one process can overwhelm, reduce accuracy, and increase the hassle factor.

■ *Eliminate steps (or data).* Consider every step in a workflow and process as if there was a price tag on it (because essentially there is). What are the critical steps? What steps add no value? Should the CDO "pay" for that step to be performed? Can steps that add no value be eliminated, or at least fully automated? (But also consider what eliminating a step could cost in light of its absence creating an error state.) Often, steps can be eliminated while still assuring that everyone has the information they need when automation occurs. Look at data collection processes closely. One of the issues with EHRs that offers great flexibility—while desirable in some cases to address user preferences—may end up causing confusion. For example, there may be a structured data entry field for capturing all elements of a medication order and a comment field where physicians may be adding notes that actually contradict their structured data entries (Ash et al. 2007). Consider patients' complaints of having to constantly repeat information to every person they encounter during their healthcare experience. This situation should easily be able to be eliminated with automation. As Case Study 7.1 on the nursing admission assessment process indicated, many new users of EHRs still do not fully trust the system to give them accurate and reliable information. A similar situation occurs when EHRs are used to task staff where previously assigning a task may have entailed leaving the patient in an exam room and physically finding a person to whom to give the task. Case Study 9.3 further explores the new tasking capability in EHR as a very important redesign opportunity.

Case Study 9.3: Was the Task Performed, or Is Socialization Needed?

A clinic has just implemented an EHR. The EHR enables a physician from the EHR to send a task to a nurse or other staff member in the clinic. This was documented in the redesigned process, and the physicians seemed to think it was going to be a great time saver. However, after a few months of go-live, the clinic administrator was seeing the physicians walking around just as much as previously. Nurses and others also reported that they were not getting tasks sent to their in-box in the EHR. A meeting of the physicians was held to ask what was happening and how the process could be improved. The physicians then revealed that they had no visual proof on their system that the task had arrived at its intended destination, whereas previously they knew it got to the intended recipient because they took it themselves. Appreciating this concern, the clinic administrator was able to get the EHR vendor to supply an "acknowledgment of receipt" back to the physicians' in-box. Once again, the physicians thought that would really help. Yet again, after several months, there was very little change. So the clinic administrator decided to spend a day out in the clinic making observations—and found that several physicians would take the opportunity to chat with staff, visit a colleague, or just "kick back" for a few minutes. These observations suggested that the primary reason for the continued manual process seemed to be one where the physicians needed to socialize a bit, or to take a timeout from the intensity of the patient visits. This was a good case for not eliminating the walking-around step, and so the office administrator decided to leave the process as it was. Anyone who wanted to take advantage of the tasking function could; and there seemed to be no great harm in not entering tasks in the in-box. However, this decision was discussed with the nurses and they were asked to verify that the absence of the task was not causing any issues of dropping tasks that would be detrimental to the patients, productivity issues for them, or accountability problems later.

■ *Empower staff and patients.* In some respects, this redesign technique is similar to adding tasks or data, or at least reorganizing work. The emphasis here, however, is on assigning tasks appropriately and effectively. Very often, CDOs feel highly constrained by the credentials of their workforce, yet actually can find opportunities for improvement—and job satisfaction—through better utilization of staff and empowering patients! As workflows and processes are being evaluated, look at which staff members are actually performing which steps. Many staff members are not utilized to the level of their qualifications and credentials, and could be given additional tasks that may contribute to better job performance. For example, many certified medical assistants learn nursing services in school that are rarely used effectively in physician offices. These staff members could be better utilized in general, and in particular to perform certain data-collection tasks. Similarly, using patients (or their caregivers) to perform certain tasks should be considered. Self-assessments on paper have been used for years in clinics, yet rarely replicated in the electronic world. Bachman (2007) has found that automated patient self-assessments not only result in productivity improvements, but also yield very effective quality-of-care results because more time can be spent on processes that make a difference in outcomes.

■ *Reorganize tasks and data.* Resequencing tasks to make them flow more smoothly, moving data entry collection fields around on a computer screen to present information more logically, and changing the physical layout are common improvement opportunities generated by looking at ways to reorganize tasks. Processes can become very complex, especially when automation is added that supports clinical decision making. Additional data collection that is required for clinical decision support systems to work properly but then yields many annoying alerts is a good example of added complexity for little or no value. However, if the thought processes behind the decision making are fully understood, it is feasible to streamline the automation to where only the most critical alerts are provided, or the sensitivity of the alerting mechanism can be set in relationship to its target user (e.g., more alerts for generalists, fewer alerts related to the specialty of an attending physician, certain types of alerts for nurses in comparison to physicians). A very common concern of clinicians as they start to use an EHR is the impression they are making on their patients. Case Study 9.4 describes clinician concerns and ways to redesign both process and physical layout to improve the situation.

Case Study 9.4: Reorganize the Environment to Improve the Use of EHR

An EHR was implemented in a physician office; but after several months, physicians continued to document their notes during breaks and at the end of the day. The office manager was very concerned but anticipated that the physicians would complain that the system would slow them down and they would not be able to see as many patients in a day as previously. However, a very unfortunate incident occurred for one of the physician's patients where a prescription for a medication that was contraindicated resulted in acute liver failure. The office manager decided to take this opportunity to observe that because physicians were not using the EHR at the point of care, they were not able to take advantage of its clinical decision support. Such support would have identified that this drug could have a severe impact on a patient with poor liver function, and that a liver function study should be performed prior to prescribing it. As expected, the physicians expressed concerns about productivity. The office manager, however, was determined to turn around the situation and asked a physician at a neighboring office, and who was known to use the EHR at the point of care, to visit with the physicians. Much to the surprise of the office manager, the physician first asked to visit the exam rooms. Second, the physician spoke to the physicians about protocols for using the EHR with patients. It was further suggested that the physicians redesign the layout of the exam rooms to better accommodate use of the EHR at the point of care. In fact, the physician used the layout provided in Figure 9.2 to describe the impact of different types of input devices on patient discussion. The physician then used a series of illustrations to describe

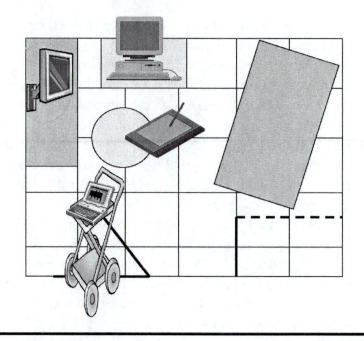

Figure 9.2 Reorganize the environment. (From Copyright © Margret\A Consulting, LLC. With permission.)

things the physicians could say to and do with their patients to engage them more in the process of using the computer at the point of care (Baker 2010). Such strategies are described in Table 9.4. Rather than hound the physicians about using the EHR at the point of care with no suggestions for doing so, shifting the focus slightly actually made the physicians more willing to try using the EHR with patients.

■ *Reuse (data).* Data reuse, often called copying and pasting in the EHR environment, is a purposeful design element of computers in general and a very common practice used in EHRs. It is a process that can be both a very effective time-saver and a huge risk (Dimick 2008; AAMC 2011). In fact, many lament the fact that physicians often do not take the time to learn how to use an EHR well, but somehow manage to find out how to copy and paste! It is very difficult to mandate that such functionality cannot be used. So perhaps the best way to take advantage of the benefits and mitigate the risk is to build right into the redesign of processes ways to reuse data effectively. The American Health Information Management Association (AHIMA 2008) provides a "Copy Functionality Toolkit" on its website that supplies many good ideas. Reuse of data must also be accompanied by information system controls. When data are copied, is there a flag for the user to customize the entry or cite the source where necessary?

Data reuse is not just about copy and paste. Auto-population, or prepopulation, is also a form of data reuse that can be very helpful in saving time but also is potentially risky (Toth, 2010a, b). Again referring to Case Study 7.1 on the nursing admission assessment process, nurses were concerned

Table 9.4 Use of EHR at Point of Care

1. At the registration desk, put up an "Under Construction" sign to ask patients for their patience. Distribute flyers about the EHR to explain its purpose, that the initial visit using the EHR may take a bit longer, and allay privacy concerns.
2. Consider asking the nurse to stay in the room or come to the room to help with some of the early documentation. This collaboration helps patients also trust the nurse who may then be used to collect more information during check-in and relieve the data-entry burden for the physician even further. When ready, position yourself for eye contact with the patients, either having them sit beside your desk with a desktop computer that includes a swivel monitor, or in front of you as you use a tablet computer that can be shown to the patient.
3. When starting to use the EHR, tell your patient you are logging on to alleviate security concerns. Explain that use of the EHR is new for you, and that it is taking a bit of time to learn—but be positive, no matter what. Patients will respond to your negativity with negativity of their own. Most patients will be sympathetic and may even offer to help you! The time this takes also enables you to get properly situated.
4. Use the EHR to explain trends or to show the patient an x-ray. Use the EHR to check the accuracy of the data you have about patients from other sources, indicating you are pleased to have such data available to help you coordinate care.
5. Observe patient response to your use of the EHR and discontinue use temporarily if there are any concerns. When appropriate to return to the EHR, discuss—up front— with the patient how important the EHR is to their safety. Note that because of the EHR, the pharmacy should have the patient's drugs ready for them when they arrive. Remain positive about the EHR to reassure the patient.
6. When ready for the patient to go, state that you are logging off and that a summary of the patient's visit will be ready for them at check-out or from the nurse. If not done so earlier and the patient appears curious or concerned, ask the patients if they have any questions about the EHR.

Source: Copyright © Margret\A Consulting, LLC. With permission.

about taking the prepopulated (i.e., reused) data as accurate. What controls can be put into the EHR to overcome this concern? Are there certain data that should never prepopulate? Are there certain data that should always prepopulate, but where the entire CDO needs to be assured that the original data are accurate, perhaps through extensive automation of edit checking as well as manual checkpoint processes? Such a process will require examination across many functions and departments. While not unique to data reuse, the following two questions are vital to be asked: Does the process redesign need to reflect that it is "ok" for professional judgment to be applied in specified situations? And similarly, does the process redesign need to reflect that it is essential for professional judgment to be applied?

Another form of data reuse relates to the use of standard templates and order sets. Such templates are widely used in capturing medical history data, documenting physical exams, performing assessments, creating visit notes, and in CPOE systems (where they are referred to as standard order sets). But each use of a template represents a set of data to be captured for a given patient. It is a unique process reflecting a decision of the user. A wrong template or order set can just as easily be used in an EHR as the wrong paragraph being copied. Just as with not changing the copied paragraph to fit the given patient, a template may have data fields left incomplete or a wrong choice can be selected from a drop-down menu. It is essential for all templates to be reviewed in advance by all intended users and customized where applicable (Toth 2010a, b). Templates should be designed carefully to ensure appropriate use and the ability to retrieve metadata that provides evidence of who did what when with them in the EHR (Goldberg 2011). The Institute for Safe Medication Practices (ISMP 2010) has created "Guidelines for Standard Order Sets" that provide a comprehensive set of recommendations for safely building and using order sets. With all these caveats, some may believe that templates and order sets should be avoided—and this is certainly not the case. If templates are built correctly, they can ensure complete and accurate data collection, and may contribute not only to patient safety and quality of care, but also improved documentation for compliance, such as for the quality measures in the meaningful incentive program and optimal coding revenue generation (AAFP 2010).

■ *Separate steps.* Just as there are steps that potentially can be combined, it is very likely there are some steps that benefit from separation. Certain people may just be doing too much and cannot get all the work performed in the allotted time, or make more errors as a result. It may be necessary to map several alternative ways to redesign a process or part of a process in order to look for natural breaks. When looking at empowering staff, it is very likely that separation of steps will be a result. Sometimes, separation of tasks creates parallel paths that can reduce cycle time. This is a benefit of separating steps, but it must be remembered that a patient is only one person and cannot be separated. Avoid separating steps only to create more work to be performed when the total work is added together.

■ *Simplify work.* Many CDOs have already taken steps to attempt to simplify work. As HIT and EHR are adopted, however, work may become more complex because of greater capabilities afforded by the automation. So, simplifying work is a key step to take in redesigning processes as aided by HIT and EHR, but also to ensure that HIT and EHR do not increase the complexity of an already-simplified process. Key questions to ask of a process may be the following: Have we already simplified this process only to make it more complex with EHR? How is each function in the EHR making work more efficient *and* effective, or at least more effective? While workarounds are often created with the idea of simplifying a process, the opposite effect frequently occurs; and can occur as easily in an automated environment as a paper-based one. Case Study 9.5 is a classic case—and frequently described in the literature.

Case Study 9.5: Beating the System

An article in the *Journal of Healthcare Information Management* by Phillips and Berner (2004) was one of the earliest of several subsequent articles highlighting issues in getting nurses to use bar-code medication administration record (BC-MAR) systems. The article describes several issues, but one in particular was that nurses really disliked moving workstations on wheels and wanding patients. They decided to print copies of patient ID-wristbands and hang them at the nurses' station. Figure 9.3 depicts such an ID-wristband list. Before going to a patient's room to administer medications, the nurses wanded the patient's ID-wristband at the nurses' station, obviously defeating the purpose of bar-coding for positive patient identification and not following the medication five rights of positive drug identification. The conclusions reached in this article were that CDOs looking for a quick fix to reducing medication errors through the use of bar-code technology need to understand that the technology alone will not solve their problem. The authors felt that shifting the nurses' focus from that of efficiency to that of operational effectiveness—and accounting for the additional time—would make the use of the bar-code technology more acceptable.

- *Standardize work (and data).* There is considerable value in using the power of the computer to "crunch" data to improve standardization of processes and utilize best practices. Applying standard terminology to achieve semantic interoperability was illustrated in Case Study 8.1 with the medication terminology "switcheroo." Adoption of best practices aids in assuring that

Figure 9.3   Beating the BC-MAR system.

evidence-based care is applied where appropriate. Workflows and processes can be simplified through the adoption of standards of practice. The potential for error is reduced through the use of standard safety alerts and reminders. Productivity is improved where calls are necessitated surrounding deviations from normal practice, especially without a rationale being documented. Finally, coordination of care can be improved if all participants in the care delivery process adhere to standards of practice across disciplines, levels of care, services, and sites of care. These are all potential workflow and process issues that can be addressed with the aid of HIT and EHR. However, it is essential that all such practice standards be collaboratively developed or reviewed and approved by their intended users and other stakeholders. Adoption of standards of practice requires communication of a clear vision to all intended users; regular, credible reports on how new practices provide better patient outcomes and how each clinician's treatment choices compare with those of their colleagues; and support from information systems that makes it easier to interact with the EHR and adhere to standards of practice (Steiner 2011). In addition as previously noted in Chapter 7, medicine is an imperfect science. Tonelli (2006) described the ethical issue of applying evidence from clinical trials to a specific patient who did not "fit" the norms of the clinical trial population. Once again, professional judgment must prevail—and should not be left out of a redesigned workflow and process map just because the assumption is that such will always be followed.

Key factors for successful redesign should always be borne in mind. The redesign process should not be rushed. The expectation should be that it will take time to completely redesign the twenty to thirty processes impacted by HIT and EHR. In fact, one hospital, NorthShore University Health System, implementing a comprehensive suite of EHR products, describes that it started out with 500 integrated high-level workflows that eventually developed into 2,000 detailed workflows (Smith et al. 2004).

It is very important to avoid redesigning only for the short term, or focusing only on redesigning symptoms and not the root causes of problems. In general, short-term solutions tend to focus on symptoms, so these factors go hand-in-hand and also are symptoms of rushing the redesign process. Alternatively, a lesson learned from NorthShore University Health System is not trying to do too much at once. New mappers forced to get very detailed can get discouraged in both their "as-is" and "to-be" mapping. Constructing high-level maps and then breaking them apart for further detail is an excellent strategy.

Perhaps most importantly, successful redesign should focus on the information payload. However, the focus should not be the technology itself, but rather the process. Looking at dataflows and how information is used keeps the focus on the process. This, after all, is the key objective of the redesign of workflows and processes as implementation of HIT and EHR occurs.

Finally, redesign is a creative process. Redesign teams should be encouraged to "think out of the box." However, the solutions must fit the problem and should not be oversimplified. Thinking too far out of the box may frustrate the team members when they find their creative solutions are not feasible within the technology constraints. Attempting to simplify, combine, reorganize, etc. too much will create solutions that in themselves are likely to have other problems, leading to unintended consequences.

Documenting the Redesigned Workflows and Processes

As with the "as-is" workflow and process, the "to-be" workflow and process must be documented. Some CDOs find it convenient to document the two process states side-by-side, such as on a spreadsheet. There are several advantages to this. First, the "as-is" map can be annotated with areas of concern that guide the redesign. Although illustrating only one "side" of a rather complicated "as-is" map, Figure 9.4 offers a methodology in which a checklist of redesign techniques is applied to the "as-is" map in order to redesign and document (not shown) a "to-be" map. Figure 9.5 offers another approach in which questions are applied directly to an "as-is" map. In this example, the questions are more focused on validating the completeness of the "as-is" map, but the process can be applied equally well to asking questions for redesign. The redesigned map can then be placed to the right of the "as-is" map.

A second advantage to side-by-side documentation of "as-is" and "to-be" maps is that it can serve as a system of checks and balances that the redesigned work-flow truly is improved, often by virtue of being shorter, containing fewer steps, or having a more streamlined flow. However, looks can be deceiving sometimes, so truly annotating the full process is necessary. For example, it may actually take longer to use e-prescribing or CPOE to enter medication orders, but many downstream steps are eliminated, thereby yielding overall time savings.

A final advantage of drawing the maps side-by-side is that it enables easier valida-tion of the redesigned process (see next section, "Validating the Redesigned Process").

"To-be" maps do not have to be drawn side-by-side. Certainly the documenta-tion illustrated in Figure 9.4 might become very large if both maps were drawn side-by-side. Sometimes side-by-side visualization is actually aided by drawing the maps separately, but viewing them simultaneously from two monitors.

Whatever approach a CDO takes, the "to-be" map is that which will direct sys-tem configuration, be used in training to illustrate to new users how their work will change with the new HIT or EHR, and can become part of a procedure document. The "to-be" map is also the guide to evaluating how successful the CDO is in achieving its goals for HIT and EHR, further discussed in Chapter 12.

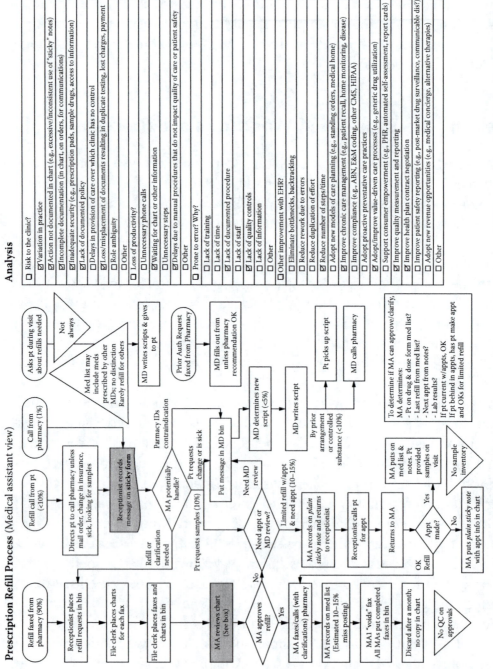

Figure 9.4 Documentation of "as-is" workflow and process map—with redesign technique checklist. (From Copyright © Margret\A Consulting, LLC. With permission.)

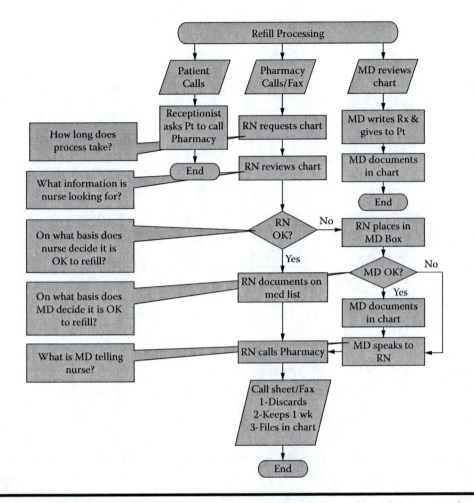

Figure 9.5   Documentation of "as-is" workflow and process map—with key questions annotated. (From Copyright © Margret\A Consulting, LLC. With permission.)

Validating the Redesigned Process

Once workflows and processes are redesigned, the new designs should be validated. While the maps should be drawn following mapping conventions and reflect the appropriate level of detail to convey the desired changes, there is no harm in validating these structural aspects of the "to-be" maps. However, the culmination of documenting the "to-be" maps should also be to validate the actual changes in the workflows and processes. There are two phases to this validation activity. The first is a paper-and-pencil exercise that occurs prior to implementation, and the second is a testing of the process that occurs during implementation.

Paper-and-pencil validation entails a validation team, such as described in Chapter 8 and referenced at the start of this chapter, reviewing each map with respect to a set of predefined criteria. The validation team can include the same types of people as the "as-is" validation team: a process auditor, a participant in the process, an individual or individuals impacted by the process (both those who will perform the process and those who will be customers of the

Table 9.5   Redesign Validation Checklist

Process:_____ Version:_____ Reviewer:_____ Date of Review:_____			
Success Factor	Accomplishment		
	Yes	No	N/A
Improves quality of care/patient safety			
Reduces likelihood of error			
Ensures timeliness of action			
Reduces practice variation/supports adherence to best practices			
Improves productivity			
Contributes to usability of HIT and EHR			
Contains cost			
Improves profitability			
Reduces hassle factors/improves user satisfaction			
Improves patient satisfaction			

process), and a systems analyst who will be responsible for the new system's configuration. It may be advantageous to also include the CDO's risk manager.

Criteria for the validation should be defined and compiled in a checklist. Ideally, the CDO's goals for HIT and EHR should form the basis for the criteria. Reviewers should compare the "as-is" map with the "to-be" map and consider how well the redesigned workflow and process will actually address the desired criteria. This side-by-side comparison, coupled with the knowledge and expertise of those accountable for performing the work today and in the future, should provide a good sense of whether the "to-be" maps represent the ability to accomplish successful workflow and process improvement. Table 9.5 illustrates a simple, yet potentially powerful checklist that can be modified by any CDO with respect to its goals for HIT and EHR, and its overall business imperatives.

In addition to the validation team members auditing redesigned workflows, the risk manager should consider the resources required to effect the changes, the feasibility with respect to how likely it is the HIT and EHR will support the change, and the measurability of success with the new process.

Implementation validation would occur simultaneously with the information system being tested. In fact, it should be a key element of the system integration testing performed on the system prior to initiating end-user training and go-live. During this phase of the process redesign validation, the "to-be" map should be compared to the "dry run" of the system. Every single step in the workflow and process map should become "visible" to the reviewer, either as a part of the technology or that requires human steps prior to and after each technical component. Figure 9.6 is an example of how to construct an

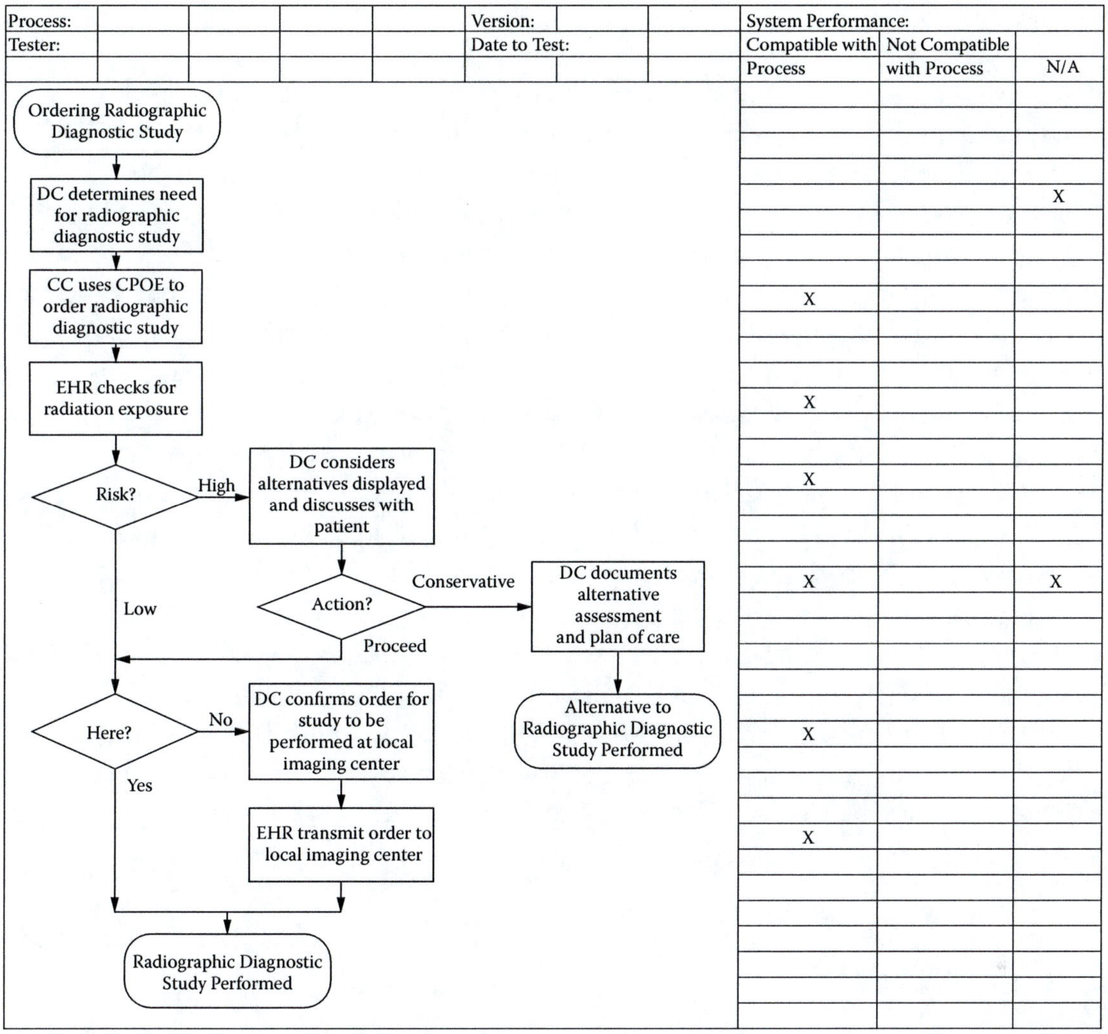
Process:
Version:
System Performance:
Tester:
Date to Test:
Compatible with Process
Not Compatible with Process
N/A
Ordering Radiographic Diagnostic Study
DC determines need for radiographic diagnostic study
CC uses CPOE to order radiographic diagnostic study
EHR checks for radiation exposure
Risk?
High
DC considers alternatives displayed and discusses with patient
Action?
Conservative
DC documents alternative assessment and plan of care
Low
Proceed
Alternative to Radiographic Diagnostic Study Performed
Here?
No
DC confirms order for study to be performed at local imaging center
Yes
EHR transmit order to local imaging center
Radiographic Diagnostic Study Performed
X
X
X
X
X
X
X
X
X

Figure 9.6 Implementation validation checklist. (From Copyright © Margret\A Consulting, LLC. With permission.)

implementation validation checklist. The example describes a chiropractor (DC) ordering a radiographic study, the EHR supporting evaluation of radiation exposure and display of alternative assessments if necessary, and transmission of the order to a remote diagnostic imaging center if the chiropractor cannot perform the modality in the office.

Of course, after go-live, the success of the "to-be" workflows and processes in achieving goals for HIT or EHR can be further validated. However, it is also important to consider the words of Isaac Asimov, former biochemistry professor at Boston University and noted science fiction author, who is quoted as saying, "It is change, continuing change, inevitable change that is the dominant factor in society today. No sensible decision can be made any longer without taking into account not only the world as it is, but the world as it will be." This is why it is essential to redesign workflows and processes—and to appreciate that they will be continuously evolving.

Key Points

■ Redesign of workflows and processes is a means to achieve their improvement. All steps leading to the redesign process support the ability of a CDO to achieve success with redesign. Most important among the steps that contribute to successful "to-be" mapping may be the **completeness of the "as-is"** maps. It cannot be emphasized enough how vital it is to include all stakeholders in identifying all "warts and workarounds" in "as-is" maps—or opportunities for improvement will just not be very apparent.

■ Redesign begins with the formation of **redesign teams,** including **process owners**, **process customers**, and **systems analysts**. Effective redesign depends on recognizing **redesign opportunities**, often through brainstorming or other **group process** activity. Redesign may require **root cause analysis** so that actual problems, not just their symptoms, are addressed. **Redesign techniques** include looking for ways to make improvements that are effective and do not introduce further risk.

■ A key element of redesign should be **validation of the "to-be" processes**—for how well the changes made will achieve the CDO's goals. Such validation should occur in "paper-and-pencil" mode prior to implementation, as well as during implementation as an actual "dry run" of the system occurs. The true test of success, of course, occurs once the "to-be" workflows and processes are implemented.

References

AAFP, 2010. Integrating Tobacco Cessation Into Electronic Health Records, Ask and Act Practice Toolkit. Available at: www.aafp.org/online/etc/medialib/aafp_org/documents/clinical/pub_health/askact/ehrs.Par.0001.File.tmp/AAEHRSheet2010.pdf

AAMC, 2011 (July 11). "Appropriate Documentation in an EHR: Use of Information That Is Not Generated During the Encounter for Which the Claim is Submitted: Copying/Importing/Scripts/Templates." Academic Medical Centers, Compliance Advisory 2, Association of American Medical Colleges.

AHIMA, 2008. *Copy Functionality Toolkit*, Chicago: American Health Information Management Association.

Ash, J.S., et al., 2007. "Some Unintended Consequences of Clinical Decision Support Systems," *AMIA 2007 Symposium Proceedings*, Bethesda, MD: American Medical Informatics Association, 26–30.

Bachman, J., 2007 (Jul.–Aug.). "Improving Care with an Automated Patient History." *Family Practice Management*: 14(7): 39–43.

Baker, L.H., 2010 (May). "Adoption of EHR Does Not Equal Implementation: Communication Techniques for the Exam Room are Key for Practitioners as EHR is Implemented." The Governance Institute, E_Briefings V7N3.

Brouillard, C.P., 2010 (July). "Emergency Trends in Electronic Health Record Liability." *For the Defense*, 39–44.

Casalino, L.P. et al., 2009 (June 22). "Frequency of Failure to Inform Patients of Clinically Significant Outpatient Test Results." *Archives of Internal Medicine*, 169(12): 1123–1129.

Cassidy, A. and K. Guggenberger, 2001. *A Practical Guide to Information Systems Process Improvement,* Boca Raton, FL: St. Lucie Press, 149.

CDC, 2006 (Nov.). "Gaining Consensus Among Stakeholders Through the Nominal Group Technique." Department of Health and Human Services, Centers for Disease Control and Prevention. No. 7.

Covey, S.R. 2004. *The Seven Habits of Highly Effective People, 2nd edition*. New York: Free Press.

DeCarlo, D., 2011. "Six Essential Facilitation Techniques for Project Managers." Global Knowledge. Available at: http://www.globalknowledge.com/training/generic. asp?pageid=1907&country=United+States

Dimick, C., 2008 (June). "Documentation Bad Habits: Shortcuts in Electronic Records Pose Risk." *Journal of AHIMA*, 79(6): 40–43.

Goldberg, D., 2011 (Feb. 1). "EHR Systems Create New Legal Risks." *Dermatology Times*.

Greenberger, M., Ed., 1971. *Computers, Communications and the Public Interest*. Baltimore, MD: The Johns Hopkins University Press, 40–41.

Gur-Arie, M., 2010 (Nov. 14). "The Ethics of EHR Vendors." *On Health Care Technology*. Available at: http://onhealthtech.blogspot.com/2010/11/ethics-of-ehr-vendors.htm.

Institute of Medicine, 2001. *Crossing the Quality Chasm: A New Health System for the 21st Century*. Washington, DC: National Academy Press, 39–40.

ISMP, 2010 (Mar. 11). "ISMP Develops Guidelines for Standard Order Sets." ISMP Medication Safety Alert! Available at: http://www.ismp.org/newsletters/acutecare/articles/20100311.asp.

Maine General, n.d. "Patient Safety Goals." Available at: http://www.mainegeneral.org/blankcustom.cfm?print=yes&id=866

Mansar, S.L. and H.A. Reijers, 2005 (March). "Best Practices in Business Process Redesign: Validation of a Redesign Framework." *Computers in Industry*, 56: 457–471.

Mellin, A., 2010. "CPOE Requires Governance Structure From Organizational Leaders to Succeed." *Performance Strategies*, McKesson Corporation.

National Priorities Partnership, 2010 (Oct. 14). "Input to the Secretary of Health and Human Services on Priorities for the 2011 National Quality Strategy," Washington, DC: National Quality Forum.

NSO, n.d. "Keeping Up with Technology: Your Risks and Responsibilites." Nurses Service Organization. Available at: http://www.nso.com/nursing-resources/article/250.jsp

Phillips, M.T. and E.S. Berner, 2004. "Beating the System—Pitfalls of Bar Code Medication Administration." *Journal of Healthcare Information Management,* 18(4): 16–18.

Smith, T. et al., 2004. Nicholas E. Davies Award of Excellence: Transforming Healthcare with a Patient-Centric Electronic Health Record System. Evanston Northwestern Healthcare (now renamed NorthShore University Health System). Available from: http://www.himss.org/davies/pastRecipients_org.asp

Steiner, C., 2011. "Using EHRs to Reduce Practice Variation." *Ambulatory Practice Newsletter,* 2(1): 2.

Stout, D., 2010 (Mar. 31). "Top Ten Electronic Health Record System Expectations/Requirements: Beyond 'Meaningful Use.'" EpsteinBeckerGreen Client Newsletters. Available at: http://www.ebglaw.com/shownewsletter.aspx?Show=12669

Straker, D. and G. Rawlinson, 2003. *How to Invent (Almost) Anything. Delphi Method*. Australia: Spiro Press.

Sutton, R., 2006 (July 26). "Eight Tips for Better Brainstorming." *Bloomberg Businessweek*. Available at: http://www.businessweek.com/innovate/content/jul2006/id20060726_517774.htm

Tonelli, M., 2006 (February). "Evidence-Based Medicine and Clinical Expertise." *Virtual Mentor American Medical Association Journal of Ethics*, 8(2): 71–74.

Toth, C.L., 2010a (February). "Auto-Population Gone Wild." *AAPC Coding Edge*, 26–30.

Toth, C.L., 2010b (June). "Is Your EMR Fueling Risky Record Keeping? *AAOS Now*, American Academy of Orthopaedic Surgeons.

Chapter 10

Step 8: Conduct Root Cause Analysis to Redesign Workflows and Processes

Do not look where you fell, but where you slipped.

—African proverb

This African proverb, according to Sommer (2003), literally means "Don't look at your mistakes, look at what caused you to make the mistakes." This philosophy about root cause analysis helps one dig deep and stay focused on finding the underlying reason for rather than just the symptoms of a problem. Unfortunately, many root cause analyses go astray. C. Robert Nelms (2003) has observed that

> Loaded with cliché and ambiguity, true root cause analysis is neither being practiced nor even desired in most areas of life. Plenty of organizations are addressing the 'physical' causes of failure. Even more seem to enjoy finding out 'who did it' so that disciplinary action can occur. But only a few seem willing to dig deeper in an attempt to understand the 'root' causes of things that go wrong.

This chapter urges those finding ways to redesign a workflow and process in need of improvement to avoid the "blame game" and truly find the fundamental elements that must be addressed to achieve success (Williams 2001). It discusses cause and effect, finding and weighing potential solutions, requirements for performing root cause analysis, and tools and techniques to aid root cause analysis.

Cause and Effect

The dictionary defines *causality* as the relationship between an event (the cause) and a second event (the effect), where the second event is understood to be the consequence of the first. The problem is that causality is rarely as simple as it seems; sometimes assumptions must be made about causality, sometimes there are multiple causes, and sometimes there are surprises when the underlying cause is determined. A few examples from outside health care and potentially outside workflow follow:

- A man eats a quarter of a pie with three scoops of ice cream every night for dessert and never puts on an ounce of weight, whereas the man's wife finds eating pretty much any dessert every night results in pounds adding up rapidly. Can it be said, then, that eating dessert is the cause of weight gain? Obviously it is not the sole factor. What other factors may contribute? A person's metabolism plays a role. Perhaps what else they eat during the day. The timing of eating the dessert—in this case, the man is a "night owl" whereas the wife is an "early bird." Does this suggest that the wife could eat such dessert for breakfast and not gain weight? Very likely, she decides the risk is not worth the experiment because she still assumes that such dessert will cause weight gain.
- Dandelion weeds are a gardener's perpetual foe. If you only cut off the top of the plant, it will grow back from the root; but if you remove the root, your chances of reducing dandelions in your yard are enhanced (Figure 10.1). Unfortunately, your neighbors—far and wide—may not be

Figure 10.1 Cut the root of the dandelion (and all of your neighbors' dandelions) to eliminate weeds. (From Copyright © Margret\A Consulting, LLC. With permission.)

quite as diligent as you about removing dandelions. The dandelions will repopulate your yard from the seeds blowing in the wind.

■ A scenario relayed by Bellinger (2004)—and slightly modified to illustrate the root cause analysis technique "**Ask Why 5 Times**" to get to the root of a problem. The story goes that a plant manager who finds oil on the floor of the plant *first* asks the foreman why there is oil on the floor and is told it is due to a leaky gasket. The plant manager *second* asks why the gasket was not replaced, and the foreman responds that the maintenance department has installed 4 gaskets over the past few weeks and they each leaked. The plant manager *third* goes to the purchasing manager to ask why the gaskets were bought from a disreputable supplier, and the purchasing manager says they went with the lowest bidder based on direction received from the vice president of finance. The plant manager *fourth* goes to the vice president of finance about this directive and is told—"you indicated we have to be as cost conscious as possible and this supplier saves us a lot of money." The plant manager then realizes that he was the reason there was oil on the floor of the plant and asks himself *fifth* why he was not more careful in giving directions!

In workflow and process management, Ishikawa is the "guru" of determining cause and effect (Pecht and Boulton, 1995). The Ishikawa diagram, also known as the cause-and-effect diagram or fishbone diagram, is a common tool used to identify possible causes for certain problems. The traditional "fishbone" cause-and-effect diagram with example is illustrated in Figure 10.2a, with a key to the meaning of the symbols; and a spreadsheet version is shown in Figure 10.2b.

A diagramming tool can be helpful to remind the workflow and process redesign team to specifically define the effect and to be guided in possible causes. Whether or not a diagramming aid is used, causal categories and considerations for health information technology (HIT), electronic health records (EHR), and

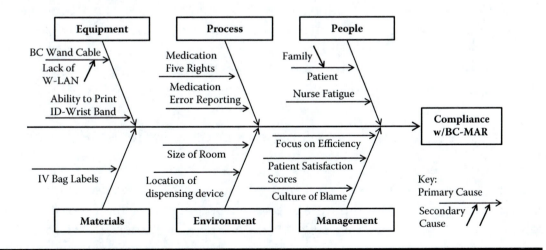

**Figure 10.2a Traditional fishbone cause-and-effect diagram. (From Copyright ©
Margret\A Consulting, LLC. With permission.)**

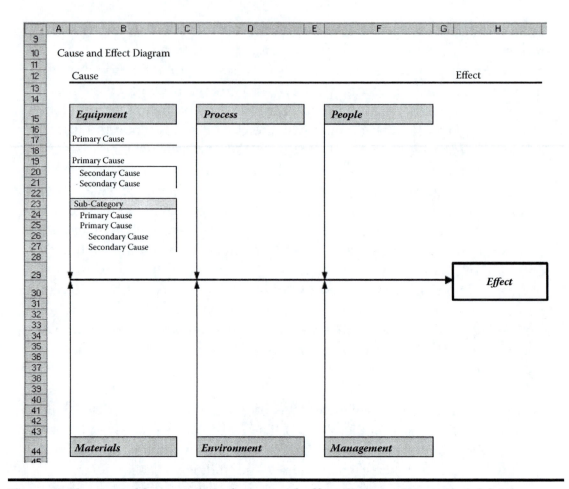

Figure 10.2b Spreadsheet version of cause-and-effect diagram. (From Copyright © Margret\A Consulting, LLC. With permission.)

health information exchange (HIE) may include those identified in Table 10.1 (Hughes 2008; Palanque 2004; Wittwer 2009; Dew 2003).

Figure 10.2a illustrates several considerations for possible causes of nurse noncompliance with a bar-code medication administration record (BC-MAR) system (see also Case Study 9.7). In the illustration, the workflow and process redesign team considered a variety of potential causes. Some were primary causes, and others secondary. In every causal category there were possible issues identified. Case Study 10.1 elaborates on the issues the workflow and process redesign team assigned to study the problem identified.

Case Study 10.1: Causality of Noncompliance with BC-MAR System

Several nurses, a pharmacist, a systems analyst, and a process analyst formed the workflow and process redesign team to determine the root cause of the nurses' noncompliance with the BC-MAR system recently implemented. Nurses expressed that they felt uncomfortable "wanding" patients, especially when family members were present, and especially in light of management's recent edicts surrounding the need to improve patient satisfaction scores. They also felt

Table 10.1 Causal Categories

Categories	Examples for HIT, EHR, and HIE

Equipment	• Information system software
	
	    • Financial and administrative systems (Billing, Scheduling, Health Information Management, Purchasing, Time and Attendance, General Ledger, Others)
	
	    • Ancillary systems (Laboratory, Radiology, Pharmacy, Others)
	
	    • Electronic health record components (Computerized Provider Order Entry, Electronic Prescribing, Electronic Medication Administration Record, Point of Care Charting, Results Management, Clinical Decision Support, Analytics and Reporting)
	
	    • Specialty systems (Intensive Care Units, Emergency Department, Cardiology, Surgery, Others)
	
	    • Health information exchange (Continuity of Care Record, Health Information Organization, Consent Management)
	
	    • Privacy and security systems (Authorization, Access Controls, Audit Logs, Authentication Processes, Encryption, Integrity Controls, Others)
	
	• Information system hardware
	
	    • Input/output devices
	
	    • Networking and telecommunications
	
	    • Servers, storage
	
	    • Others
	
	• Medical devices (Smart Infusion Pumps, Glucometers, Physiologic Monitors, Automated Dispensing Machines)
	
	• Furnishings (Wireless on Wheels, Carts, Robots, Smart Beds, Others)
	
	• Malfunction
	
	• Insufficiency
	
	• Absence
	
	• Professional judgment
	
	• Others

Process	• Workflows • Methods • Procedures • Controls (timeouts, checkpoints, duplication, statistical processes, others) • Protocols • Best practices • Evidence-based care guidelines • Lack of specificity

continued

Table 10.1 (continued)   Causal Categories

Categories	Examples for HIT, EHR, and HIE
	• Too detailed • Automation • Others
People	• Patients • Families and other caregivers • Physicians • Staff (Staff Nurses, Phlebotomists, Laboratorians, Pharmacists, Therapists, Visiting Nurses, Systems Analysts, Coders, Billers, Others) • Travel nurses, locum tenens, other temporary staff • Government, public health, and other oversight officials • Payers • Employers • Public health officials • Vendors • Suppliers • Skills • Credentials • Training • Education • Experience • Leadership • Engagement • Accidental acts posing threat (Inattention, Errors of Omission/Co-mission, Waste, Fatigue, Burnout, Other) • Work stoppage • Deliberate acts posing threat (Insubordination, Misuse, Theft, Fraud, Other) • Others
Materials	• Knowledge sources and other reference materials • Medications • Medical equipment (Stethoscopes, Blood Pressure Monitors, Ultrasound, Magnetic Resonance Imaging, Others) • Medical supplies (Syringes, Test Strips, Bandages, Others) • Paper charts, forms, schedules, other • Food and nutrition • Linens and clothing • Others

Table 10.1 (continued)   Causal Categories

Categories	Examples for HIT, EHR, and HIE
Environment	• Building architecture • Campus design • Maintenance, HVAC • Contamination • Furniture (Nurses' Stations, Chairs, Tables, Shelves, Other) • Case mix • Population served • Mother nature • Others
Management	• Governance structure • Culture • Policy • Price • Promotion • Product • Supervisors • Managers • Executives • Board of Directors • Mission • Vision • Goals • Regulations • Others

Source: Copyright © Margret\A Consulting, LLC. With permission.

management focused exclusively on efficiency, not effectiveness, and so they felt their workaround of printing copies of ID-wristbands and "wanding" them at the nurses' station was more expeditious. They felt there was a culture of blame, so that if the nurse did not administer the medication at the precise minute it was called for, the computer would spit out a report identifying medication timing errors and those would impact the nurses' performance reviews. While nurses wanted to adhere to the process espoused in the "medication five rights" (i.e., right patient, right drug, right dose, right route, right time), they also felt that the medication error reporting policy associated thereto was not flexible and in some cases led to dangerous patient care practices. The size of the room (not easily accommodating the wireless on wheels [WOW] cart) and the distance of the medication-dispensing device from the nurses' station were identified as issues.

Finally, nurses noted that the cable to the bar-code wand was not long enough to reach the patient's wristband comfortably, and intravenous (IV) bags to supply medications were not yet bar-coded. The systems analyst reported that the hospital had not yet fully deployed a wireless local area network (W-LAN), hence the need for the bar-code wand cable. The pharmacist indicated they were working on a solution to create bar-code labels for IV solutions, but were not yet ready for deployment.

Weighing Potential Solutions

It has been observed that root cause analysis is intended to get to the root of a problem so it can be fixed, so as to not just address symptoms. Very often there is not "one and only one" cause of a problem, as illustrated well by Case Study 10.1 (and several others previously included in this book). Healthcare processes are generally too complex for there to be only one cause. In fact, virtually every issue identified in Figure 10.2a could be addressed in some way. And, of course, the purpose of a root cause analysis should not be to merely identify the issues, but to find solutions for them.

Table 10.2 provides a simple tool to help a workflow and process redesign team identify solutions, describe their feasibility, prioritize them, and plan for implementing them. The tool offers an example of suggestions for possible solutions to one of the issues identified in Case Study 10.1 and the cause-and-effect diagram in Figure 10.2a.

NOTE: The "Plan" in this illustration is only moderately described. Ideally, the plan would include

- Identification of solution owner
- Start and end dates for implementing solution
- Budget for solution
- Review date for determining improvement
- Applicable metrics to measure improvement
- Link to overall goal or organizational initiative

Requirement for Root Cause Analysis

The Joint Commission has probably been one of the biggest proponents of root cause analysis since it began requiring such analysis for all sentinel events in 2001. The Joint Commission defines a sentinel event as "an unexpected occurrence involving death or serious physical or psychological injury, or the risk thereof. Serious injury specifically includes loss of limb or function. The phrase "or risk thereof" includes any process variation for which a recurrence carries a

Table 10.2   Solutions Analysis and Plan

Issue	Possible Solutions (With Brief Explanation)	Feasibility			Priority (Sum of Risk, Cost, and Difficulty)[d]	Plan*
		Risk[a]	Marginal Cost[b]	Level of Difficulty[c]		
Patient and Family	Ignore	5	3	1	9	X
	Too much risk to ignore					
	Educate through nurse explanation on admission	2	2	3	7	X
Patients have too many things to think about on admission; nurses have too many things to do on admission.						
	Post education program on hospital's intranet and make available on patient TV	2	1	1	4	Do in 1 mo.
Not every patient or their family will watch TV, but easy and relatively low cost.						
	Distribute pamphlets about medication safety to patients and or caregivers	1	2	2	5	Do in 3 mo.
Every patient/family can receive, and can include other patient safety tips. Nurses can remind patient/family at time of first med administration; can answer questions as time permits.						

Source: Copyright © Margret\A Consulting, LLC. With permission.

[a] Very high = 5; high = 4; mod = 3; low = 2; very low = 1.
[b] Low = 1; mod = 2; high = 3.
[c] Easy = 1; mod = 2; diff = 3.
[d] Lowest # = highest priority.

significant chance of a serious adverse outcome. Such events are called "sentinel" because they signal the need for immediate investigation and response. As of September 30, 2009, The Joint Commission has had reported to it 6,428 sentinel events, with the most common being wrong-site surgery, suicide, operative or post-operative complication, delay in treatment, medication error, and patient fall.

Since they introduced the requirement for root cause analysis, The Joint Commission has been recommending tools and techniques to ensure that all important details surrounding any error or variance are identified, as soon as possible after such occurs, and by all personnel involved. In its *Root Cause Analysis in Health Care: Tools and Techniques*, now in its fourth edition (2010), The Joint Commission outlines the type of plan a care delivery organization (CDO) should have for addressing sentinel events. Their steps are listed in Table 10.3.

Similarly, the National Quality Forum has used the term "Never Event" in reference to particularly shocking medical errors (such as wrong-site surgery) that should never occur. Over time, the list has been expanded to signify adverse

Table 10.3   The Joint Commission's Steps for Root Cause Analysis of Sentinel Events

1. Organize a team
2. Define the problem
3. Study the problem
4. Determine what happened
5. Identify contributing factors
6. Identify other contributing factors
7. Measure: collect and assess data on proximate and underlying causes
8. Design and implement immediate changes
9. Identify which systems are involved—the root causes
10. Prune the list of root causes
11. Confirm root causes and consider their interrelationships
12. Explore and identify risk reduction strategies
13. Formulate improvement actions
14. Evaluate proposed improvement actions
15. Design improvements
16. Ensure acceptability of the action plan
17. Implement the improvement plan
18. Develop measures of effectiveness and ensure their success
19. Evaluate implementation of improvement efforts
20. Take additional action
21. Communicate the results

Source: Root Cause Analysis in Health Care: Tools and Techniques, fourth edition (2010). Edited by Richard J. Croteau, MD, Oak Brook Terrace, IL: Joint Commission Resources, iii–iv. With permission.

events that are unambiguous (clearly identifiable and measurable), serious (resulting in death or significant disability), and usually preventable. These Never Events are categorized as identified in Table 10.4.

Tools and Techniques to Aid Root Cause Analysis

Whether performing root cause analysis when required by the occurrence of a sentinel event, or never event, or studying root cause to redesign workflows and processes in light of opportunities and threats HIT and EHR implementations may afford, there are a variety of tools that can be used for data collection (Table 10.5), data display and analysis (Figure 10.3), and idea generation, problem

Table 10.4 National Quality Forum's Never Events, 2006

• Surgical events (e.g., wrong-site surgery)
• Product or device events (e.g., death or serious disability associated with the use of contaminated drugs, devices, or biologics provided by the healthcare facility)
• Patient protection events (e.g., infant discharged to wrong person)
• Care management events (e.g., stage 3 or 4 pressure ulcers acquired after admission to a healthcare facility)
• Environment events (e.g., patient death or serious disability associated with a fall while being cared for in a healthcare facility)
• Criminal events (e.g., abduction of a patient of any age)

solving, and risk assessment (Table 10.6) that have not been covered extensively elsewhere in this book. Tools have been listed only once in the category in which they are most commonly used, although several tools have multiple uses. Tools for workflow and process mapping are not included as they are the primary focus of this book.

Case Study 10.2 describes an interesting dilemma in a clinic with a new work-flow adopted as a result of its EHR acquisition. The case study illustrates the use of a movement diagram as illustrated in Figure 10.4.

Case Study 10.2: New Workflow Results in Construction Project

A clinic with six physicians had just acquired an EHR. One of the primary goals for its use was to encourage patients to have their lab results performed in advance of the visit with a physician. The clinic had a small lab and, in addition to believing this process change would improve patient satisfaction and reduce repeat visits for treatment plan development, it would also generate more revenue from more lab tests being performed in the clinic. This would be accomplished by the EHR (integrated with a practice management system) displaying to the registration clerk whether or not lab tests were required for the next visit. (The clinic did not feel it was necessary for the clerk to know or be able to discuss what lab tests were required—largely as a privacy concern. If asked, the clerk was to tell the patient the lab tests were previously discussed, the lab would know what tests were necessary, and if further information was requested, the clerk would refer the patient to a nurse.) Many patients took advantage of this and were very happy with the change because they no longer had to wait to hear about their lab results—all would be discussed with a physician as soon as they became available. However, the clinic discovered it had created a traffic jam in its waiting room and an escort issue because patients would arrive early or sometimes even days prior to their visit to have the lab tests performed and would need to be escorted through the office. As a result, the clinic decided it would redesign its office, first studying the current movement and then plotting

Table 10.5   Tools to Collect Data for Root Cause Analysis

Tool	Description
Cognitive Task Analysis (a.k.a. Mind Mapping)	Means of capturing the way the mind works, including in decision-making, reasoning, and how information is processed.
Cognitive Walkthrough	Technique typically used for evaluating the design of a user interface (web site, EHR screen layout), with special attention to how well the interface supports "exploratory learning," i.e., first-time use without formal training.
Focus Group	Form of qualitative research in which people are invited to share, in an interactive session with others, their perceptions, opinions, beliefs, and attitudes surrounding a specific topic, such as why an error occurred or how to solve a problem. Made popular in the retail industry for product analysis.
Force Field Analysis	A technique for looking at all the forces for and against a decision that enables weighing pros and cons of a change. A group identifies driving and restraining forces by their strength. Upon analysis, ways to strengthen forces supporting a decision are identified and ways to reduce the impact of opposition are found.
Movement Diagram	An architectural drawing on which the flow of work requiring physical movement is illustrated to identify potential bottlenecks that may require physical reconstruction of space.
Physical Layout	An architectural drawing of a space, such as an exam room, operating room, or other location, is evaluated for optimal placement of equipment, supplies, computer access, staff positioning, etc. See Chapter 9.
Rounding	Similar to physicians making rounds to check on their patients, rounding is a structured process of targeted questions used by managers and executives to build relationships with their staff and customers, often to spot potential problems.
Time and Motion Study (a.k.a. Stop Watch Time Study)	A direct and continuous observation of a task, using a stopwatch (or videotape camera) to record the time taken to accomplish a task in order to reduce cycle times, define reliable time standards, and improve efficiency.

a change that would provide a central area that had one door to the clinic and another door to the lab so that patients could be directed accordingly. While not inexpensive, the lab revenue and patient satisfaction effect covered the cost.

Tools and techniques to aid root cause analysis can be very helpful. If nothing else, they help move participants in the investigatory process away from the personal blame, bias, and subjectivity to greater objectivity and focus on finding solutions. Caution should be applied as any of the tools are used, however, to avoid "analysis paralysis." This is a situation where over-analyzing or over-thinking occurs such that a decision or action is never taken, or at least significantly delayed, thus potentially compounding the original issue.

Affinity Diagram (a.k.a. Jiro Kawakita Method)	Tool to help synthesize a large number of ideas by finding relationships between them. May be used to organize information from a brainstorming session.	
Control Chart (a.k.a. Shewhart Chart)	Statistical tool used to monitor quality, where a Run Chart with a center line representing the mean value of the process is used with an upper control limit and lower control limit to monitor where a process has gone out-of-control and needs correction.	
Histogram (a.k.a. Bar Chart) and Pie Charts	These charts graphically demonstrates the frequency with which various values of a particular variable occur in a set of data. The Histogram shows comparisons among categories while the Pie Chart shows relative proportions of various items in making up a whole. These charts can be used in defining problems or choosing solutions.	
Pareto Chart (a.k.a., Distribution chart)	Named after the 19th century Italian economist Vilfredo Pareto who made famous the principle that 80 percent of the problems come from 20 percent of the causes, a Pareto chart shows bars in decreasing length from left to right and where the bar length corresponds to time, frequency, or amount. This identify factors that have the greatest cumulative effect on a system.	
Radar Chart	Chart that graphically shows the size of gaps among five to ten organizational performance areas, illustrating strengths and weakness performance areas. This radar chart shows 7 performance areas, with that at the 12:00 o'clock position being the strongest and the area at the 10:00 o'clock position the weakest.	
Scatter Diagram	Tool for analyzing relationships between two variables to determine, through use of correlation, the likelihood one variable causes the other. The illustration here shows a high correlation between the two variables plotted on the X and Y axes because the data are closely clustered in a linear shape.	

Figure 10.3   Tools to collect data for root cause analysis.

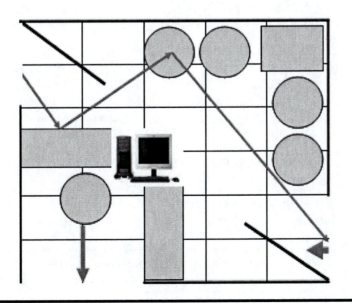

Figure 10.4   Movement diagram. (*Source:* Copyright © Margret\A Consulting, LLC. Reprinted with permission.)

Table 10.6   Tools for Idea Generation, Problem Solving, and Risk Assessment for Root Cause Analysis

Tool	Comments
5W2H	Tool that provides the guiding questions who, what, when, where, why, how, and how much to generate ideas for occurrences to be overcome.
Ask Why 5 Times	Process of repetitively asking "Why?" in order to determine root cause
Benchmarking	Process of evaluating metrics or best practices from other organizations and applying them to a specific organization's process improvement strategy.
Brainstorming	Group process technique used to generate ideas simultaneously and without judgment until all idea generation is spent.
Cause-and Effect-Diagram (a.k.a., Fishbone diagram, Ishikawa diagram)	Visual means of conveying all suspected and possible causes and consequences of a specific problem.
Contingency Diagram	Technique for generating ideas concerning and issue or concern that capitalizes on negative thought. By thinking of all the ways a problem can be caused or worsened, the basis for development of an action plan to overcome these barriers can be constructed. Mosaic and Parquet Diagrams are contingency diagrams combined with statistical measures, such as Pearson's goodness-of-fit *chi*-square for prioritization.
Delphi Method	Idea generation technique where anonymous voting is used to generate and reach consensus on an idea or solution.
Failure Mode and Effects Analysis (FMEA)	Tool to prospectively identify process risks in an organization, analyze the ways in which the process can fail, prioritize those failure modes, and take corrective action before failures have occurred.
Fault Tree Analysis (a.k.a. Causal Tree, Dandelion Diagram, Murphy Diagram)	Top-down, deductive analysis in which an undesired state is analyzed using Boolean logic to determine the probability of a safety accident or particular functional failure. Similar to Cause-and-Effect Diagram, but includes the application of statistical probability.
Multi-voting	A means of reducing a large list of options to a smaller list of best options by sequential voting on subsets of the list.
Nominal Group Technique	Structured brainstorming method where all members of a group are encouraged to participate, at first silently, and then to critique ideas.
Simulation Modeling	Dynamic tool that models the behavior of a process over time to show how random variation affects intricate, time-based events.
Use Case	A tool to describe what a user does to interact with an information system.

Often in health care, a group will attempt to seek the optimal or "perfect" solution, fearing that anything less would be harmful, lead to poor outcomes, create further errors, or result in other unintended consequences. The saying "Don't let perfect be the enemy of good" is very applicable here. This does not advocate for a decision to be made in haste; but the longer the wait, the more likely the situation will worsen. If at least an interim solution can be found—it should be implemented with the thought that further and potentially better solutions can follow.

Key Points

- **Redesign of workflows and processes** in light of HIT and EHR should be focused on determining how to use technology to the advantage of the patient, providers, and all other stakeholders. This requires understanding of the current workflows and processes, knowledge of how HIT and EHRs function, and having a healthy desire to use technology to transform health care. A clinical transformation with HIT and EHR is not just changing the way providers document, but fundamentally how they use information to improve the practice of medicine.
- Very often, current processes contain workarounds or limitations due to lack of information. These issues have resulted in problems, including sentinel (or never) events. This is not to say that there will never be unintended consequences from the use of new technology, but getting to the **root cause** of the workflow and process—as it is today and improving upon it for use with technology will make a significant contribution to reducing error and waste and improve the value of health care.
- Tools and techniques are available and should be used to understand **cause and effect**. Collecting data about the issues, understanding the data, and using them in a way that identifies potential solutions and then evaluating and implementing the solutions—even in a stepwise approach—contributes to an efficient and effective redesign of workflows and processes to enable technology to best serve the healthcare industry.

References

Bellinger, G., 2004. "Root Cause Analysis." *The Way of Systems*. Available at: http://www.systems-thinking.org/rca/rootca.htm

Croteau, R.J., 2010. *Root Cause Analysis in Health Care: Tools and Techniques.* Oakbrook Terrace, IL: Joint Commission Resources, iii–iv.

Dew, J.R., 2003. "Using Root Cause Analysis to Make the Patient Care System Safe." *ASQ Health Care Division Newsletter.*

Hughes, R.G., 2008 (April). "Patient Safety and Quality: An Evidence-Based Handbook for Nurses." AHRQ Publication No. 08-0043.

Joint Commission, The, 2009 (Sept. 30). "Sentinel Events Most Frequently Reported to The Joint Commission." Available at: http://psnet.ahrq.gov/primer.aspx?primerID=3

Nelms, C.R., 2003 (July 28). "Root Cause Analysis—NOT What You Might Think." *Maintenance World*.

Palanque, P., 2004. *An Introduction to Root Cause Analysis in Healthcare*. New York: Kluwer Academic Press.

Pecht, M. and W.R. Boulton, 1995 (Feb.). Chapter 6. "Quality Assurance and Reliability in the Japanese Electronics Industry." *Electronic Manufacturing and Packaging in Japan*. WTEC Hyper-Librarian. Available at: http://www.wtec.org/loyola/ep/c6s1.htm

National Quality Forum. Never Events 2006. Available at: http://psnet.ahrq.gov/primer.aspx?primerID=3

Sommer, J.I., 2003 (May 13). "Root Cause Analysis." *Thoughtable Quotes*. Available at: http://www.jsommer.com/tquotes/?p=4

Williams, P.M., 2001 (April). "Techniques for Root Cause Analysis." *Proceedings of Baylor University Medical Center,* 14(2): 154–157.

Wittwer, J.W., 2009 (Oct. 29). "Fishbone Diagram/Cause and Effect Diagram in Excel." *Vertex42.com*.

Chapter 11

Step 9: Implement Redesigned Workflows and Processes

Which of the following quotes most represents how you feel about change brought about by health information technology (HIT) and electronic health records (EHR)?

A. Technological change is like an axe in the hands of a pathological criminal.

—Albert Einstein

B. Any change, even for the better, is always accompanied by drawbacks and discomforts.

—Arnold Bennett, English novelist

C. You must welcome change as the rule but not as your ruler.

—Denis Waitley
Motivational, writer, consultant, and best-selling author

D. If nothing ever changed, there'd be no butterflies.

—Author Unknown

All the above statements are motivational quotes about change, but it is likely that every person will answer differently—depending on their tolerance for change and how their organization approaches implementation of HIT and EHR. This chapter covers implementation of redesigned workflows and processes. It also urges care delivery organizations (CDOs) to be proactive in putting attention on change management, making change management a priority, creating change agents, and using specific change management tools to help manage change during implementation of HIT and EHR. There is a tremendous body of knowledge on change management. There is no absolute silver bullet, but this chapter is intended to explore approaches to change management that have been effective when dealing with knowledge workers adopting information technology.

Implementing Redesigned Workflows and Processes

It is often suggested that if an organization plans thoroughly and takes all the necessary steps to design a right solution, then implementing the solution will be easy. While there is no guarantee that this will be true, the case can be made that up-front planning at least diffuses the intensity of the implementation. Planning enables the organization to "breathe" during implementation, ideally being clearer of mind and able to more effectively overcome the "haste makes waste" syndrome.

Anyone implementing major HIT or EHR technology will have a project plan for doing so. This book has walked through a ten-step methodology for managing workflow and process changes. Ideally, the plan for managing workflow and process changes is incorporated within the overarching project plan for the HIT or EHR. If not or not fully, CDOs would be well served to follow the steps in Table 11.1.

In their workflow and process redesign implementations, CDOs should pay particular attention to the testing and training aspects where new workflows and processes can be validated and introduced.

Table 11.1 Steps in Implementing Redesigned Workflows and Processes

1. Use the Process Inventory to identify what redesigned workflows and processes connect to each aspect of the HIT and EHR implementation.
2. Stage redesigned workflow and process changes in concert with the deployment of the HIT or EHR.
3. Incorporate redesigned workflows and processes into the testing plans for the technology deployment in each process area.
4. Conduct validation of redesigned workflows and processes as part of system integration testing.
5. Further redesign any workflow and process that does not pass the validation phase.
6. Add workflow and process elements to the training materials for each component of HIT or EHR that is deployed.
7. Check that training competencies for use of HIT or EHR include redesigned workflows and processes.
8. Include workflow and process changes in the dress rehearsal for HIT or EHR go-live.
9. Reassure new HIT or EHR users that workflow and process changes support their use of HIT or EHR and that such changes will be closely monitored to ensure fit.
10. Monitor workflow and process changes as part of the overall monitoring of goal achievement for the HIT and EHR adoption.

With respect to testing, many HIT and EHR vendors perform system testing during their original product development but then perform only limited testing of each implementation—possibly only testing new interfaces. Many HIT and EHR systems enable configuration to the CDO requirements through toolboxes that reside above the source code. As a result, the belief is that because the underlying source code is not touched, there is no need for testing beyond what the vendor did when the product was first released. Unfortunately, there can be carry-over design flaws, flaws in newer versions not tested thoroughly, or the configuration issues themselves do not work properly. And, of course, without the system testing process at the specific product delivery site, there is no opportunity for testing workflows and processes concurrently. The result has been that CDOs often find software flaws during the training period. Because new users are nervous enough about the impending change, subjecting them to a potentially flawed system during the time they are expected to focus on learning the system seems to be a flawed approach to gaining new user trust. Just the same, this may be the only opportunity the CDO has to also validate the redesigned workflows and processes. One way to partially overcome this issue is to construct a "pilot" project wherein a small number of new users very committed to the project and with a high tolerance for change are trained first so they are the ones to work out issues with the software and the redesigned workflows and processes.

Training on the new HIT or EHR is another area where vendors could, but often do not afford sufficient opportunity to introduce new workflows and processes. Most HT and EHR vendors only train users on their product—how to log on to the system, navigate a screen, enter data, etc. Most vendors do not perceive that workflow and process changes surrounding the use of the HIT or EHR are their responsibility. Often there is no time for workflow and process considerations to be included with the technical training. In fact, sometimes CDOs run out of money, steam, or both when it comes to training, and so they budget for only a minimum amount. In fact, some vendors encourage CDOs to rely on the product being "so intuitive" that training is not necessary. Unfortunately, this is often not the case, or the intuition that is applied is used to find a workaround! CDOs that put great attention on training and require it for every user, while also mandating use, are finding that they are able to gain better adoption (Whiting and Gale, 2008). Case Study 11.1 provides an example of consequences on training without workflow and process management.

Case Study 11.1: Consequences of Training without Workflow and Process Management

A hospital implementing a barcode medication administration record (BC-MAR) system brought nurses to a classroom to receive instruction. They were shown a bar-code reader. It was passed around so that each nurse could touch it, find the button to perform the reading, and learn how to position the reader for the most accurate reading. The nurses were then told how close the bar-code reader needed to be in proximity to the bar-coded wristband and that a tone would be heard when the reading had occurred. It was reiterated which button on the reader to press to perform the reading. The trainer then discussed the contents of the screen, showing the nurses what they will see, how it will change when the wristband is scanned, how to make any changes if necessary, and where the Help button is for additional information. As part of this training, however, no one took a nurse with the wireless-on-wheels (WOW) cart to an actual patient room to demonstrate how to use the bar-code reader to read a patient's wristband. No one suggested to the nurse that the first time this is performed, it is a good idea to tell the patient what is being done and why. There was no reminder that the nurse should check the computer monitor to make sure the wristband had been read correctly. No one addressed the steps to be taken before or after this part of the process. There had been no data collected on how long the medication administration process took prior to implementation, or the distance the nurse had to travel in the "as-is" process, or the force the nurse must use to push the WOW. Finally, once implemented, no one evaluated how the patients responded, what the nurses were concerned about, whether or not the cable on the reader was long enough to reach the patient's wrist, or how many tries the nurses had to make to get a read on the wristbands. After a year of deployment and many complaints by nurses, administration was surprised to find the many workarounds the nurses had created and reprimanded them for doing so.

The scenario painted in Case Study 11.1 is a sad situation, which unfortunately has been repeated in many hospitals. To improve upon this situation, CDOs are encouraged to not only conduct workflow and process redesign prior to implementing the HIT or EHR and to incorporate such changes directly into the implementation, but also to make it a requirement that managers and supervisors consider how people will be and are reacting to change. Managers and supervisors need to understand how reactions will vary, and to prepare how to respond to each type of reaction. Table 11.2 provides a summary of reactions to change, along with some recommendations for overcoming each type of reaction.

Making Change Management a Priority

What Case Study 11.1 and Table 11.2 highlight is the need for an organization to make managing change a priority. It is not enough to tell people about an impending change, train them, and then expect that adoption will occur. Even where many new users have been engaged in workflow and process documentation and redesign, there still need to be reminders about the new workflows and processes and support for making the change. Furthermore, reprimanding people who have not been trained properly is inappropriate and inexcusable. If there

Table 11.2   Reactions to Change and Responses

Characteristic	Reaction	Potential Responses
Active support	Supportive, energetic, volunteers for and performs tasks well. They may almost be too willing to take on the challenge of change, jumping the gun and not learning about the change adequately— although they tend to overcome this deficiency on their own.	Express appreciation and continue to channel energies into constructive help, such as using them on redesign teams or as super-users.
Acceptance	Positive about change with no evidence of resistance. These are early adopters who recognize that change is inevitable, whether or not desired. They generally will do as they are told. They will not be encouraging or discouraging to others.	Express appreciation, encourage partnership, and cultivate as many of these people as possible.
Acceptance/ modification	States support but continually seeks to modify change back to existing ways. These may be pragmatists who have seen so many changes in the past that they become skeptical of the value of change. They may initially resist use until it is proven to them that the system works as intended, has value, and will not be changed again soon.	These individuals could derail the project if not counseled on the underlying reason for modifications. Clearly make the case for the need for the change and follow up with specific feedback on how the change is helping the organization. Set appropriate expectations for them directly and follow up with each regularly.
Acquiescence	Not at all involved, but no evidence of resistance. This will probably be the silent majority. Some will comply fully, but others could take it upon themselves to create a workaround if something is not working properly or if they believe an alternate way is more convenient. They will not tell anyone about this workaround.	These people could prove to be adequate users, or introduce issues with any workarounds they may create. Engage as many as possible in some aspect of the workflow and process redesign, if only to put the redesigned process where they will see it every day. Use rounding to ask about the change and to check that workarounds have not been created.
Active resistance	States opposition and continually complains about impending changes. May or may not adopt the change.	Establish expectations and follow up regularly; channel energies into constructive help.

continued

Table 11.2 (continued)   Reactions to Change and Responses

Characteristic	Reaction	Potential Responses
Opposition	Does not state opposition but refuses to get involved. May appear to be making the change when they are actually not (getting others to use the system or perform the new task on their behalf).	Hardest to identify and turn around; counseling is required. Peer pressure helps.
Leaving	Seriously threatens to leave/retire, or actually leaves.	Acknowledge accomplishments and let go.

Source: Copyright © MargretA Consulting, LLC. With permission.

is any fault, it is actually leadership failing to provide the resources necessary to learn how to use the HIT or EHR correctly, conduct rounding, and provide support. Making change a priority stems from a culture where blame is removed from the equation and replaced with root cause analysis and finding solutions.

Creating Change Agents

Many change management experts recommend going a step beyond managers and supervisors giving change a priority to empowering everyone in an organization undergoing a major change to become change agents. Mahatma Gandhi is widely quoted as saying, "Be the **change** you want to see in the world." An empowered workforce does not require only certain persons to "crack the whip." In fact, there should be no whip, or no ruler as Denis Waitley's quote at the start of this chapter suggests. Knowledge workers, especially, need to feel they are empowered.

Writing in the *Healthcare Financial Management* journal, Kazemek (1989) described successful management for a CDO as one where managers have the "power to empower." He observed that while "many managers do not view themselves in terms of their power—which carries a negative connotation, all managers possess some degree of power by virtue of the positions they hold." He then noted that "what [managers] do with this hierarchical form of power will make the difference between successful and unsuccessful managers…." Some tips to empower workers summarized from Kazemek's article are provided in Table 11.3

Interestingly, in 2007, the Institute of Medicine (IOM) started conducting roundtables on value- and science-driven health care, which they called the "Learning Health System." The purpose of the roundtable was to serve as "a neutral venue for cooperative work among stakeholders in order to help transform the availability and use of the best evidence for the collaborative healthcare choices of each patient and provider; to drive the process of discovery as a natural outgrowth of patient care; and to ensure innovation, quality, safety, and value in health care." The roundtable found the most pressing needs for change

Table 11.3   Tips to Empower Workers

• *Trust people.* Most people really want to do the right thing and especially when allowed to do so, will do so.
• *Let go.* Many managers in health care are in the position they are in because they were good at their line jobs. It is often difficult to allow others to find their own way.
• *Give others the opportunity to be successful.* Sometimes managers believe that they will shine if their workers fail; but the exact opposite is true.
• *Accept mistakes.* This is especially difficult in health care and with knowledge workers. But an employee who fears making a mistake typically makes more than those who understand that they happen and they can be a learning experience. Kazemek observed that "The healthcare industry needs innovations and solutions from its workers. Mistakes are a natural by-product of innovative, changing organizations."
• *Avoid dependency.* Just as managers often find it difficult to let go, they may unwittingly make employees dependent on them such that they do not feel empowered. This may be the result of constant hovering, asking if the employee needs help, or even offering to lend a hand in a difficult situation. Instead, managers should keep an open door and respond fully when asked.
• *Talk straight.* Managers should not "sugar-coat" discussions about mistakes. Honesty is important, and can be communicated without blame.
• *Fail to praise effective performance.* In health care, the assumption that all must be and will be perfect often leads to failing to acknowledge the good work everyone is doing. Celebrating the routine good work performed will encourage more of the same.
• *Become vulnerable.* Managers who learn to trust, to let go, and to not make their employees dependent upon them are learning to live with uncertainty and anxiety. Workers do learn from managers—both the good and the bad. It is better to display the good so those will be the traits learned, or expected.

Source: Summarized from Kazemek, E.A., 1989 (Nov.), The Power to Empower—Successful Management. *Healthcare Financial Management.* http://findarticles.com/p/articles/mi_m3257/is_n11_v43/ai_8130427/

to include adaptation to the pace of change; stronger synchrony of efforts; new clinical research paradigm; clinical decision support systems; tools for database linkage, mining, and use; notion of clinical data as a public good; incentives aligned for practice-based evidence; public engagement; trusted scientific broker; and leadership. Ultimately, the IOM had conducted eleven such roundtables, publishing the results in 2011 as *The Learning Health System Series.*

Pascale and Sternin write in the *Harvard Business Review* (2005) that managers need to find their company's "secret change agents." They write about finding the groups of people who are already doing things differently and better. They described these as areas of "positive deviance" and urge managers to "fan their flames," including "making it safe to learn." The SC Partnership to Advance Patient Safety and Quality Healthcare (2010) must have learned of such secret change agents when they created a clean hands campaign as further described in Case Study 11.2.

Case Study 11.2: Grime Scene Investigators Focus on the Hand Hygiene Process

Recognizing that MRSA (**methicillin-resistant** *Staphylococcus aureus*) infections cost the US health system $2.5 billion per year and were both increasing not only in hospitals but schools and athletic programs as well as contributing to the H1N1 influenza spread, South Carolina looked to empower the community to eliminate the spread of preventable infections and related loss of lives through an innovative approach to promoting proper hand hygiene. Persons they dubbed "grime scene investigators" (GSIs) utilized a philosophy of collaboration and shared accountability to reach out at malls, schools, festivals, industries, athletic events, fairs, and other locations. They engaged local media in active communication and knowledge sharing, inserting pop-ups on frequently visited websites, using glow boxes to show people how dirty their hands were, and conducting skits with crime scene tape and chalked outlines of improper hand hygiene. They built their educational campaign around effective use of quality improvement tools and methodologies and an active learning model, demonstrating how to wash hands, how to sneeze into your upper sleeve or elbow, etc. They also had fun, while focusing on measurable process and outcomes performance indicators. They literally created an environment that encourages innovation.

Change Management Tools

The South Carolina campaign was highly innovative and fun—while very serious about taking specific, formal steps in preparing for a transformative change. Case Study 11.2 also illustrates that empowerment does not mean there should be no guidance or accountability for actions. Leaders in change management thinking, such as John P. Kotter (1995), urge organizations to take responsibility for managing change by creating a vision and setting goals; communicating broadly; empowering action; generating short-term wins, or milestones; encouraging determination and persistence; and reinforcing the value of successful change. Change must not be imposed on people, but they do need and want help to make change successful.

There are many models that have been created to help managers help workers in the change process. A few are included here as those that seem to resonate with healthcare knowledge workers.

Force Field Analysis, originally created by Kurt Lewin (Change Management Coach.com n.d.), may be useful for initiating communications about an upcoming significant change, such as the implementation of HIT or EHR. Figure 11.1 provides an example of a force field diagram.

Lewin's model assumes that in any situation there are driving forces and restraining forces that influence human behavior; and that the goal of an organization should be to move people toward the positive behaviors that help drive

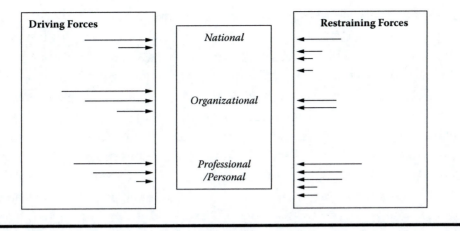

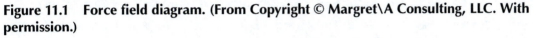

Figure 11.1 Force field diagram. (From Copyright © Margret\A Consulting, LLC. With permission.)

the change and away from the negative ones that hinder change. In the diagram, the lengths of the lines denote the strength of the force. The tool is often used in a discussion where stakeholders to a change are encouraged to identify all driving and restraining forces—without judgment by the facilitator or group present. Once forces are identified and attendees agree upon the forces, discussion ensues about how to mitigate, or weaken, the restraining forces and how to improve upon, or strengthen the driving forces. The forces identified by the group may be completely free-form, or they may be categorized as illustrated in the greyed-out area on the diagram. Case Study 11.3 describes how the force field diagram in Figure 11.1 was used.

Case Study 11.3: Forces Impacting EHR Adoption

A large, integrated delivery network (IDN) had been extensively implementing information technology, including many of the components of an EHR. It had not yet, however, implemented computerized provider order entry (CPOE) due to physicians' concerns. When the federal incentive program for making meaningful use of EHR technology was announced and it included the requirement for CPOE, the IDN knew it had to "bite the bullet." The IDN also knew it had to engage its physicians at every step of the way. As an early step, the IDN decided to hold town-hall meetings to bring physicians together to talk about CPOE and the broader EHR initiative. At the first meeting, physicians harangued about the federal "mandate" and how it was unfair, etc. Organizers were deflated, felt they had lost control of the situation, but also felt they had to persevere. At the next meeting, they decided to try getting physicians to talk first about the positive factors from already-implemented HIT and then to document the negative factors they were concerned about. The IDN told the physicians they would seek their help in reaching equilibrium where—together and to the extent feasible—they would attempt to mitigate the restraining forces. The IDN also decided to focus at the national level first, then the organizational level, and last the personal level—in an attempt to remove any possible individualization. They did not want physicians to feel they personally were being targeted; and they did not want any physician to feel that his or her negative statements would put that person in a bad light. The result was a much more effective meeting, where the physicians left feeling more empowered. The IDN felt it got many excellent ideas that it would not otherwise had considered.

Lewin's Change Theory is another time-tested model. The model encompasses three stages of change: identified as unfreeze, change, and refreeze. Others may use newer terms, such as Campbell (2008) who describes "endings, the neutral zone, and beginnings." Lewin's Change Theory is illustrated in Figure 11.2.

The assumption in Lewin's Change Theory is that just talking about change will not get people ready to make the change (Changing Minds n.d.). Some "push" method is required. This may entail exposing a crisis, such as the "wake-up call" the IOM provided in its 1999 report, *To Err is Human*, where the number of deaths that occur in hospitals due to errors was exposed. For healthcare knowledge workers, however, the crisis must be true, with specific, legitimate evidence. Many, for instance, questioned the IOM's figures, although they acknowledged that errors were a serious issue. Education is also essential. There is much lack of knowledge and many myths about EHR in particular. Again, however, education must show evidence of reality. Physicians have heard so many times that there is a significant loss of productivity with EHR that every

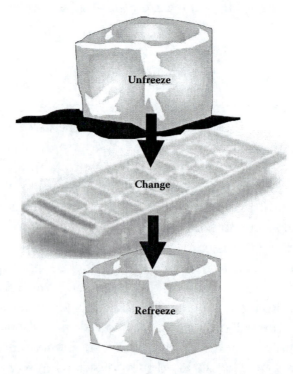

Figure 11.2   Lewin's Change Theory. (From Copyright © Margret\A Consulting, LLC. With permission.)

physician is convinced this is true and that the loss lasts forever—even though there are strategies to reduce the loss and quickly return to full productivity. Visioning is another tool that can help push knowledge workers to be ready for change. Visioning may be done through education and scenarios, or—often in the case for physicians, visioning may require site visits to see the EHR being used by physicians just like them in a real-life setting. Other "push" techniques have been described extensively in the early chapters of this book.

Once ready for change, the change does not happen automatically. There needs to be a transition in which specific steps are taken to introduce the change, engage and inspire, carefully design the change, test it, provide training, and, most importantly, phase in the new technology and its associated workflows and processes.

Finally, the new state must be established and stabilized. This typically is performed by a "push" technique. Ensuring there is no way to go back to the state prior to the change, a reward program, and even starting people to get ready for the next change can be effective ways to freeze the new behavior into place. For example, many CDOs decide to turn off the print capability in their HIT or EHR after a certain period of time. Others remove dictation devices or charge for transcription services. Some withhold a salary increase or give workers bonuses for adoption.

The re-freezing phase must be orchestrated carefully. Some suggest that there are two types of EHR adopters: those who want to yank the band-aid off rapidly, causing only a short time of pain, and others who want to peel the band-aid off slowly, thinking the pain will be lessened even though they will feel pain for a greater amount of time (Nocella, 2010). While both strategies have been used, each with some success; the more likely scenario is one that finds a middle ground. No one wants the transition stage to last forever, but it cannot be turned off like a switch. Case Study 11.4 provides an example of the effects of both.

Case Study 11.4: Physician Strategy Impacts All

A hospital had heard horror stories about getting physicians to use the EHR. As a result, it developed a strategy whereby physicians could ease into use—starting with lab results review and ultimately ending with using CPOE. They initially made viewing lab results available to any physician who chose to use the functionality, but would continue to respond to office phone calls for verbal results, faxes, or copies put in the physicians' mailboxes at the hospital. After nearly a year and with the sense that not many physicians were using the system, they asked a physician focus group what would enable better use. The physicians noted that only viewing the results could lead to errors. They could get distracted during the review and forget the exact values, perhaps recording in their notes wrong data. The physicians said they really needed to be able to receive a copy of the results. So, the hospital decided to offer classes on using the lab results viewer for physicians to retrieve the data and put it into their own EHR or practice management system. At that time, they notified physicians they would have three months to get acclimated to the process and work out any bugs, and that after that the hospital would stop supplying the view-only capability. They implemented this policy at the time indicated. However, nearly immediately they started to receive complaints from both the lab and the nurses on the floor that physician offices were calling for the results to be faxed. Office staff were stating they did not have access to the system, they had not been trained, they could not find the patient on the system when they did access it, and many other excuses. Because the immediate change not only did not accomplish its goal, but also presented an additional burden on the hospital's staff who felt they had to take the time to walk all the callers through the process of retrieving the results, they had to reinstate the previous policy until they could figure out what to do next.

So, while theoretically following Lewin's Change Theory, the hospital attempted to re-freeze behavior too rapidly and without planning the proper workflow and process changes or really how to manage the change fully.

There are many success stories, however, when Lewin's Change Theory is applied carefully. One of the key ingredients to pushing the re-freeze stage is to not only manage the workflow and process changes, but also to provide continual feedback. Workers who see the difference being made by the change are much more apt to want to take advantage of the change. Chung and Nguyen (2005) describe using Lewin's Change Theory to improve pain outcomes—where the key form of "push" was tracking the changes. Healthcare workers see a lot of pain—and knowing they were making a difference with newly instituted workflows and processes made a significant difference.

Kübler-Ross and Kessler's (2005) **Five Stages of Grief**, which include denial, anger, bargaining, depression, and acceptance, is another change management theory that can be applied to major changes as a means to understand how people react to change and what support structures may be applicable during each stage. It is often said that time heals, but Kilcrease (2008) notes that "it's what you do with the time that heals." Lewin's Change Theory helps prepare people for making the change and establishing the change as the new way; but during that time all the stages of grief are often exhibited—and some people will not get past the early stages without specific intervention. For many, moving away from the familiar paper-based record and the "thought-flow" habits that accompany it is a significant loss. Baker (2010) has observed that for many clinicians this is literally a frightening experience—even for those who know how to use a computer. In addition, adopting an EHR and the proposal that it should effect a clinical transformation adds extremely high expectations to a loss situation. Table 11.4 reviews the five stages of grief with some suggestions for helping clinicians move through the stages as they are faced with adopting HIT and EHR and their accompanying workflow and process changes.

From these great works and others come a number of lessons directly applicable to workflow and process management, including Peter Senge's comment that "people do not resist change; they resist being changed" and Prochaska's

Table 11.4   The Five Stages of Losing the Familiar

Stages of Grief and Their Signs	*Actions to Help*
Denial: rejects use of EHR, withdraws from colleagues, makes child-like demands	"Bagel breakfasts" and "pizza lunches" are good ways to informally get people together to open up about what is bothering them and to see that everyone is in the same situation; be proactive about providing one-on-one coaching to openly discuss the habits that must be changed and to encourage talking with others.
Anger: blaming others for the EHR and even other trivial issues, venting to anyone who will listen	Encourage people to channel this powerful emotion into something positive, such as volunteering at a free clinic or a soup kitchen, serving as a host at a holiday event held by the CDO, or enrolling in a course.
Bargaining: threatening to leave, asks for something in return for use of EHR	Avoid giving in to any bargaining situation; but provide evidence of the good the EHR has already achieved. Statistics such as the fact that no patients have had to be seen without a chart, or 100% of lab results have been available to clinicians as soon as they had been processed can be helpful.
Depression: distrust of the EHR and even loss of trust in staff, weight loss/gain, alcohol/drug use, fatigue, and talking about early retirement	Bring EHR users together to talk about their likes and dislikes—and follow up on every issue prior to the next session. Encourage people to talk about and agree to publish in the CDO's newsletter or bulletin board even the smallest of positive stories about their use of EHR. Provide visible means of celebration—both to individuals and all stakeholders. Give medals of different colors for reaching milestones, even including a bronze medal for turning on the computer. Be aware of how the depression may be impacting other aspects of performance and encourage formal help if necessary.
Acceptance: agreeing to use the EHR for limited functions, experimentation with EHR	Slowly there should be signs of willingness to use the EHR. Acknowledge this, express appreciation, but also be very available for questions, help, etc.—while not hovering, and hence not empowering people.

Source: Copyright © Margret\A Consulting, LLC. With permission.

(Prochaska, Norcross, and DiClemente 1995) observation that "change is a process, not an event."

In fact, Prochaska and colleagues may be some of the most relevant change management experts with respect to adopting EHR technology. In *Changing for Good: A Revolutionary Six Stage Program for Overcoming Bad Habits and Moving Your Life Positively Forward* (Prochaska, Norcross, and DiClemente 1995), the authors describe six stages and the average time frame that people spend in each stage (such as for a smoking-cessation program). Its relevancy to the initial five-year/three-stage federal government incentive program for meaningful use of EHR technology is illustrated in Table 11.5.

Table 11.5   Prochaska Stages of Change versus Federal Incentives for Meaningful Use of EHR

Time Frame	Prochaska Stages of [Behavioral] Change	Federal Meaningful Use of EHR Stages
6 months	Pre-contemplation	Stage 1 Requirements and full amount of incentives (2011–2012)
6 months	Contemplation	
1 month	Preparation	
6 months	Action	
6 months		
5 years	Maintenance	Stage 2 Requirements and reduced amount of incentives (2013–2014)
		Stage 3 Requirements and further reduced amount of incentives (2015)
	Termination (or Relapse)	(Downward) adjustment in Medicare reimbursement if hospital or physician has not made meaningful use of EHR

Source: Copyright © Margret\A Consulting, LLC. With permission.

Key Points

- Implementing workflows and processes that have been redesigned to support improvement through the use of HIT and EHR is a significant undertaking. It is also one often not well-supported by vendors. In an age where everyone wants instant gratification or at least the anticipated benefits from use of HIT and EHR as soon as possible, taking the time to institute change is difficult. Working through the issues that arise out of a significant change can be as overwhelming to a CDO as the actual change is to the individual knowledge worker.
- Proactively addressing the impending changes and carving out specific time for the redesigned workflows and processes to be **tested**, staff to be **trained** on, and each to be **phased in** is as important as—and some say more important than—similar functions for the technology itself.
- Managing the change brought about by moving from paper to technology and its associated workflows can represent a significant **loss**. Coupled with **expectations** for clinical transformation, the level of change may be akin to the death of a loved one. CDOs must be able to read people's behavior and take appropriate steps to turn **resisters** into **adopters**, remove **restraining forces** to **drive** use, **freeze** new behaviors into place, and overcome the very real **stages of grief**.

References

Baker, L.H., 2010 (May). "Adoption of EHR Does Not Equal Implementation: Communication Techniques for the Exam Room are Key for Practitioners as EHR is Implemented." The Governance Institute, E_Briefings V7N3.

Campbell, R.J., 2008 (Jan.–Mar.). "Change Management in Health Care." *Health Care Management*, 27(1): 23–39.

Change Management Coach.com, n.d. "Force Field Analysis—Kurt Lewin." Available at: http://www.change-management-coach.com/force-field-analysis.html

Changing Minds, n.d. "Lewin's Change Management Model: Understanding the Three Stages of Change." Available at: http://www.mindtools.com/pages/article/newPPM_94.htm

Chung, H. and P.H. Nguyen, 2005 (Mar./Apr.). "JHQ 161—Changing Unit Culture: An Interdisciplinary Commitment to Improve Pain Outcomes." Available at: www.nursing-informatics.com/N4111/Chung.pdf

Institute of Medicine, 2007. "The Learning Healthcare System, Workshop Summary." Available at: http://www.iom.edu/Reports/2007/The-Learning-Healthcare-System-Workshop-Summary.aspx

Institute of Medicine, 2011. *The Learning Health System Series*. Washington, DC: National Academies Press.

IOM, 1999. *To Err is Human: Building a Safer Health System*. Washington, DC: National Academy Press, 2, 4.

Kazemek, E.A., 1989 (Nov.). "The Power to Empower—Successful Management." *Healthcare Financial Management*, 43(11). Available at: http://findarticles.com/p/articles/mi_m3257/is_n11_v43/ai_8130427/

Kilcrease, W., 2008 (Apr.). "Time Heals All Wounds, or Does It?" *Psychology Today*. Available at: http://www.psychologytoday.com/blog/the-journey-ahead/200804/time-heals-all-wounds-or-does-it

Kotter, J.P., 1995 (Mar.–Apr.). "Leading Change: Why Transformation Efforts Fail." *Harvard Business Review On Point*, Product Number 4231.

Kübler-Ross, E. and D. Kessler, 2005. *On Grief and Grieving*. New York: Scribner, 7–24.

Nocella, K.C., 2010. "Physician EHR Adoption: A Report from the Trenches." Presentation to HITEC/LA Regional Extension Center. Available at: http://www.pptsearch.net/details-physician-ehr-adoption-a-report-from-the-trenches-336027.html

Pascale, R.T. and J. Sternin, 2005 (May). "Your Company's Secret Change Agents." *Harvard Business Review*, Reprint R0505D.

Prochaska, J.O., J.C. Norcross, and C.C. DiClemente, 1995. Changing for Good: A Revolutionary Six-Stage Program for Overcoming Bad Habits and Moving Your Life Positively Forward. New York: Avon Books, Inc., 218–219.

The SC Partnership to Advance Patient Safety and Quality Healthcare, 2010 (June 15). "Creating Change Agents for Safer Care at the Community Level." Presentation available at: http://www.marylandpatientsafety.org/html/collaboratives/hand_hygiene/documents/SCHA_Presentation.pdf

Whiting, S.O. and A. Gale, 2008 (July–Sept.). "Computerized Physician Order Entry Usage in North America: The Doctor Is In." *Healthcare Quarterly*, 11(3): 94–97.

Chapter 12

Step 10: Monitor Goal Achievement with Redesigned Workflows

You can't accomplish anything unless you have some fun.

—Charles F. Knight
Chairman Emeritus of Emerson Electric Co.

This final chapter on monitoring goal achievement with redesigned workflows is an essential element in "closing the loop" to achieve safety, effectiveness, patient-centeredness, timeliness, efficiency, and equitable care—the Institute of Medicine's (2001) six quality aims—with the support of health information technology (HIT) and electronic health records (EHR). It stresses the importance of measuring goal achievement and then celebrating success and correcting course where needed. The quote from Charles Knight was chosen to emphasize the importance of creating a positive work environment, one of six key elements of the power of process in which he fervently believed.

Monitoring Goal Achievement

Once a redesigned workflow and process has been implemented, continuous monitoring and feedback are necessary to ensure that they are working as intended. If the care delivery organization (CDO) has committed to adopting a culture that enables it to build a safer healthcare *system* within its organization, engaged all stakeholders in setting S.M.A.R.T. goals for quality improvement through HIT and EHR, and proactively attended to workflow and process redesign, it should then be in a good position to measure results.

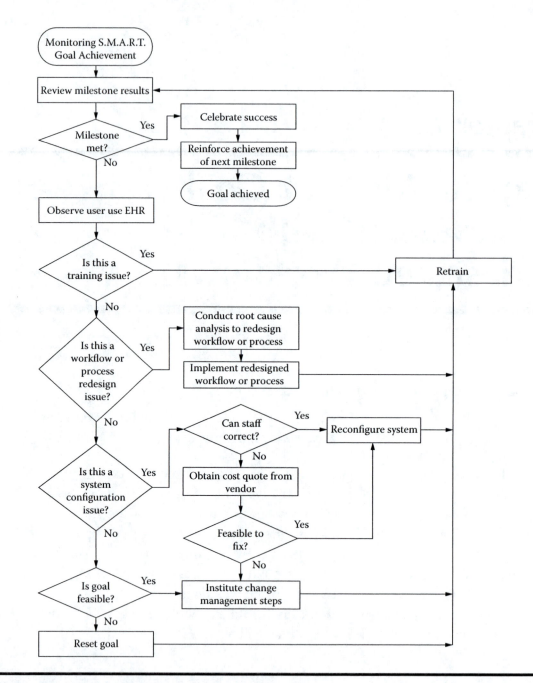

Figure 12.1 Monitoring S.M.A.R.T. goal achievment. (From Copyright © Margret\A Consluting, LLC. With permisson.)

A tool to demonstrate the process that will be taken going forward to monitor goal achievement and design appropriate actions therefrom is depicted in Figure 12.1. In fact, showing this process to stakeholders in the planning for HIT and EHR and as part of S.M.A.R.T. goal setting helps them appreciate that goals are not "cast in concrete" and that the CDO is committed to a process to ensure they can be met. (It also provides yet another way to introduce flowcharting as a means of workflow and process mapping!)

Measuring Results

Monitoring and measuring are sometimes used synonymously; but while closely related, they do have an important distinction as identified in Figure 12.2.

Planning for Monitoring and Measuring

Monitoring goal achievement and measuring results of redesigned workflows and processes associated with HIT and EHR takes some planning. Some considerations include

1. *Timing.* Even for an organization that continuously performs process improvement, time must be given for a new process to stabilize. Attempting to measure results too early will yield highly skewed results and great disappointment. Performed too late, new habits that may not be consistent with desired ones will become ingrained. In an EHR environment where components are implemented over the course of considerable time, measuring results must be performed at milestone intervals, potentially with intermediary goals. To some extent, timing is a matter of sensing when the time is right and applying some trial-and-error principles. When it appears that the

Monitoring is a process of observing the environment to determine changes that may have occurred over time. Monitoring tends to be qualitative and subjective. It may use tools such as rounding, focus groups, and others described in previous chapters to get a sense of what is going on. Impressions or experience gleaned through monitoring often suggest the need for more quantitative and objective measurement. Although seeing the same experience over and over again in every location in the CDO would seem to yield a pretty objective finding, a formal process of taking such observations, ensuring they are randomized over time and place, and that there is inter-rater reliability may be important to perform before drawing conclusions.

Measuring is a process of ascertaining the extent, dimensions, quantity, capacity, etc. of something by comparing it to a standard. For example, the extent to which a standard procedure has been followed might be measured by observing a process and checking off that every step has been performed. Obviously, dimensions are measured in inches or centimeters, capacity in quarters or liters, etc. It has been observed that measuring processes are easier than measuring outcomes in health care. Measuring outcomes may be improved using standard protocols developed through scientific research processes, but will still be influenced by confounding variables.

Figure 12.2 Monitoring versus measuring.

steepest part of the learning curve is over is probably about the right time to start measuring. If cues have been missed, document these and apply lessons learned to the next process and its milestones.

2. *Pulse taking.* While timing is important, a CDO should not wait for what it thinks is the right cue if it becomes obvious that a redesigned workflow and process is not working. It may be that the right time for the planned measurement to take place is four to six weeks after go-live of a major application. But if on the second day after go-live there is a huge bottleneck, delay, or other issue, immediate investigation and corrective action is necessary. In fact, this may suggest that an even longer time is needed before the formal measurement of goals should take place.

3. *Data availability.* Chapter 7 focused on collecting baseline data and described that in the absence of baseline data a CDO might use external data to benchmark its performance, encourage anecdotal evidence of improvement, or even use surrogate data as a measure that change has been successful. Some CDOs that do not have data for comparison purposes define go-live as "ground zero" and measure from that point going forward. While data collected on go-live will likely demonstrate results that would be significantly lower than the past normal, a fast increase in improvement may be inspirational. A CDO must understand the culture of its stakeholders to anticipate whether starting at this point will indeed help or cause people to question the validity and reliability of the measure. Another caveat is that such measurements are often taken that relate to the *process* of HIT or EHR adoption, not the *outcomes* of its adoption. Measuring adoption is not bad, but it is not the same as measuring outcomes. As long as it is clear what is being measured, both measures can be very appropriate.

4. *Management commitment.* Even in a CDO with empowered change agents, management must be present to guide and support, to be the conductor of the orchestra. For quality measurement to truly result in quality improvement, managers must be devoted to measurement and a posture of learning, not blame. Measurement requires a degree of flexibility. Certainly if results demonstrate that desired goals have been met and further goals are not anticipated, the CDO may significantly scale back on measurements and only monitor for potential issues. Likewise, a serious deviation from the desired goals should signal stepped-up measurement and monitoring as redesign of workflows and processes occur and are implemented. Finally, results of measures taken should be evaluated in the same manner as current workflows and processes. They are what they are—and they may not be what is desired, but the focus must be on helping people move forward, with root cause analysis, redesign, testing, training, and go-live.

5. *Resources.* Monitoring improvement is not easy. It must be a purposeful process that takes time and attention. While some (objective) measurements may be automated or readily tallied, counted, etc., as described in Chapter 7, other (subjective) measurements will require more time and a deliberate

approach. Both are necessary. Objective measures will form the trusted evidence knowledge workers require. But subjective measures can point the quality improvement process toward areas needing attention. Resources must also be available to celebrate success and correct course, which will also require time and effort.

6. *Feedback.* Achieving goals requires a three-pronged approach: measurement, reporting, and improvement. Much like a three-legged stool (Figure 12.3), if one leg is missing, the stool will not hold up. Interestingly, while a number of quality improvement initiatives (e.g., The Joint Commission, CMS Hospital Compare or Physicians Quality Reporting System, the incentives for meaningful use of EHR technology, and many state programs) have focused on public reporting, in many CDOs, the focus is on measurement and improvement often with inadequate reporting. A vague generality of "the need to improve" is inadequate, especially for knowledge workers. Report cards should be specific and focused. While they can be aggregated so that a group of stakeholders can see how the group is performing, report cards must get to the individual. These should include the specific measure, how and when it was measured, the specific goal that was agreed upon in advance, the source of any benchmark data applied, and the action anticipated to be taken.

Table 12.1 provides an example of such a report card template. Each section may be repeatedly used to account for individuals who are engaged in performing multiple processes and accountable for several outcomes. The source of baseline data may be internal baseline data collection performed before HIT or EHR was implemented, or may be benchmark data from an external source. Milestone results should also identify the source of how the data were collected. For example, the EHR may generate the number of times an alert was overridden. The day's patient schedule matched against time logged by the receptionist would identify the number of patients seen and the length of each patient's (overall) visit. Results may be reported for both

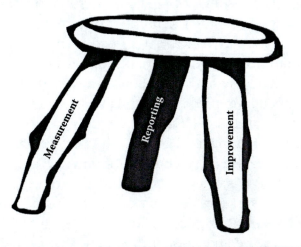

Figure 12.3   Three-pronged approach to goal achievement.

Table 12.1 Sample Report Card Template

Name:											

Group:

Process:

Baseline				Milestone Results				Goals			
		Results				Results		Goal for Period	Overall Goal	Action
Date	Source	Indv	Grp	Date	Source	Indv	Grp			

Outcome:

Baseline				Milestone Results				Goals			
		Results				Results		Goal for Period	Overall Goal	Action
Date	Source	Indv	Grp	Date	Source	Indv	Grp			

Source: Copyright © Margret\A Consulting, LLC. With permission.

the individual and the group to which the individual belongs (e.g., Nurse Jones and Med/Surg Nurses). Action to be taken should identify needed retraining, workflow and process redesign, addressing system configuration issues, resetting goals for the individual or group, or some form of change management strategy (see final section, Correcting Course, in this chapter).

7. *Celebration.* Health care is very serious business, but the old adage "laughter is the best medicine" truly should apply despite the nature of the environment. The next section in this chapter stresses the importance of celebration and describes some modalities.

8. *Course correction.* The Institute of Medicine's 1999 report, *To Err is Human*, was a landmark work revealing the number of errors made in hospitals that resulted in deaths. This report was not named by mistake. Indeed, it would be wonderful to never make a mistake, but that is not the human condition. However, humans have the ability to reduce their mistakes—which is the purpose of quality measurement, reporting, and improvement. Mistakes can be reduced by many means: technology, workflow and process improvement, education and training, and others. The last section in this chapter, Correcting Course, offers some techniques to aid in course correction.

9. *Standardization.* Once it is determined that goals are being met on a consistent basis, the new workflows and processes should be considered the standard for all subsequent practice—at least until such time that other factors influence the practice and cause it to require change, perhaps as a result of new technology, regulations, research, etc. The standard workflows and

processes should be incorporated into the CDO's policies and procedures or medical staff bylaws, rules and regulations, or practice guidelines as applicable.

10. *Continued monitoring.* Once things stabilize and a workflow and process is standardized, it implies that the frequency of measurement and intensity of monitoring can be reduced. Before this step is taken, it may be desirable for the stakeholders to convene and agree that the goal has essentially been met with the new workflows and processes, technology, etc. It is a good idea for this group to make a formal recommendation for subsequent monitoring and measurement activities. In this way, stakeholders have an opportunity to see the fruits of their labors and will be more likely to take accountability for alerting of the need for stepped up monitoring and measures where they are deemed appropriate.

Celebrating Success

Charles Knight, who was quoted at the start of this chapter, is a business leader who was only one of three chief executives in the hundred-year history of Emerson Electric Co. Today, this company is a global business; but in the 1980s, it was caught off-guard by foreign competition. To respond, Knight implemented an enhanced quality improvement program, emphasizing higher quality than its competitors, which he believed was actually a way to reduce costs over time. In his book *Performance without Compromise* (2005), Knight describes his management philosophy as one with a unique and singular belief in the power of process. He identifies six key elements of that process as

1. Keep it simple
2. Commit to planning
3. A strong system of control and follow-up
4. Action-oriented organization
5. Operational excellence
6. Creating a positive work environment

Creating a positive work environment is not always easy. As noted above, health care is a very serious business. Healthcare stakeholders tend be very conservative. But finding time for fun is not unheard of and, if done properly, can contribute significantly to a positive culture in an organization. Case Studies 12.1 and 12.2 serve to illustrate where celebration may not work and where it did work.

Case Study 12.1: Celebration Gone Awry

A hospital provided an open parking garage for patients, their family members, and certain others (e.g., members of the clergy, the coroner, the Employee-of-the-Day, and physicians covering the emergency department). This garage provided direct access to the hospital, thereby enabling people to avoid long walks and inclement weather. However, it was known that many staff took advantage of this, such that an increasing number of patients were unable to find space. The hospital considered requiring anyone who was using the garage to obtain a pass and show it at the entrance or exit—but did not want to inconvenience their patients or delay access to specified others. The hospital instead tried posting announcements in employee-only areas, asked managers to remind staff about the parking prohibition, and many other tactics—still with little lasting success. As Halloween was approaching, members of management got the idea that they would dress in costume and inspect cars as they approached the entrance. They told employees in advance that they would be providing a trick-or-treat opportunity at the garage, and that it was designed to reduce prohibited parking. On Halloween day, everyone was asked for his or her employee badge, and those who were employees were told they could go in and back out to get a treat (i.e., taffy apple) at the exit, or they could park if they accepted a parking ticket. Not fully understanding what the "parking ticket" meant, some employees accepted the ticket—finding that it was an actual parking ticket as legitimately offered by the city police. Unfortunately, this use of what is typically a fun holiday in an unscrupulous manner cost the hospital a union complaint and a number of angry employees. It also cost them the opportunity to use "fun" in other ways that would have been very effective—as now employees became leery of any such activity.

Case Study 12.2: A True Celebration for Learning

A consultant had been engaged by a highly prestigious hospital to conduct an assessment of its compliance with the Health Insurance Portability and Accountability Act (HIPAA) Privacy and Security Rules. The engagement was set to begin in mid-April. Considering the reputation of the organization, the consultant approached the engagement conservatively. Immediately upon entering the lobby, however, the consultant was surprised to find a huge Easter bunny display and an announcement that there was a "HIPAA Hunt" occurring and that the department finding the most eggs would get an ice cream social held for them in their department. There were also pamphlets distributed to visitors to explain HIPAA. Asking about this, the consultant was told that the "eggs" were anything that an employee observed that might be a violation of the HIPAA Privacy and Security Rules. They were only to describe the violation—such as "sticky note with password under keyboard." They were specifically told not to identify where they found the violation. The organizers, who were members of the hospital's compliance committee, stated that they wanted to educate people in a fun way without getting anyone in trouble. HIPAA was new and this was intended to be a learning experience. At the conclusion of collecting all the "eggs," a list would be published to help people learn about HIPAA. Over the course of the year's engagement, the consultant found the hospital to be very serious about its obligations, but continuing to use fun activities to educate their stakeholders.

Celebration obviously needs to be performed in a manner consistent with the organization's culture and resources. It may literally only be the distribution of gold stars, ribbons, or "medals" that amazingly do get attention and make people feel proud of their accomplishments. Consideration should also be given to the recipients. Some people really do not like having attention drawn to them. Celebration for them might be a letter of commendation from the CEO that goes in their file. It might as simple (but well-orchestrated) as the CEO rounding with physicians and shaking hands to appreciate use of an EHR. At a small hospital that had a residency program, the dietician baked chocolate-chip cookies when she learned about a positive outcome in particularly troubling cases. Everyone in the building could smell the cookies and shared in the appreciation—often without really knowing who or what it was all about, only that something good had happened. The proverbial "bagel breakfasts" and "pizza lunches"—whether bagels and pizza or breakfast bars and snacks—fall back on the notion that "breaking bread" provides food, fellowship, and support, perhaps in this case to those who find computers scary and new workflows and processes deterring.

Correcting Course

As suggested by the flowchart in Figure 12.1, correcting course requires study to fully understand why new workflows and processes may not have been fully mastered or effective. Although any sequence of training, workflow and process design, system configuration, goal setting, or change management as issues is feasible, the sequence depicted in the flowchart tends to be the most likely.

Training as an issue may literally include the need for further instruction, more careful explanation, or additional demonstration. Additional training may encompass issues not initially considered, such as for those for whom English is a second language, or where there may be ethnic or religious norms that were unknowingly violated during the training. "Training" may also mean "coaching," "counseling," "cheerleading," or other personal change management technique. Finally, if many need additional training, the training process itself might need to be evaluated. The training may have been too short, not timely, missing certain elements, too quickly delivered, or not fun! Redesign the training for improvement.

Workflows and processes may not have been appropriately redesigned. Aside from issues with lack of attention to workflow and process redesign, it is certainly possible that the most well-intentioned redesign does not work out in real life. Figure 2.1 depicts workflow and process management as a continuous cycle not only to take advantage of new opportunities (or mitigate new threats), but also to ensure that there is corrective action when something is not working properly. Use root cause analysis to redesign workflows and processes that are not working. Conduct pilots to validate their improvement before rolling out to all.

System configuration refers to the need to make an adjustment in the information system. This is a relatively common occurrence, where certain settings may not have been made properly, or there has been a planned phase-in of certain functions such as alerts. Workflow issues may need to be addressed, such as described in Case Studies 1.1 and 1.3. System configuration is listed third in the sequence of corrective action considerations because not all systems are fully customizable. Some are easily customized by staff at the CDO—although caution should be exercised in making such changes. A formal change management process should be undertaken, where the change and its potential impact on other functions in the system should be thoroughly evaluated. Such changes should be reviewed and approved, and fully documented. Other changes may require the vendor to make the change for the organization or even to reprogram the system. Some changes can be made as part of ongoing maintenance and support, while others will incur programming costs or may be delayed for a new version of the software. Finally, for products acquired through a subscription, there are often very few customization opportunities. Subscription services are priced low because they follow economies of scale. Special requests that a CDO may be willing to pay for may not even be feasible. Ideally, these should be considered by the vendor for subsequent product versions—although they will require a sufficient number of such requests to be adopted.

Goal (re-)setting may be needed if the above considerations do not yield evidence of sufficient need or correction. Sometimes goals have been set too high. Consider the benefits realization study depicted in Figure 7.1. The hospital established two very lofty goals of zero over- or under-dosing errors in one year, and only 5 percent of charts with a verbal order by the end of six months. Considering just the verbal orders, the hospital did make progress from 80 percent of charts with verbal orders as their baseline to 65 percent at the end of the first three months, but only 60 percent at the end of six months. The fact that the rate at which the decrease occurred fell off suggests that this goal may not have been feasible from the start. By the end of the period in which the goal was to have been met, they were not close at all. Not only did a new goal need to be set because time had run out, but very likely a number of corrective elements may have been needed. While CDOs should attempt to set realistic goals, it is not always easy to determine what is realistic.

Change management is the last step in the considerations for corrective action in light of less than desirable goal achievement. As with all the above corrective action strategies—while shown in the flowchart and discussed here sequentially—several if not all may be required in a different sequence or simultaneously. This is especially true for change management, wherein several strategies were described in Chapter 11. Change management may also need to be applied to specific groups or individuals, whereas many of the other corrective actions apply more globally.

Summary

As this concludes the steps in workflow and process management, it is time for celebration. While the context of workflow and process management to support the adoption of HIT and EHR is set in the very serious business of health care where documentation has typically been considered a distasteful, albeit necessary task, the success of such efforts truly requires an appreciation for the scope of change brought about by such technology and its associated workflow and process changes. Any continuous quality improvement (CQI) methodology can support and enhance workflow and process mapping and redesign. But the organization must be ready and open to adopting the change that is inevitable from new technology and which is intended to make a clinical transformation that changes fundamental thought processes, coordination and collaboration, and empowerment. Sometimes a shift in the culture of the organization is necessary to enable goal-setting to occur in an environment in which knowledge workers can trust.

Embarking on the workflow and process management journey may be aided by a workflow and process management governance structure. Identifying the processes that will be impacted by HIT and EHR helps establish the scope of a workflow and process management project. Selecting and training on the tools that are comfortable for all stakeholders to create, review, approve, and adopt is a necessary precursor to actual mapping of current (or "as-is") workflows and processes. It was noted that it is especially important to consider those mental processes that cannot be visualized as a critical part of the depiction of current workflows and processes. "Thought flow" is the fundamental process that a knowledge worker uses to make decisions. As these decisions can be added by clinical decision support in HIT and EHR systems, they must be fully understood. Knowledge workers who perform these mental processes must be encouraged to expose these processes not so that they can be replaced, but so that they can be more fully supported and enhanced.

The purpose of workflow and process management is to effect improvement—whether in quality of care and patient safety, or personal productivity and reduced hassles. It is often helpful to understand the current state of affairs with respect to workflows and processes in order to appreciate the need for improvement and to help envision the future. This includes collecting baseline data to use later in benefits realization studies. As attention is turned to redesigning workflows and processes, the current maps, often depicted through flowcharts although also in more user-readable forms such as use cases, must be validated as being true to the actual processes. Depicting "warts and workarounds" in current workflow and process documentation was identified as being the only way to truly have the tools necessary to redesign workflows and processes. Such opportunities for improvement often require increased collaboration with other departments or types of users—an activity that is often not typical in health care, but which is growing in importance as coordination of care is urged as a means to reform health care and generate better value (quality and cost). It is often necessary also to determine the root cause of the issues presented by current workflows and processes. Finding the best solution or solutions may also require a risk analysis and prioritization in light of CDO resources.

Finally, implementing redesigned workflows and processes, especially as they occur simultaneously with the loss of "old ways" represented by paper processes, can represent a significant challenge to management. Change management strategies and approaches should be proactively applied. And to "close the loop," monitoring and measurement of success provide opportunities for corrective action that continuously provides improvement to be celebrated. It is very likely that the result of successful workflow and process improvement will breed many other successes as well. Workflow and process management is not an easy or one-time task. But it is a task that has been increasingly recognized as one of the most important of the critical success factors in gaining user adoption of HIT and EHR.

References

Institute of Medicine, 2001. *Crossing the Quality Chasm: A New Health System for the 21st Century*. Washington, DC: National Academies Press.

Institute of Medicine, 1999. *To Err Is Human: Building a Safer Health System*. Washington, DC: National Academies Press.

Knight, C.F., 2005. *Performance Without Compromise: How Emerson Consistently Achieves Winning Results*. Boston, MA: Harvard Business School Publishing.

Index

copying and pasting, 188
determining attitudes and beliefs toward,
    53–55
educating stakeholders about, 55–58
expected clinical transformation, *See*
    Clinical transformation
factors affecting efficacy, 17
human factors and success, 44–45
meaningful use incentives, 2, 20, 43–44, 72,
    122, 225, 229–230
as medical device, 9, 23
patient perspective survey, 153
process characteristics, 72
productivity loss and, 142, 151, 166
related metrics, 145*t*
return-on-investment, 142–143
sequencing of data in, 12
system components, 8*f*
unintended consequences from using, 4, 32
use at point of care, 187, 189*t*
vendor stakeholders, 34
workflow and process management
    definition, 5, 17
workflow and process management timing,
    28–30
Electronic medication record administration
    (EMAR) systems, 31, 90–91, 184–185,
    191, 204, 207–208, 219–220
Eliminating steps or data, 185–186
Empowering staff and patients, 185–186, 223*t*
End users, 30, 36
    clinical transformation readiness
        assessment, *See also* Readiness
        assessment
    readiness assessment, 52–55
    stakeholder education about EHR/HIT, 57
Entity-relationship diagram (ERD), 97
E-prescribing systems, 11, 32, 91–92, 114–115,
    121, 126, 144, 193
Essential use case, 98–100
Evidence-based guidance software, 121
Evidence-based medicine (EBM), 3–4
Executive leadership, *See* Leadership
Executive management education, 55–58
Exercises, organizational culture assessment,
    47*t*
Expanding scope of process, 80, 113
External validity, 155

F

Facility design, 30–31, 184, 211–212
Failure mode and effects analysis (FMEA), 214*t*

Fault tree analysis, 214*t*
Feedback on goal achievement, 237–238
Fishbone diagram, 203–204, 214*t*
Five S, 26
Five Stages of Grief model, 228–229
Flowcharting, *See* Systems flowchart; Workflow
    and process mapping tools
Flowcharting conventions, 128
Flowcharting software support, 130–131
Flowcharting symbols
    process diagram, 87*t*
    systems flowchart, 92
Flow documentation, 126–128
Focused interviews, 46*t*
    questions for, 49*t*
Follow-up tracking, 111
Food and Drug Administration (FDA)
    oversight, 9, 23
Force field analysis, 224–225
Frequency documentation, 125–126

G

Gandhi, Mahatma, 222
Gebhardt, Joan E., 109
Gemba walks, 26
Generic lists of processes, 75–79
Generic metrics for benefits data, 143–144
Goal achievement celebration, 39, 105, 238,
    239–241
Goals and goal setting, 18, 30, 138, *See also*
    Monitoring goal achievement
    goal re-setting for course correction, 242
    setting S.M.A.R.T. goals, 58–62, 138, 233–234
    software tools, 96
    three-pronged approach, 237
Godin, André, 138, 143
Governance, 36, 62–67
    project charter, 62–67
    structure, 62
Grief and loss stages, 228–229
Grime scene investigators (GSIs), 224
Group-facilitated workflow and process
    mapping, 104

H

Hale, P. L., 121
Hammer, Michael, 85
Hand hygiene, 224
Hand-offs
    combining steps, 185
    process expansion, 113

Printed by Publishers' Graphics Kentucky